THE SHARED SOCIETY

A VISION FOR THE GLOBAL FUTURE OF LATIN AMERICA

Alejandro Toledo

REDWOOD PRESS
Stanford, California

Stanford University Press
Stanford, California

Printed in the United States of America on acid-free, archival-quality paper

Library of Congress Cataloging-in-Publication Data

Toledo Manrique, Alejandro, author.
  The shared society : a vision for the global future of Latin America / Alejandro Toledo.
     pages cm
  Includes bibliographical references and index.
  ISBN 978-0-8047-9551-7 (cloth : alk. paper)
     1. Latin America—Economic policy.   2. Latin America—Social policy.   3. Latin America—Politics and government—21st century.   4. Latin America—Economic conditions—21st century.   5. Latin America—Social conditions—21st century.   I. Title.
     HC125.T59 2015
     320.6098—dc23

                                                                    2014043520

ISBN 978-0-8047-9565-4 (electronic)

Typeset by Newgen in 10/15 Sabon

Contents

THE SHARED
SOCIETY

CHAPTER I

Latin America's Historic Opportunity to Achieve a Shared Society

IN THE PAST TWO DECADES, Latin America has gone through a major transformation. You could even call it a renaissance. This renaissance could continue for many decades, transforming most Latin American countries into highly developed, socially more equal and deeply democratic societies. In these societies, today's poor and lower middle classes would be full participants in vibrant, socially progressive, diverse national cultures, both part of and very influential in shaping the global knowledge economy. Yet, there is no assurance that the renaissance will continue. Latin America is at a crucial moment. The enormous economic and political progress being made could be halted by social strife. Economic growth rates could slow, and democracy could deteriorate into well-known forms of populist *caudillismo*.

I have been an active participant in Latin America's renaissance, and in my Andean homeland, Peru, I played a part in helping to make it happen. I am proud of that and am optimistic that it can be the beginning of a long cycle of Latin American development.

I am writing this book because I believe Latin America is at a crossroads. Hard work, planning, and serendipity have led us to a time and place where we have a historic opportunity to make a giant leap forward. I believe that by 2050, we could be a region that leads the world in human development, economic development, and equity of opportunity. We could be a region without poverty, with low levels of inequality, with a diverse economy based on the minds of our people rather than commodities—a region enjoying sustainable development based on social and economic responsibility and technological innovation.

MY VISION FOR A SHARED SOCIETY

My vision is of a Latin America that is an inclusive, shared society—economically, socially, and politically. Recent research by the World Bank and others suggests that shared societies enjoy considerably higher economic growth. If we understand economic well-being to be a combination of sustained economic growth with equitable distribution of its gains for all, then shared societies are more likely to achieve it. Shared societies also create a virtuous and self-reinforcing cycle that generates more economic dividends by ensuring that everyone shares (and reinvests) the gains from economic growth. Shared societies' economies also have reduced costs related to intersocietal tensions, like law enforcement, security, and the repair of damage caused by violence or protests.

I am a member of the Club de Madrid, a nonprofit organization of over 90 former leaders of democratic countries. The Club de Madrid has led the way in pushing for the creation of global and local shared societies through the shared societies project. I believe that if we actively work to construct a shared society, our vision for Latin America's future will be achieved. By our Club de Madrid definition:

A "shared society" is a socially cohesive society. It is stable, safe. It is where all those living there feel at home. It respects everyone's dignity and human rights, while providing every individual with equal opportunity. It is tolerant. It respects diversity. A shared society is constructed and nurtured through strong political leadership.[1]

A number of basic principles are essential for building shared societies and critical parts of the vision we put forward in this book. They include:

- Respect for the dignity of every individual.
- Equality and fairness. True equality and fairness do not really exist where there is still discrimination, marginalization, or a lack of opportunity for all.
- Respect for human rights and the rule of law. This means that political leaders, business owners, workers, field laborers, and all members of society alike must adhere to the rule of law.
- Democracy. I believe that strong, functioning democracies enable people to overcome their own self-interest and work toward the benefit of all. In true democracies, individuals can express their aspirations and needs, while simultaneously building social cohesion.

It should be evident by now that I am not concerned only with economic growth. Economic growth is a means to an end. Economic growth alone is not sufficient to improve people's well-being, to give equal opportunity for all, or to ensure the possibility of future growth and stability. In my vision of a shared society, Latin Americans would enjoy the benefits of economic growth that are created from focusing on sustainable development and investing in the minds and health of our people and societies to ensure equal opportunities for all.

We would have evolved from being dependent on the export of raw materials to being exporters of knowledge-based products and services. With healthy citizens who are well versed in science, technology, and innovation through a quality education, our economy will be strong, resilient, and less vulnerable to exogenous shocks.

This would be a Latin America in which a child's future does not depend on her gender, her family's income, where she lives, what language she speaks at home, or the color of her skin or the shape of her nose.

We would be aware of the incredible resources we are blessed with in the cultural diversity of our people and encourage this diversity because we know it will inspire new and unique perspectives on our challenges and spark creativity in the development of solutions. Latin America is a cradle to ancestral, millenary peoples and can brag of a rare explosion of cultural diversity that manifests itself in the over 400 different indigenous peoples who survive and thrive there despite the dramatic pulse of extermination brought about by the Spanish conquistadores (and their diseases) in the sixteenth century. This compendium of diverse cultures represents approximately 7 percent of the total population of the subcontinent and 1.6 percent of the global population. Such an amalgamation of peoples constitutes a disproportionately high grouping of cultures in comparison with other parts of the world and is reflected in the existence of some 600 different languages, hailing from about 34 uniquely distinct linguistic families. This in turn allows for an equally impressive and vast constellation of cultural, ideological, and social perspectives that without a doubt are of singular global relevance, both qualitatively and quantitatively.[2]

We must ensure that all citizens have the opportunity to develop the capabilities they need to succeed in the life of their choosing. To do this, we must invest in the health and minds of our people. We must ensure equitable and universal access to basic services like water, sanitation, and electricity; health care services; and quality education. Without basic utilities or health services, children cannot develop to their full potential physically or mentally.

Providing equitable and universal access to quality education is non-negotiable. Education can set you free. (It set me free.) Thanks to education, I never had to live in poverty. While we have made great strides in providing equal access to education, our educational quality is low across the board, and, in addition, it is inequitably distributed. Education frees us from "the noises of the stomachs and the noises of the streets" because education helps individuals become active, productive, engaged members of our society and our economy. Quality education is an essential part of a shared society, and in my vision, by midcentury we will have developed a high-quality school system that serves all of our children. Commodity prices might drop tomorrow, but what we have invested in our children's minds can never be taken away.

This would be a Latin America that is conscious of how our decisions about growth and development affect our environmental and social sustainability. We would be a region fully aware of climate change, and we would make active decisions to reduce or offset our contribution to it. We have been blessed—or cursed, depending on how you look at it—with bountiful natural resources. I say possibly cursed because as a result of our easy access to revenues through our natural resources, we have tended to ignore the need to invest in our people. We now know that in the long term the knowledge and capabilities of our citizens will be more important to the health of our society than natural resources, especially if we continue to deplete the natural wealth from our lands. But natural resources can also provide the funding we need to invest in our people. By midcentury we will be striking a balance between protecting our lands and resources and investing in our people.

We would be a region in which the money we spend on weapons is inversely related to the investment in health care and education. As we become more integrated, our enemies would no longer be at our borders or frontiers but in the midst of our society; these enemies would be poverty, inequality, discrimination, and exclusion. In 2009, we spent $48 billion on weapons. Just imagine what we could do with $48 billion invested in the minds and health of our people! I believed this should be a goal when I was president of Peru, and I practiced what I preached: on my first day in Congress, I reduced military expenditures by 25 percent and reallocated the funds to health care. I believe this change is even more important today.

Real human security—economic and physical—will not come from buying more guns. It will come from building shared societies in which social cohesion is strong, in which everyone feels that they are a part of the community, and in which each individual feels responsible to his or her fellow community members.

We would be a Latin America that accomplishes all of this through deeply democratic institutions. We would spend time and energy building institutions that have the capacity to deliver real results. Our high-quality educational system would feed a vibrant, informed, deliberative democracy—a democracy that produces a concrete, measurable, tangible, and powerful sense of well-being and identity for all members of our diverse societies.

But to do this, we need to commit ourselves. Many would say that we do not need to change, that our current course is good enough. It is true that today's economic development is reaping some benefits: I am proud that we have reduced poverty and that we are the only continent to have reduced income inequality since 2000. We have done a better job of getting our economic house in order (the latest economic crisis was not driven by us, and we were less affected by it than other regions). However, we still live in the most unequal region in the world. And, although we have made progress, we still face huge challenges in our efforts to provide basic services, health services, and a quality education to all of our children. Tens of millions of our children are denied the opportunity most important to all humans: the chance to develop the capabilities they need to be proactive, productive members of their society.

So, alternatively, we can make the effort to take a sharp turn and a giant leap. We can begin to focus on actively creating shared societies and establishing positive, self-reinforcing cycles of economic growth, equity, and democracy that will nourish healthy and productive individuals, societies, and nations. I believe if we take this leap, by 2050, we will have eliminated poverty, reduced inequality, and provided equitable access to basic services, health, and education to all of its citizens. In this vision, which I believe is achievable if we act now, Latin America will have developed a diverse economy that is based on the well-educated and creative minds of its people and that plays a crucial role on the world stage. In this vision, Latin America will also share the benefits and profits of its advanced economy more equitably, incorporating the high fraction of Latin Americans now living in poverty into a vibrant and expanding middle class.

Latin America today has an enormous and unique opportunity. No other region has our abundance of natural resources and macroeconomic flexibility, combined with high levels of national language homogeneity and cultural and historical commonalities. All this gives us the ability to integrate ourselves in terms of infrastructure and trade and to develop comparative and competitive advantages that enable us to compete in the global economy. We are also fortunate to be well positioned geographically to collaborate with the fastest-growing region in the world: the Asia-Pacific rim. If we make this leap, Latin America will be a region that stands on its own feet. We will have learned from our own mistakes and cultivated independence, health, and knowledge at the individual and community levels, which will lead to economic independence, growth, and a horizontal relationship power-wise with the rest of the world at the national and regional levels.

With the right set of policies and politics, I am sure that Latin America will be an economic powerhouse by the middle of this century. The great mass of Latin Americans can attain the economic and personal security now enjoyed only in the highly developed countries. I want to underline the beginning of that last sentence: with the right set of policies and politics. Accomplishing the bright future that I believe is possible for the people of the region requires real discipline and willingness by governments and private businesses to think long term. As I explain throughout this book, despite the impression given by political bickering, we already know what will work. We also know what has to be done. Getting it done is the hard part, and that is where politics comes in.

THE STAGE IS SET

Beginning in the late 1980s and early 1990s, Latin American countries implemented national development strategies based on economic reform and democratic governance. In the 2000s, these reforms helped the region attain sustained economic growth of almost 4.5 percent per year since 2003. With hardly a ripple, Latin American economies just kept expanding through the economic crisis of 2008–2009. Two of the big economies, Argentina and Peru, have had much higher annual growth rates of about 7 to 7.5 percent.

Achieving these levels of economic expansion has opened up tremendous opportunities for changing Latin Americans' lives and for further strengthening democracy in the region. Declining population growth has also helped. Population growth in Latin America has dropped from 2 percent annually in the 1980s to just over 1 percent in the past five years. This means that if economic growth were distributed equally over all income groups, the average Latin American would have seen his or her purchasing power increased by 25 percent in eight short years. In my country, Peru, the economic growth I helped get underway in the early 2000s has increased average per capita purchasing power since 2001 by about 70 percent.

The sustained nature of this growth has had a major impact on poverty reduction, at least in terms of how many people earn less than $2 per day, which is the way international agencies measure poverty, or $1 per day, which is the way these agencies measure extreme poverty. According to the Economic Commission for Latin America and the Caribbean (ECLAC), based on these measures, the percentage of people living under the poverty line decreased from 42 to 29 percent in 2000–2011, and those in extreme poverty decreased from 18 to 12 percent. The good news is that Brazil has reduced its poverty rate to 20 percent, Chile to only 11 percent, and Argentina and Uruguay to about 5 percent. Thanks to the high economic growth rate in Peru over the past decade, the poverty rate dropped from more than 50 percent to 25 percent, and extreme poverty from 24 to just 6 percent. The rates in Peru are still high, but the decline is a tribute to what sustained, rapid economic growth can accomplish, at least in terms of this measure of poverty.

The bad news is that in the *rural areas* of Latin America, and in many of the larger countries such as Brazil, Colombia, Mexico, and Peru, the poverty and extreme poverty rates are still very high: 36 percent poverty and 15 percent extreme poverty in Brazil, 46 percent and 22 percent in Colombia, and 43 percent and 21 percent in Mexico. In Peru, an astronomically high 56 percent of people in rural areas are poor, and 20 percent are extremely poor, even after a decade of record economic growth. In the low-income Central American countries, more than half to three-quarters of people in rural areas are still poor, and one-fourth to one-half are extremely poor. In other words, sustained growth in Latin America has accomplished a lot, but there is still a long way to go.

That is not the only bad news on the poverty front. The figures I just cited only tell us that the percent of people in each country earning $2 or $1 per day is falling because economic growth is increasing their income. Welcome as that is, it hardly captures the various dimensions of poverty that do not change for poor people in Latin America even when their incomes rise. When a poor person makes $2.50/day instead of $2.00, she probably does not get access to good water or indoor plumbing or decent education and health care for her children. She probably does not get access to better housing or get empowered politically. She is still treated as a second-class citizen in the courts. On all these counts, the fundamentals of being poor in Latin America remain and, with them, the frustration and despair that accompany poverty.

Latin America's renaissance is not just about economic growth and increasing the incomes of Latin America's poor. We have had periods of rapid economic development and poverty reduction before. Yet, these past two decades have witnessed an even more important change: the region is enjoying its longest period of uninterrupted democracy and succession of popularly elected governments, whose elections have largely met international election standards. All this is a huge change from a generation ago when military governments ruled in countries like Argentina, Brazil, and Chile. Some of today's governments are "leftist," some are conservative, and some can be seen as authoritarian populist. Nevertheless, elections are taking place when they are scheduled, and leaders are subjecting themselves to the verdict of the voters. In almost all Latin American countries, this means every eligible adult, because voting is a legally required act. The voters have elected governments with different ideologies, but those of all ideological stripes are, so far, subjecting themselves to the voters' decision as to whether or not they stay on.

For all the drama associated with electoral conflict, electoral democracy signals a "basic fundamental" of political stability for investors and economic markets in general. And even though electoral democracy has not eliminated corruption, it may have helped to contain it. When my political party, Perú Posible, led the movement in 2000 to prevent then president Fujimori from taking on dictatorial powers, the Peruvian government was infested with corruption. Drug money ruled the Peruvian political system and the economy. Economic growth had stagnated. By reestablishing democracy and containing corruption, we were able to unleash a decade of growth that is still in full swing.

So Latin America has come a long way toward creating the political stability needed for economic growth. But the region suffers from a low *quality* of democracy. Low-quality democracy does not include citizens sufficiently in the decision-making process and the exercise of power. Combined with poverty rates in most of Latin America that still remain relatively high, low-quality democracy has meant significant levels of marginalization and exclusion, which constantly test the stability of the political system. This situation is exacerbated by extreme inequality in income distribution. Latin America, along with Africa, is the most economically unequal region in the world. Income inequality is declining in some countries from very high levels in places such as Brazil, Chile, and Mexico, but as long as it remains as extreme as it is now, it could set off a vicious cycle of political instability, breakdowns in the democratic rule of law, and a slowing of economic growth.

In our past, when leaders talked about democracy, there was an assumption that this meant a government elected by the majority that works for the majority. But what we have realized is that simply holding elections is not enough to make sure that the government works for the people.

Leaders who have been working for the benefit of themselves and their friends, weak institutions with little capacity to deliver results, and the insidious challenges posed by powerful narcotrafficking networks have meant that while we hold democratic ideals, our ostensibly democratic elections have not delivered the concrete and measurable results we wanted and expected. If we do not create shared democratic societies that deliver concrete and measurable results, there will be unrest. Empty stomachs, unequal opportunity, inequitable distribution of resources, and inefficient and insensitive institutions will beget societal tension, conflict, and violence. A democracy that does not serve the majority of the people is not a functioning democracy.

A UNIQUE, HISTORIC MOMENT

Why is this moment different from other moments? For the first time in Latin America, four major factors have converged to facilitate the leap forward toward inclusive growth and sustained development.

The first factor is that we have learned from our own mistakes in the twentieth century. I call this an "endogenous" factor—something we can generate and control by ourselves. Some 40 years ago, other countries considered us a continent that generated chaos, violence, import substitution industrialization, low levels of economic growth and high levels of unemployment, inflation (and hyperinflation), and foreign debt. As a result, we had social unrest, which at the same time scared investors away from the region. We were the source of crises for the world. Maybe we needed to hit bottom in this way as a mysterious path to where we are now. We have learned how to put our house in order. Latin America is one of the fasting-growing regions in the world in democracy. Our inflation levels are low nowadays, except in outlier countries; our countries' fiscal deficits are manageable; our central banks are independent; and we have learned that authoritarian populism does not pay off in the medium term.

There is other concrete evidence that we have learned from our mistakes. In 2008, Latin America was subjected to world scrutiny. The financial crisis at the end of the past decade was caused not by Latin America but by banks, including Lehman Brothers, JP Morgan, Merrill-Lynch, and banks in Europe. Yet, in this interlinked world, we paid part of the cost. As a consequence of the crisis, 6 million people failed to emerge from poverty in the region. Fortunately, the region recovered from this financial crisis faster than the United States and Europe because of its previous years of macroeconomic discipline.

In many ways, Latin America has already started down the road to change. We have democratically elected governments, and almost all of our economies are governed by rules that foster competition and promote trade and investment. These democratically elected governments are also universally conscious of the need to use conditional cash transfers (CCTs) to incentivize our lowest-income citizens to take advantage of health services and to get their children to attend schools, while providing them additional cash to improve their basic nutrition. Many governments are already taking steps to equalize income distribution, both through CCTs and other programs. Our average level of education has risen dramatically in the past two decades, and many of our governments have begun serious initiatives to improve educational quality at the primary and secondary levels. Some Latin American governments have even begun—just begun—to confront issues of pollution, deforestation, and safeguarding water quality. The "good inertia" that helps us move in the right direction helps us move faster, too.

The second reason I think the time is ripe to make big changes is that currently Latin America's economy is fairly flush. As is well known, the prices of all the commodities exported by our region (soybeans, oil, gas, fishmeal, and copper, among others) are still high in the international markets and will likely remain so for many years. I call this an exogenous factor because we cannot control it; this is an opportunity that the region must take advantage of, but we do not generate it and we cannot regulate it.

It is crucial to invest the income that the region is earning from trading those commodities at high prices in developing the minds of our people. We need to reinvest in human capital, drinking water, sanitation, health care, quality of education, decent jobs, and infrastructure, particularly in rural areas. Through all these investments, particularly those that amount to investing in our people's minds, the region will be able to make the shift from exporting raw materials with no or limited value added to manufactured products. For that, we also need to invest in technology, science, and innovation.

Brazil and Chile have government debt that is only half their GDP. Peru's government debt is even smaller: one-fourth of GDP. Compare that to France, the United Kingdom, and the United States, where the debt is more than four-fifths of GDP, or Japan, where it is almost twice GDP. Latin American countries' populations are also relatively young, so the labor force will continue to grow relative to the nonworking older population. Rising incomes and a growing labor force in Latin America will make it possible to increase government revenues and public spending rapidly, particularly through income taxation. This is in sharp contrast to developed countries and even China, where already high taxes and the rising health care costs and pensions associated with an aging population are putting public investments in education and infrastructure under strain.

The third reason for this unique opportunity is also an endogenous factor: now, more than ever, we must capitalize. The region has been blessed or cursed with many natural resources. Latin America has 23 percent of the world's $250 trillion worth of crude oil reserves (the second biggest crude oil reserves); 50 percent of the world's $22.6 trillion worth of copper reserves; 47 percent of the world's $522.5 billion worth of silver reserves; 18 percent of the world's $2.7 trillion worth of gold reserves; 37 percent of the world's $5.6 quadrillion worth of freshwater reserves; 42 percent of the world's soybean production; 54 percent of the world's sugarcane production; 58 percent of the world's coffee production; 12 percent of the world's wheat production; 18 percent of the world's chicken production; 22 percent of the world's cattle production; and 6 percent of the world's pork production (see Figures 1.1–1.6).

In addition, Latin America is characterized by the exuberant diversity it houses. Such diversity manifests itself in many forms, and one of the best examples is the region's biological diversity: the plethora of biological resources it contains, which is vital for the survival of humanity itself. Indeed, the value of Latin America's contribution to the world's biodiversity can hardly be understated, as it represents, for example, an estimated one-third of all the plant life diversity on the planet.

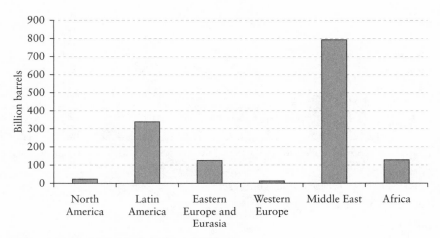

FIGURE 1.1 *International crude oil reserves*

Source: ECLAC (2014).

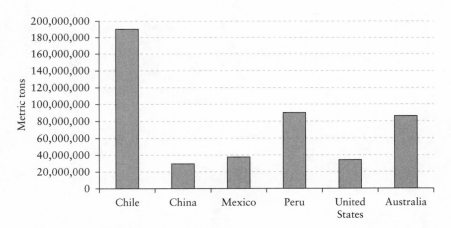

FIGURE 1.2 *International copper reserves*

Source: ECLAC (2014).

In addition, Latin America boasts one of the most extensive groups of ecosystems on earth, including the entire range of elevations—from the mangrove forests at sea level to the chilling peaks of the Andes over 4,000 meters above sea level. Similarly, this region of the world also harbors ecosystems adapted to the most diverse climates, ranging from the hyper-wet jungles of the Amazon in Peru and Brazil to the most arid

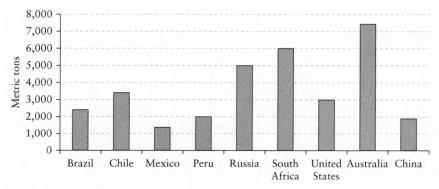

FIGURE 1.3 *International gold reserves*
Source: ECLAC (2014).

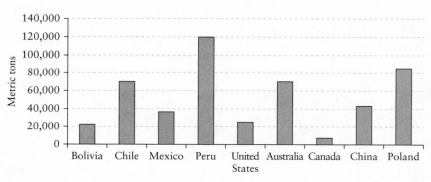

FIGURE 1.4 *International silver reserves*
Source: ECLAC (2014).

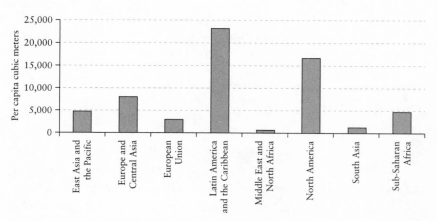

FIGURE 1.5 *Renewable internal freshwater resources*
Source: ECLAC (2014).

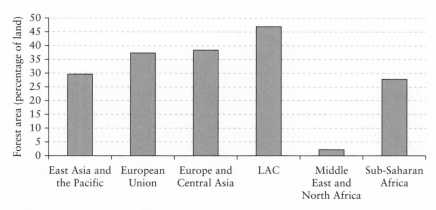

FIGURE 1.6 *Regional forest area*
Source: ECLAC (2014).

expanses of land anywhere in the world, overlapping the borders of Chile and Peru. The variety of environmental services that such rich biodiversity contributes to all of humankind is beyond estimation. The Amazon basin is, for instance, by far the largest freshwater storage and circulation system on the planet.

In short, approximately one-third of all the biological capital in the world, along with the ecological services that come with it, is to be found in Latin America. At the same time, we need to acknowledge that it is our responsibility to protect all this natural wealth because it belongs to the world; it is a crucial part of our vision of a "shared society."

It is no surprise, then, that both of these expressions of diversity—cultural and natural—intermingle in a sort of anthropo-biological co-evolution by way of the patient and ever-constant interactions among ethnic groups and their natural resources. The result is a plethora of crafts, music, dances, and many other products and cultural and artistic expressions that combine with the region's biological riches and define a singular "biocultural diversity" of global relevance.

Thanks to this biocultural diversity, humanity has benefited, for instance, from the domestication (through trial and error) of herbs and shrubs that resulted in such treasures as potatoes, corn, beans, and peppers; forest trees turned into sources of cacao; wild vines modified to produce vanilla; and even the discovery and application of penicillin-producing mushrooms, just to name a few. After all, it is hard to imagine what our world might be like without foods like potatoes and corn. Yet, these treasures are but one component of the contributions of Latin America, and they go hand in hand with the wisdom and knowledge achieved by the peoples who first encountered this natural capital.[3]

The fourth reason why this moment is so special is the existence of a considerable stock of highly trained Latin American human capital, now in a diaspora around the world fostered, since the 1960s, in part by the vision of the Ford Foundation, the United States Agency for International Development (USAID), and several European countries. Some professionals now living abroad were evicted from the region because of military dictatorships, violence, or terrorism; others left because they wanted to explore the world.

It is crucial now that we take advantage of this stock of human capital outside of our region. There are around 5.5 million Latin Americans holding BA, MA, and PhD degrees in the diaspora around the world.[4] I am convinced that many highly trained Latin Americans are willing to forgo part of their salaries and the comforts of living in a developed country to return to their respective countries and use their new knowledge and skills in different disciplines to help make this leap forward a reality.

I am one of them. Although I have already had the privileges of studying in some of the best universities in the world; working in international organizations such as the World Bank, the International Labour Organization, the United Nations, and the Inter-American Development Bank; and directing the destiny of my country for five years, I am aware that I still have much work to do in Peru. And I am sure that millions of other Latin Americans have the desire to complete their unfinished business with their societies.

We need to build human capital not only to make the bureaucracies in the capitals of our respective countries more professional but to boost the decentralization of the state that some countries have already embarked on. Partnerships with institutions in the United States and Canada can reinforce reform that is essential if Latin American states are to begin delivering concrete, measurable, and tangible results to the poorest of the poor in our respective countries. The lack of capacity to deliver progress outside the capital cities in most Latin American countries means that significant levels of economic growth will coexist with increasing social discontent, an outcome fraught with risks, as I mentioned above.

Add to this the challenge of providing equality of opportunity to all Latin Americans by eliminating today's high levels of early malnutrition and providing quality health care, education, infrastructure, and electricity in rural areas. We need to prioritize science, technology, and innovation and create our respective countries' Silicon Valleys (scientific and technological cities).

All these four converging factors—learning from past economic and social mistakes; the current growth and rising revenues; a plethora of resources; and abundant, well-trained Latin American human capital—could help trigger unprecedented synergy, enabling Latin America to make this historical opportunity a reality within the next 35 years. It is this interrelationship among human capital, technology, R&D, and natural resources that gives ground for optimism. Time, here, is of the essence. It is an opportunity we dare not waste.

THE CHALLENGES

Latin America is not a homogeneous continent but shares social, economic, technological, and political challenges. First, the region needs to continue stimulating investment in natural resources, with which—as I explained in the previous section and will do again in Chapters 5 and 7—we are vastly and diversely endowed, taking advantage of the high price of commodities. We cannot stop these investments; we need these resources.

Second, we need to begin a drastic shift to diversify the composition of economic growth and escape our vulnerability to a fall in the demand for, and price of, commodity exports. The diversification process needs to extend to all sectors in the economy, particularly agriculture, manufacturing (including small and medium-sized enterprises), and ecotourism. It should also stimulate the generation of decent and well-remunerated jobs, particularly for youth.

Third, Latin America requires aggressive investment in science, technology, and innovation. Here, the relationship between the region and its neighbors in the Northern Hemisphere is important. We need to increase technology transfers for all the different sectors in our economies.

Fourth, we need highly trained human capital to continue implementing the decentralization plans that our countries have already embarked upon in provinces, districts, and communities.

Fifth, the region needs to meet the challenges for sustainable development: clean water, full security, climate change, protection of biodiversity, and an end to nuclear proliferation.

Sixth, we need to reduce military expenditure and reallocate the funds saved to social investments aimed at eliminating poverty and reducing inequality. In 2008 and 2009, paradoxically, Latin America spent US$48 billion on weapons purchases.

Seventh, Latin America needs to respect and celebrate its cultural diversity, particularly in this permanently dynamic and changing world. Our pluralism is our strength, not our weakness.

CONFRONTING THE CHALLENGES

Accomplishing these goals is a tall order. It will take extraordinary effort and inspired leadership to make the decisions required to put Latin America on the path to inclusive development and a shared society. The difficult part is that inclusive development and a shared society require continued economic growth, preservation of the environment, public policies that focus more on investment in the poorest 40 percent of the population, and building political structures that empower all Latin Americans, not just the privileged.

The fact that we are one of the fastest-growing regions in the world should not make us complacent. Economic growth is an indispensable component of development, and we need to create the economic, social, political, and legal stability to attract capital investments for sustained economic growth with a medium- and long-term vision. Economic growth is, of course, a means, not an end. We need to know what kind of economic growth we are searching for in order to take advantage of this unique opportunity. We can choose mediocre and weak economic growth or sustainable and diversified growth—as I mentioned before. And as I said before, we cannot miss the train of history. We need to start facing the challenges to make the leap forward now.

Diversification of the products of our respective economies will lead us to be less vulnerable to fluctuations in commodities prices. Without a doubt, this will reduce our vulnerability to external factors. The time has come for the region to take charge of its own destiny.

It is also important to opt for inclusive growth—growth that does a better job of distributing the benefits of economic growth by providing equal opportunities for all Latin Americans, beginning with the poorest of the poor. I am not advocating taking money from the rich and giving it to the poor. I am saying that we need to give the most disadvantaged people in our region equal opportunities.

The time has also come to bring education, science, and technology to our young people, while at the same time harvesting the human capital we have already helped to build, only to see it fly away and benefit the developed world.

As the World Bank and the Inter-American Development Bank have shown, there has been a substantial decline in poverty in the region over the past decade. We are not the poorest part of the world, but we are the most unequal one, precisely at a time when cyber-technology makes even the most marginalized segments of society acutely aware of that inequality. For the sake of our children and grandchildren, the region's number one task is to eradicate poverty, reduce inequality, and generate decent jobs, particularly for youth.

Let me share a personal reflection: I am a man free of poverty, able to travel around the world sharing my personal and professional experiences because I received a quality education. Nothing, in my experience, is a more effective weapon for eradicating poverty, reducing inequality, and eliminating discrimination than quality education. From a purely business perspective, too, investing in poverty eradication, reducing inequality, and sharing the benefits of growth through social inclusion and sustainable development are highly profitable.

Data from the World Bank show that of a world population of 7 billion, 2.3 billion (35 percent) live below the poverty line. Even worse,

75 million of these are young people. From an entrepreneurial perspective, investing in those 2.3 billion people means that, once they have a job and a decent salary, they will have money in their pockets to purchase the products that those entrepreneurs produce. In Latin America, 180 million out of 600 million people live under the poverty line; taking them out of poverty is a huge expansion of the market. Moreover, if these people get a decent job, the likelihood of social turmoil decreases. That, in turn, lowers country risk and, consequently, the interest rate. Therefore, the rate of return on these entrepreneurs' investments would rise. The workers would be entrepreneurs' partners, and capital investments would be less risky. Poverty and inequality would decrease, and the benefits would be shared by everyone.

This means, for example, that private investors need to have confidence in Latin American nations' political stability and in the consistency and fairness of their legal systems. At the same time, private investors—both domestic and foreign—cannot expect to do business in Latin America on terms that do not contribute—by paying fair taxes via a progressive tax structure where the richest pay the most—to the general welfare or that destroy the environment and exploit the local population by wasting its resources and not contributing to its development.

This has been a historically problematic issue in the region, but it is a two-way street. Latin American governments have historically been too compliant in granting investors concessions at the expense of their people. These same governments have also been notoriously corrupt, and they have been extremely ineffective in using available resources to invest in better education, better health care systems, and an infrastructure to make their populations more productive, healthier, and happier.

Such improvements clearly cannot happen without major changes in the work of governments. Latin America will not achieve the goals I have laid out here unless the Latin American state reinvents itself. Politicians have to develop a different set of reflexes in dealing with the conflicts that will continue to pervade current relations between the haves and the have-nots in Latin America. Their reactions should be framed by the ultimate goals of promoting more investment and economic growth, yet making the economic system fairer and more inclusive. Each decision should be judged in terms of how well it meets those goals.

Democracy has proved to be the best way of keeping up the social pressure needed to guarantee sustained and inclusive economic growth with corporate, social, and environmental responsibility. We need to strengthen our institutions and make them more accountable to their citizens so they fight corruption, drug trafficking, and other crimes. Obviously, this is no mean feat. Walking this path and meeting these challenges demand courage and vision over the long haul.

Some of the state policies they require will be opposed by vested interests, but they will be remembered in the collective memory of future generations as the first steps toward making the leap forward to inclusive growth and sustainable development in 2050.

This book takes a realistic look at how we can achieve this vision of shared prosperity. It outlines the opportunities and challenges we face and the policies we need to develop to keep our renaissance growing. I will start in Chapter 2 by spelling out the three basic propositions on the need to achieve economic growth under environmental constraints, deepen democracy, and increase economic and social equality— underpinning my view of progress toward the shared society. In Chapters 3, 4, and 5, I assess the current status in Latin America of these three fundamental components of my vision for the region, beginning with the present state of our Latin American democracies. In these chapters, I discuss both progress made and the potential threats facing each component. In Chapters 6, 7, and 8, I present a series of concrete ideas—mostly based on programs already tested in our region—that would bring us much closer to my vision of more equitable and inclusive Latin American societies. Some of these ideas would be quite simple to move forward; others are more difficult. In Chapter 9, I take on the hardest nut to crack: how to increase the capacity of Latin American states to carry out the many programs I propose. Finally, in Chapter 10, I discuss how a reinvented Latin America can reposition itself in a global economy and polity, and, in turn, how the United States, Europe, and Asia should anticipate very different relations with the region than they have today.

CHAPTER 2

The Unavoidable Challenges

LATIN AMERICA'S economic and social potential can already be glimpsed in the burgeoning middle class in our many mega-cities. Sharing the same values, drives, and global outlook as their counterparts in the highly developed economies elsewhere in the world, some 150 million Latin Americans are already beginning to experience middle-class levels of health, education, economic security, and political empowerment. Although they continue to be surrounded by extreme poverty and their democracies are still fragile, they set standards and encourage aspirations that could raise the quality of life of the rest of the population and change the face of our region.

However, just as there are many signs of the highly developed and democratic society that Latin America can become over the next four decades, a good argument could be made that this vitality is only skin deep and that the vision I hold for my region could be thwarted by its many ingrained social, political, and economic weaknesses. These weaknesses could halt progress in its tracks. As I spelled out earlier, we Latin Americans are not going to realize our potential without making some major changes in the way we organize our political, economic, and social institutions.

Why aren't the past 10 or 20 years of progress proof that we can achieve high levels of development just by continuing to follow our current path? Recalling Mark Twain's famous quote about predicting the future length of the lower Mississippi River based on past changes,[1] there are many reasons why the progress we have made recently may be the result of particular conditions and not a permanent feature of Latin American development.

My experience of and in the movement to restore democracy to Peru in the late 1990s and my years as president fostering economic growth and rebuilding an almost destroyed civil society in my country have given me many insights into the pitfalls, as well as the opportunities, we face.

Those experiences shaped my view of progress in Latin America, which is founded upon three basic propositions:

1. Sustained economic growth is crucial for eliminating poverty and improving the conditions for furthering democracy.
2. We need to "deepen" our democracies if they are to become legitimate and durable.
3. Long-term economic growth and durable democracy in Latin America are inexorably linked to reducing economic, social, and political inequality.

PROPOSITION I: THE FUNDAMENTAL ROLE OF SUSTAINED ECONOMIC GROWTH

My first basic proposition is that sustained economic growth is crucial for eliminating poverty and improving the conditions for deepening democracy. I realize that this is a controversial proposition. Why should economic growth and increasing consumption be such an important measure of progress when human happiness and even longer-term economic well-being may not be served by focusing so heavily on economic growth?

The main argument I make for continuing to focus on good economic policies that foster economic growth is a simple one: sound macroeconomic policies can be the basis for helping all individuals in society to contribute effectively to their own economic well-being. For individuals in any society to have a sense of self-worth, they need to have the opportunity to earn a decent livelihood.

My view is crystallized in an excellent article in *World Development* in 2008. In that article, Brian Snowdon, an economics professor at North Umbria University in England, interviewed Harvard economics professor Benjamin Friedman—a leading expert on macroeconomic policy—about the role of economic growth in improving the human condition. Friedman stated, "Economic growth—meaning a rising standard of living for the clear majority of citizens—more often than not fosters greater opportunity, tolerance of diversity, social mobility, commitment to fairness, and dedication to democracy."[2]

Friedman, as Snowdon notes, shows there is an enormous disadvantage to living in a low-growth, static economy—that is, a zero-sum society where the progress of individuals and groups depends on taking resources away from other individuals and groups. With economic growth, the potential for conflict engendered by low growth is reduced, and the potential for "openness of opportunity, tolerance, economic and social mobility, fairness, the creation of liberal democratic institutions, and political stability" increases.[3]

Friedman's condition for realizing these positive outcomes of growth is one I will stress again and again in these pages: the "moral" benefits of economic growth will accrue to society "providing that growth positively affects the material living standards of the vast *majority* of a country's population."[4] This is crucial. Economic growth accompanied by increasing inequality (the US case), or even economic growth that continues to be distributed unequally (the Latin American case), does not fulfill this condition. Rather, as I argue below, continued unequal distribution of the fruits of growth may reduce political stability, maintain low rates of social mobility, undermine democracy, and maintain intolerance.

Not everyone agrees that human happiness can be improved by focusing on policies that foster economic growth. A focus on the consumerism and accumulation that, after all, are the driving forces behind economic growth is associated with increased stress, family breakdown, and accentuating the here and now rather than long-term benefits to society.

On the other hand, the United Nations Human Development Index (HDI) is a measure that is much broader than just GDP per capita, and it shows how much—in just one generation—many Latin American countries have improved by that standard. The increase in their HDI is due largely to economic growth and some equalization of income distribution. Table 2.1 shows the trend in the HDI for seven of the largest Latin American countries plus Uruguay. The United States and Canada are shown as reference points. All eight of the Latin American countries shown gained relative to those references but still remain much lower on the HDI. Chile and Mexico advanced the most during the 30 years from 1980 to 2011, and Venezuela's population made the least progress.

TABLE 2.1 *Human Development Index, 1975–2011*

Country	1975	1980	1990	1995	2000	2005	2011	2012
Argentina	0.669	0.687	0.697	0.726	0.749	0.765	0.797	0.811
Brazil	0.549	0.575	0.600	0.634	0.665	0.692	0.718	0.730
Chile	0.630	0.654	0.698	0.722	0.749	0.779	0.805	0.819
Colombia	0.550	0.568	0.594	0.628	0.652	0.675	0.710	0.719
Mexico	0.546	0.572	0.618	0.648	0.672	0.703	0.728	0.775
Peru	0.574	0.597	0.612	0.644	0.674	0.691	0.725	0.741
Uruguay	0.658	0.660	0.686	0.705	0.736	0.748	0.783	0.792
Venezuela	0.623	0.627	0.629	0.646	0.656	0.692	0.735	0.748
United States	0.837	0.853	0.870	0.883	0.897	0.902	0.910	0.937
Canada	0.817	0.834	0.857	0.870	0.879	0.892	0.908	0.911

Source: United Nations (2008), UNDP, *Human Development Report, 2013*, and http://hdr.undp.org/en/data/trends/.

Thus, the HDI suggests that even in a broader index of well-being, Latin Americans are better off today than they were 30 years ago. Chile closed about 43 percent of the gap between it and the United States; Mexico reduced a larger initial gap by almost 45 percent. But this still leaves even Chile considerably behind the highly developed countries, mainly because of its large income inequalities.

Conservatives argue that we should just leave economic growth to markets and to private capital investment. That is a naive view of the relationship between private capital and government. In modern, globally interdependent economies, economic growth requires sound macroeconomic policies, including market regulation and fiscal policies, as well as public investment in research, education, health, and physical infrastructure.

In this book I emphasize how the "right" public policies can contribute to sustained economic growth in a world of justifiably increasing demands for economic, social, and political justice. With economic growth, the possibility for individuals to overcome poverty and to earn decent wages or income from self-employment steadily increases. In addition, economic growth increases the resources flowing into public coffers available for investments in improving individuals' lives—more and better education, health care facilities, roads, energy, communication facilities, and research and innovation.

A second key question I address is the task of achieving economic growth while preserving the environment. Preserving the environment in Peru and the rest of Latin America requires changing the way we expand the economy. Many of the big conflicts over environmental degradation involve populations now marginalized—the indigenous peoples in Latin America who are trying to preserve their possibilities for economic betterment and social and political inclusion. We have had a long-running conflict in Peru's Amazon region between the oil companies and our native population over the pollution caused by oil drilling.

Similar conflicts have broken out in our Peruvian gold mines, where the local populations are battling with the mining companies over the pollution of their scarce water supply. For many years, Peruvian government policy let Big Oil and Big Mining have their way out of fear that without such enabling policies, these companies would not invest and economic growth would be reduced. Whether that assumption is correct has not been tested, but in any model of sustained development, environmental factors must be a major factor, and at times they may require us to reduce short-term profits so we can maintain long-term development. We just need to adopt a mind-set that includes the environment as part of overall growth accounting and a mind-set that includes local populations most directly affected in the decision processes that rectify environmental degradation.

I can go even further: we need to develop a mind-set that measures economic growth and development in terms of improvements in the overall quality of human life. Most of us implicitly understand this. When we think of economic growth, we think of full employment, better-paying jobs, being able to live more comfortably, and being able to acquire many of the things we would like to have and we would like our children to have. But economic growth can also facilitate the less tangible contributions to a higher-quality life, such as the health of the population, access to knowledge, access to information (and the ability to interpret it), the quality of the water and air, day-to-day security, the aesthetic beauty of the surroundings, and a people's sense of identity and empowerment.

All these are real, highly valued benefits that shape people's individual assessments of their quality of life, and most are not traded in the market.

Realizing these as part of the economic growth process requires intelligent, effective public policies at the local, national, and global levels. Later in the book, I make some specific proposals for achieving these goals.

PROPOSITION 2: DEEPENING DEMOCRACY

The second proposition motivating my view of progress is that—in the words of my friend and colleague Larry Diamond—deepening democracy is a "moral good, maybe even an imperative," and that reforms are needed in societies such as Latin America's if democracy is to become legitimate and durable.[5] Yet, how do we tell what "quality democracy" is? I can go out and proclaim that Latin America needs to deepen democracy, but I still need to define the meaning of "deepening."

Part of that definition is easy: Latin America has achieved almost universal electoral democracy, one in which regimes change peacefully through electoral means. But many Latin American countries have judicial systems that are corrupt and treat individuals from different walks of life very differently. Most Latin Americans do not live with confidence in their physical security, and political participation is often subject to coercion. The minimal conditions of equal political participation are therefore not met. Some Latin American presidents manipulate the electoral system and the weak civil society institutions in our countries to try to stay in power forever, just as my predecessor, Alberto Fujimori, tried to do in Peru.

Today, every one of the 33 states of Latin America and the Caribbean, except Cuba, is a civilian, constitutional regime with multiparty, competitive elections. In almost all of these states, except for perhaps Venezuela and Haiti, the electoral playing field is sufficiently free and fair that these systems can be termed at least "electoral democracies." In at least 30 states of Latin America and the Caribbean, then, electoral democracy prevails: government leaders are selected and can be—and frequently *are*—replaced in regular, more or less free, and fair elections.

A number of Latin American countries have also made significant progress in institutionalizing other dimensions of "liberal democracy," such as an independent judiciary, extensive protection for civil liberties and the rule of law, a free press, and a pluralistic and open civil society. In order to avoid any misunderstanding on the concept of liberal democracy,

I explain my interpretation of it in Chapter 3. Even in many countries where the rule of law remains tenuous and partial, civilian regimes have made significant progress in rolling back the prerogatives of the military and institutionalizing an ethic of civilian, constitutional rule.

These are huge accomplishments, without precedent in the history of Latin America. But they remain only partial accomplishments. Only a few Latin American countries can claim to have democracy that is truly consolidated—that is, the attitude that the normative and behavioral commitment to democracy is "the only game in town" is now so deeply rooted and broadly shared at all levels of society, and among all key political and social actors, that a reversal of democracy is perceived to be unthinkable.

A stable and high-quality democracy requires not only that the military coup and the *autogolpe*[6] be permanently banished as options for political change but also that all political actors commit to respecting the constitutional norms of democracy and the right of opposing political voices and parties to have their say. Democracy will not be truly stable and effective in Latin America until the culture of democracy—including tolerance for differences and mutual respect between opposing political forces—takes hold among political elites, parties, and broader societal groups. Additionally, it is not enough for leaders to be democratically elected; they also must govern democratically and preside over a peaceful transition of power at the end of their terms.

If the free and peaceful struggle for power through the ballot box is becoming entrenched in Latin America, other dimensions of democracy are not. In much of the region, crime and violence are rampant, the police demand bribes and abuse individual rights, the state is corrupt and unresponsive, the judiciary is feeble and horribly backlogged, and justice is almost always partial and agonizingly slow, if it comes at all. In short, democracy is real but shallow. Until it becomes deeper, more liberal, and more accountable, it will continue to be vulnerable to the temptations of authoritarian populism, which promises to meet immediate material needs at the long-term (hidden) cost of individual rights, democratic checks and balances, and sustained quality economic growth.

The Pervasive Problem of Crime, Violence, and Institutionalized Violence

More than anything else, democracy in Latin America continues to be degraded and disfigured by a weak rule of law. To be sure, the region has come a long way from the days of brutal military dictatorships and even from tentative regime transitions. Yet, a vexing syndrome of violence, criminality, and abuse persists, driven by poverty, unemployment, inequality, and the weakness and corruption of state social services and criminal justice systems. Over the past decade, the nexus of poverty, crime, violence, drug trafficking, and state abuse has intensified with the rise of youth gangs, drawn primarily from the ranks of the unemployed and undereducated. Homicide rates have soared to the highest in the world, while corrupt and ill-equipped police struggle to cope with myriad problems. The strength of organized crime networks underscores that the most serious challenge for democratic governability in Latin America is not the overpowering strength of states but rather their incapacity to implement policies effectively and their lack of effective authority.

As in the United States, it is mainly poor communities that are victimized by government policies that strongly favor elites or policies that are ineffective in reaching the poor. This victimization feeds demands (or tolerance) for vigilante justice and countervailing public and media pressure for get-tough policing guidelines that trample civil liberties and incarcerate growing numbers of troubled, deprived, and violent young people in dysfunctional and overcrowded prisons, which are the equivalent of "gangland finishing schools." In prison, detainees face physical abuse, sexual assault, and torture. Moreover, police and prosecutors do a poor job of investigating crimes, as well as state abuses. The state does an even worse job of giving the weak and the accused access to justice, including legal representation.

Pervasive Corruption

High levels of corruption undermine every dimension of governance and undermine the rule of law. Corruption makes it more difficult to spend resources effectively on social needs. It reduces the efficiency of public investments. It distorts investment priorities and discourages investors from risking their capital in the face of rigged awarding of contracts, pervasive demands for bribes, and uncertain legal protection for property rights. In the political arena, corruption can generate cynical deals between disparate parties to provide legal immunity for past wrongdoing, as in Nicaragua.

The result is the widespread cynicism about parties and politicians that has taken hold in Latin America, a cynicism that in turn exacerbates the fragmentation and volatility of the party system. The combination of an angry, disaffected public and a weak, personality-driven party system makes it exceedingly difficult to build the political coalitions necessary to enact bold state and economic reforms, and it can bring down a presidency very quickly.

Between 1985 and 2004, a dozen Latin American presidents had their terms ended prematurely by impeachment or mass demonstrations that forced their resignations. Since then, presidents have again been "abruptly forced out of office" by mass street protests in Bolivia (for the third time in 20 years), in Ecuador (for the third time in a decade), and in Paraguay, through the impeachment in 2012 of President Fernando Lugo led by the opposition party. When Nestor Kirchner took office in May 2003, he was the sixth Argentine president in an 18-month period. While public opinion considered many of these presidents to be corrupt or incompetent, it is also true that a distinctly Latin American social and political dynamic has been at work contributing to this string of failed presidencies.

Toward Deepened Democracy

Thus, we should not fall into the trap of arguing that participation in regular elections means a society has a "deep democracy." The notion of deep democracy is a work in progress. A deep democracy implies an inclusive political system—one that includes space for peaceful social movements and mobilizations for change, for devolving more power to local communities, and, in today's world, for greatly expanding communication of information through social networks accessible to all parts of every society.

Deepening democracy means extending the rights of all individuals in society to participate in the political process, the protection of those rights in a fair and just way by the rule of laws *designed* to be fair and just, and access to information and local structures of participation that allow local communities to protect their interests through mobilization and political action. In some Latin American countries, this work in progress is likely to produce new forms of democracy. For example, deepened democracy in Peru, Ecuador, and Guatemala could and should reflect indigenous conceptions of community and property rights.

As I discuss in Chapter 4, public opinion survey data show that Latin American publics are among the world's most cynical and alienated from their political systems. They exhibit some of the lowest levels of trust in political parties and national assemblies, on average, compared to democracies anywhere else. Political reform of democratic governance must therefore address the cynicism that Latin Americans feel about their politics, politicians, and political institutions. To the extent possible, political reforms must substantively address the problems of corruption and abuse of power that drive this cynicism; these reforms *must be seen to be visibly* addressing these problems.

If democracy is to survive, prosper, and become consolidated in Latin America, it must work for and respond to all social groups—not only for the rich and the middle class. Latin American countries must therefore strengthen the political participation of the extreme poor, the working poor, the informal sector, and marginalized minority groups as well, while simultaneously respecting cultural diversity. Access to quality health care and education must be democratized.

However, the reverse is also true: if democracy is to work for the poor and marginalized of Latin America, the institutions of the entire society must also be strengthened. That is to say, any strategy to address poverty and inequality in Latin America through democracy must also have, as a significant component, a set of reforms to improve the quality of governance and to deepen democracy, transparency, and the rule of law.

PROPOSITION 3: THE IMPERATIVE OF EQUALIZATION AND INCLUSION

My third proposition is that achieving deepened democracy and improved economic well-being requires continued movement toward more equal (and equitable) income distribution and more equal social and political treatment of the diverse groups in Latin American society.

Although we can argue about how much equalization is needed, there is little doubt that even today, with considerable progress made, Latin American societies are incredibly diverse societies in terms of ethnicity and, at the same time, profoundly unequal and inequitable societies with very large income and wealth gaps between the top 20 and bottom 40 percent: where individuals are located socially and economically is highly related to their ethnicity and the wealth of their parents. From my own experience as an indigenous person in Peruvian society, the degree of social discrimination I faced, even as a professor at an elite university in the 1990s, was palpable.

Overcoming ingrained social attitudes about class, ethnicity, and race takes a long time, but one factor that feeds those attitudes is extensive "economic distance" between higher- and lower-income groups. In Latin America, as in many other societies, that economic distance is highly correlated with ethnic and race differences. The greater the percentage of indigenous peoples in a Latin American country, the higher the percentage of people living in poverty, other factors being equal. In societies with relatively high percentages of single-parent heads of household (such as the United States), poverty is also correlated with gender because women are significantly less well paid than men and more likely to head a single-parent household.

Without a doubt, ethnic and race income differences are also related to differences in the amount of education by race and ethnicity. One of the ways to help close the income gap between, say, indigenous peoples in Latin America and those of European origin is to close the gap in educational attainment and educational quality. However, this is not as easy as it sounds, and, further, unless job discrimination and other discriminatory attitudes toward indigenous and African-origin peoples change, income gaps and social treatment differences will remain.

Are more economically equal countries more democratic? Not necessarily. Communist countries such the Soviet Union and Cuba, or even today's more market-oriented China and Vietnam, are examples of authoritarian and notably undemocratic societies. Yet, democratic societies that are more economically equal are, on average, notably more deeply democratic than those that are more economically unequal. Examples such as the Scandinavian countries come to mind, as well as more diverse societies such as the United Kingdom, Canada, the United States, and postwar France, Japan, Germany, and Italy. What happens to democracy in such countries when they become more economically unequal—as is currently occurring in the United States and the United Kingdom—is an important phenomenon. The degree of economic and political polarization in the United States has visibly increased in the past 30 years and, with it, both antigovernment feeling and government gridlock. It is hard to say how all this will play out in the next decades. Democratic institutions in the United States are strong, but they are clearly suffering under the stress of increasing inequality.

In Latin America, we do not have the long history of democracy that characterizes some of the developed countries. We are working toward that history, so we need to pay attention to the features of societies that help that process mature. The lesson I take away from the United States, for example, is that the political process over the past 250 years has been fueled by the ideals of equality that founded that nation and has, at the same time, been on a long trajectory of working out the severe race and gender inequalities that existed at its founding and still linger today.

Latin America can learn from the United States that severe inequalities are major impediments to the democratic process, and hopefully, the conflicts that have marked the gradual resolution of overt racial discrimination can be avoided in our region. Were conflicts to occur, they would be very different, of course. They would likely end up bringing populist nationalists with authoritarian streaks to power, as they have in the past. This would likely disrupt the process of economic growth, particularly in the present global environment, and they would therefore reduce the likelihood of transitioning toward greater tolerance and political stability.

Yet, even if conflict resulting from continued severe inequality does not bring in populist authoritarian regimes, economic growth could be negatively affected for other reasons. Continuous conflict weakens democracy and increases economic insecurity, which means lower levels of investment and lower growth rates. This is why, many years ago,

University of California at Berkeley and Columbia University economist Albert Fishlow argued that high levels of income inequality can negatively affect economic growth.[7]

Whether or not a strong empirical case can be made that high income inequality actually slows economic growth, there is little doubt that with high inequality, economic growth has a much smaller effect on reducing poverty than in more equal income distribution economies. It will not be, or feel like, a shared society. This will reduce many people's sense of the country "making progress," even if the economy is growing according to the official numbers. In other words, members of a society measure their sense of well-being not only in absolute terms but also relative to how others are doing. The impact of the economic growth that does occur will have a much smaller effect on most people's sense of well-being and thus on the state's political legitimacy. In Benjamin Friedman's terms, the "moral effect" of economic growth will be much smaller than it could be were there greater economic equality or even a reduction in income inequality. In that last scenario, the mass of low-income Latin Americans would see their relative economic position improving. The sense of progress in these groups would, in turn, be highly positive, and that could permit state actions that would promote even higher economic growth.

The last point I want to make on the relation between more equal income distribution and growth is that by gradually fostering greater income growth at the bottom of the income distribution, Latin America also fosters more rapid growth of consumption, particularly of goods and services produced locally: better housing, education, and local consumption goods. Many economists would argue that this reduces savings rates and therefore could reduce economic growth. But I think it could very well stimulate high rates of investment by local entrepreneurs willing to tap into this growing consumption market; it could stimulate a domestic market–driven growth that would also make Latin America a more attractive place for foreign investors interested in supplying a rapidly expanding market.

A NEW ROLE FOR THE LATIN AMERICAN STATE

The bottom line of the analysis presented here is that market-driven growth is crucial for continued development in the region, but it is not enough.

Government must not only ensure that the benefits of economic growth reach traditionally excluded groups on the lowest rungs of the socioeconomic ladder but also that these groups are active in generating growth and participating in an expanded democracy at the local and national levels. This goal requires a new kind of responsibility for the Latin American state—one that views itself as a champion of free markets and also as an active stimulator and regulator of those markets, with the aim of achieving democratically agreed-upon social goals.

When the low real-interest bubble of the 1970s collapsed in the early 1980s, Latin American economies went through a major transformation. They largely abandoned the high-tariff protection system of the post–World War II "import-substitution" model of development and expanded their private sectors relative to their public sectors. Many shifted from depending almost entirely on traditional commodity exports to expanding manufactured exports and more sophisticated, higher-value-added primary exports. Most of the region's economies have modernized their telecommunications systems and greatly expanded their use of computers. Many entered into regional free trade agreements and bilateral free trade agreements with developed countries.

Thus, with the advent of the new global economy, the typical Latin American government, like governments in more developed countries, had to give up considerable control over determining which industries would flourish in their economy. The new role given to the government was to *enhance the economic environment* for domestic and foreign investment in a highly competitive global economy.

A favorable investment environment includes a well-functioning democracy and political stability, a sound and well-developed banking system, relatively low levels of corruption, and a fair and transparent system of justice. Beyond these characteristics, however, the state can contribute greatly to economic development, under these new conditions, by making public investments aimed at creating a high-quality labor force, a modern telecommunications infrastructure, a better transportation system, and reliable sources of energy that rely less on fossil fuels.

Latin American states also have to help "construct" a strong civil society that can energize economic and political development at the local level. Ultimately, unless Latin America's national populations believe that the economic and political system is working for them, only part of the vast potential for economic and social improvement will be realized.

Some Latin American governments adapted quite well to these new conditions after a number of false starts. However, most have hardly tackled the threat to their "stable" political environments represented by the serious underdevelopment of human and social capital in the bottom 40 percent of their populations.

Furthermore, in the last ten years, the specter of global warming puts government at the forefront of shaping economic development policies to achieve global environmental goals. Countries such as Brazil, Peru, Ecuador, Colombia, and Venezuela, as well as the smaller countries of Central America, all have rain forests, which are key to decelerating climate change and thus important to the entire global community. And as the price of fossil fuels inevitably rises, fostering the development of low-income communities by providing them with access to clean and affordable energy requires concerted government effort to stimulate investment in alternative sources of energy.

All of these objectives point to the ever-increasing importance of well-organized and efficient governments at the national, regional, and local levels. These are needed to implement policies that reach even the most marginalized social groups with public investments and access to private resources that help them participate in national development. They are also needed to use instruments of public policy for environmentally sound economic growth. Many studies suggest that the payoff for such policies and investments is very high.

The new recipe for success means that the Latin American state has to adapt again, this time to become a major investor in new, high-payoff infrastructure that stimulates private investment in value-added goods and services. These twenty-first-century goods and services will mainly be based on human ingenuity and produced by small and medium-sized local enterprises oriented toward national and international markets. These enterprises will also need to respond to the new constraints of climate change, but they will be enhanced by the possibilities of major technological advances in information and communications technology.

For this adaptation to occur, Latin American governments need to take much more responsibility for investing in the lowest-earning 20 to 40 percent of their populations and be much more accountable for subsidizing their elites. Today's Latin American elites are already well positioned to tap into networks for investing private funds in the acquisition of relevant skills and know-how, including in the higher education of their children. Most governments in the world greatly underinvest in the poor and greatly overinvest in elites, and this is especially true in Latin America as compared to Europe or the United States. Yet, those developing countries that have invested more in the poor have been highly successful in the new global environment. Korea and Taiwan, for instance, exemplify the success of this strategy (in contrast to the Philippines).

Investing in the poor will require significant public resources. Latin American states have two important sources for such funds. The first is more rational and equitable fiscal policies. Latin American countries collect unusually low revenues from income taxes and have unusually inequitable distributions of public spending. There is ample capacity for using fairer fiscal policies to substantially redistribute currently unequal pretax income and public spending.

The second source of funding for investing in the poor is reducing wasteful military expenditures. Many Latin American countries spend scarce resources on unnecessary armaments that could go to investing in better education, conditional cash transfers, better health care, potable water, access to electricity, and credit for decent housing. Spending on weapons to fight imaginary wars does not help Latin America's poor and may even do little to improve internal security.

This new role for the state also requires that Latin American societies develop the human resources and the will to implement such policies. Investments in training highly skilled public officials at all levels are part of the public infrastructure investments demanded by the new model. Many societies in Latin America are profoundly corrupt, and highly skilled public administrators, from central government officials to school principals, are in very short supply. For many years, international agencies and US foreign policy responded to this situation by deprecating central governments as inherently incompetent and arguing for increased decentralization of public funds to local administrators and private, non-government groups to invest locally. Unfortunately, this strategy never adequately addressed the need to simultaneously develop crucial administrative skills in regional and local institutions. Now the policy focus needs to shift to developing governments at all levels (national, regional, and local) that work to make their societies more inclusive.

I address this state capacity issue later in the book when I discuss the specific actions governments need to take to deliver social services, shift toward sustainable development, and develop the institutions needed for a society ruled by laws rather than violence. I argue that these actions will fall short without the needed state capacity to carry out such an ambitious program.

Before I do that, however, I want to flesh out the three underlying propositions I introduced in this chapter: economic growth, democracy, and greater equality. I hope the reader will indulge my professorial side as I try to define in greater detail what I mean by these propositions. As a social and political activist who led the successful fight against former president Fujimori's steady march toward dictatorship in my country, my primary concern was preserving our fragile democracy. When I became the democratically elected president, my main goal was to rebuild civil society and the democratic institutions that my predecessor had systemically undermined and almost destroyed. I was also concerned about restoring economic development—but I knew that without revitalized democratic institutions, rapid economic growth would be difficult. And it was only near the end of my presidency that I turned to the reduction of inequality. I still consider the work of creating an inclusive society my unfinished task, and unfortunately, it was not taken up by my successors.

Therefore, I discuss the issues that are so fundamentally important for Latin America in the following order: economic development (Chapter 3), democracy (Chapter 4), and social inequality (Chapter 5). Chapter 3 focuses on the challenges that the region faces to ensure inclusive growth and sustainable development. In particular, I highlight the importance of moving away from a dependence on commodity export growth; reforming fiscal policy so it is more focused on investing in the poor and promoting growth; learning from the convincing effects that conditional cash transfer have had on fighting poverty; promoting microfinance; and providing decent jobs, especially for our youth.

CHAPTER 3

Ensuring Economic Growth
with Greater Equity

THERE IS NO ESCAPING the hard fact that Latin America has to stay on a path of reasonably rapid and sustained economic growth if it wants to join the family of highly developed nations and reduce its persistent poverty. However, economic growth is a necessary but not a sufficient condition for inclusive development—the kind of development that assures economic and social mobility for the whole of Latin American society and the creation of a truly participative political democracy, a shared society.

I have already argued that poverty in Latin America is much more pervasive and profound than revealed by income measures of poverty alone. The same can be said for the distribution of political power and the narrowness of participation in the political decisions that deeply influence Latin Americans' daily lives. Voting data and contested elections obscure the overwhelming control over political power by deeply entrenched elites in most Latin American countries. In Chapter 7, I discuss the institutional capacity of Latin American political systems to make much-needed decisions concerning economic and social policy.

As I spelled out in my vision of a future Latin American shared society, we can easily imagine, based on the past 30 or so years, that under the right conditions, Latin America could attain very high levels of economic development, deepen its democracies, greatly reduce income inequality, and greatly reduce poverty. Since population growth has slowed significantly, Latin America should be able to increase the productivity of its labor force by steadily improving the quality of education and the health of its young people. It should be able to reduce its dependency on commodity exports by turning increasingly to its already burgeoning production of more sophisticated agriculture, manufacturing, and services.

Latin America is a region rich with tradition and resources. Its population is highly diverse, with large groups of indigenous peoples, the descendants of the Spanish and other immigrant Europeans and Asians, and the descendants of African slaves. Today, almost 600 million of these Latin Americans live between the Rio Grande and Tierra del Fuego.

In 2012, Latin Americans produced about 6 trillion 2005 PPP$ (purchasing power parity dollars) worth of goods and services, about one-half the amount produced in the European Union and the United States combined. A PPP$ measures how much a nation's output could buy at US consumption goods prices. When we measure output for various years in 2005 PPP$, we are measuring output in each country in each year in terms of what it could buy in US prices in the year 2005, which means that it is adjusted for inflation from year to year.

Because of its larger population, Latin American GDP on a per capita basis—PPP$(2005)10,500—was much lower than in the United States (PPP$30,500), the European Union (PPP$28,000), or Japan (PPP$42,500). Depending on how we look at it, Latin America is a big potential market, with PPP$6 trillion to spend on consumption and investment, or a relatively small market, where each individual has an average of only PPP$10,500 to spend. Remember, PPP$(2005)10,500 has to be seen as what an individual earning US$10,500, or about $5 per hour, could buy in the United States in 2005.

Average per capita income only tells a piece of the story, however. We know that a significant fraction of national product does not go to labor income—wages paid to salaried or hourly workers—but to capital owners—people who own businesses, privately or through shares. In the United States, it used to be that 70 percent of income went to labor, but that percentage has been falling. In Latin America, the figure is lower. So that means capital owners—mostly higher-income individuals—get a high share of income right off the top. The higher the share of output going to capital, the more unequal the distribution of income because most income from capital goes to higher-income groups.

Latin American economies, compared to the rest of the world, have very unequal income distributions: the bottom 40 percent of the population earns, on average, about 12 percent of total income, and the top 20 percent earns about 54 percent of total income. In contrast, in the United States, which has a fairly unequal income distribution among developed countries, the bottom 40 percent of the population earns 16 percent of income, and the top 20 percent earns 46 percent. In Spain, a European country with close ties to Latin America, the bottom 40 percent earns 19 percent of total product, and the top 20 percent only 42 percent.[1] Other countries, such as Korea, have even more unequal income distributions. We will come back to this topic in Chapter 5.

A big part of the social problem in Latin America, then, is not just that average income per capita is much lower than in developed countries but that the proportion of total income earned for those in the top-earning 20 percent of the population is so much greater compared to the bottom 40 percent than it would be if Latin America's national output were distributed somewhat more equally. So, although average per capita GDP is PPP$10,500, the bottom 40 percent had average earnings of only about PPP$(2005)3,000. Remember, this is not what they actually earn but how their earnings translate into equivalent buying power for someone living in the United States. At the same time, Latin Americans in the top 20 percent earned an average PPP$(2005)29,000, which was the same as the average individual income in 2005 in the United States.

Just to illustrate what could happen in Latin America's future under "average" growth rates of the past 20 years, I did some "back of the envelope" projections to 2050 of GDP per capita in Latin America, Europe, and the United States in 2005 purchasing power dollars. The average Latin American would have $24,000, versus $50,000 for the average European and $82,000 for the average US North American. But if Latin America continues to grow at the higher rates of the past ten years and its population growth stays at the much lower level of this past decade, the average GDP per capita in Latin America could be as much as $38,000 annually (in 2005 dollars), which is much higher than the average in the United States today.

Now I want to go one step further. Let's imagine that we could take the concrete steps I outline in this book to greatly increase public investment in the poor. Latin American income distribution is now very unequal compared to other countries. The bottom 40 percent of the population in Latin America only gets 12 percent of total GDP, and the top 20 percent gets 54 percent. If that income distribution remains unchanged to 2050, the average GDP per person for the bottom 40 percent of the population would be about $7,000 in 2050, and the top 20 percent would each get $67,000.

But let's say that Latin America gradually continues to equalize income distribution, so it looks more like the United States' income distribution or, even better, Spain's, a former colonial power in Latin America. In the United States, the bottom 40 percent of the population gets 16 percent of the GDP, and the top 20 percent gets 46 percent. In Spain, the bottom 40 percent of the population gets 19 percent of GDP, and the top 20 percent gets 42 percent. In the scenario where Latin American income distribution becomes more like Spain's over the next 40 years, the share of each Latin American in the bottom 40 percent of the population would be $11,000 and that of Latin Americans in the top 20 percent would be about $50,000 (see Figure 3.1).

There are many reasons why we would want a family of four to have a $44,000 (four times $11,000) share of GDP in 2005 prices instead of $28,000 (four times $7,000), which in 2005 US dollars would be considered working poor. A family with access to $44,000 would be

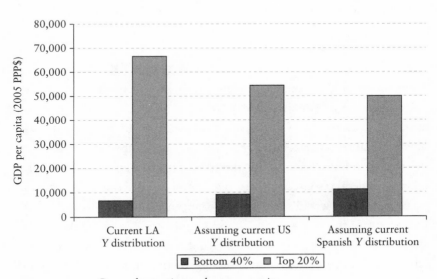

FIGURE 3.1 *Gross domestic product per capita*

Source: World Bank, World Development Indicators (database).
Note: Average projection to 2050 for bottom 40 percent and top 20 percent of population under three assumptions of income distribution (thousands of 2005 PPP dollars).

a lower-middle-class family with a considerable stake in the stability of the society in which they live. They would be able to consume a wide range of domestic products and probably afford to own a modest home. I am not worried that in this growth scenario the GDP share of the top 20 percent of the population would decline. A family of four with access to PPP$(2005)268,000 (four times $67,000) is upper middle class and a family of four with access to PPP$(2005)200,000 (four times $50,000) is also upper middle class. Reducing the ratio of the upper 20 percent to the lower 40 percent from almost 10:1 to less than 5:1 would make Latin America a more participative, democratic society with more commonly held points of view and more willingness to support similar types of development policies.

In this chapter, I address the kinds of economic policies that could and would work to continue the economic growth that has characterized Latin America in the past 10 to 15 years but would also create new opportunities. Specifically, I consider macroeconomic policies and particular programs that could continue to achieve high rates of economic growth, while at the same time gradually reducing income disparities and increasing economic inclusion for currently marginalized groups.

MOVING AWAY FROM DEPENDENCE ON COMMODITY EXPORT GROWTH

Latin American domestic growth has traditionally depended on the value and volume of its commodity exports—for instance, oil, minerals, and agricultural crops. Many Latin American countries are blessed with valuable mineral resources and the capacity to export agricultural goods to developed and developing countries (such as China in recent years). The region's mineral resources are vast. Latin America and the Caribbean hold 10 percent of the world's oil reserves, 5 percent of the world's natural gas, 60 percent of the world's copper and lithium, 50 percent of the world's silver, and 20 percent of the world's gold and iron ore. These resources have fueled much of the region's rapid growth in this century, and they may continue to do so. But at the same time, relying only on these resources unnecessarily exposes Latin America's economic development to a great deal of risk. Despite many changes in the structure of national economies, much of the boom of the 2000s still comes from large increases in traditional commodity exports—products such as soy, gold, silver, copper, and some rare metals—and those in turn have depended on incredibly high economic growth rates in China and China's ever-expanding needs for food and metals to fuel that growth.

But dependence on commodity exports also has its downsides. For one, extractive industries are not very employment intensive. In many countries they are owned by foreign companies, and their value-added is usually concentrated in a few hands. In other words, similar to the labor/capital discussion earlier, very little money makes its way into the hands of average Latin Americans. Additionally, these industries are often heavy polluters, and in the past they have not borne the costs of their environmental degradation.

Many Latin American countries, such as Argentina, Chile, Colombia, Mexico, and Peru, depend heavily on exports for GDP growth. Exports for a country such as Brazil, with its huge internal market, are less important. Being dependent on exports is no sin: China, Korea, and Germany are even more export oriented than the most export-dependent economies in Latin America. It is also a two-way street from another point of view. Latin American growth has been spurred in the past decade by the rapid growth of China's huge economy. Exports of minerals and agricultural goods from Latin America to China have boomed. With rising prices for commodities generally, exports have been a leading source of output growth for our economies. However, Latin America should not count on high commodity prices or 10 percent growth rates in China lasting forever. Relying exclusively on the price of commodities would mean opting for mediocre economic growth, and that is a decision Latin America must avoid.[2]

In 2009, primary products and natural resource–based manufactures made up 75 percent of Latin American exports to the European Union and 85 percent of exports to China. They accounted for only 46 percent of exports to the United States and exports to regional partners. Because of the tremendous increase in exports to China over the past ten years, this means Latin America is more natural resource base dependent for growth than at the beginning of the 2000s. The proportion of all Latin American exports going to Asia (mostly China) from Latin America jumped from 5 percent to 17 percent in this period, largely driven by exports from five South American countries, and the much more diverse exports from the region to the United States dropped from 60 percent to 40 percent of total exports (Economic Commission for Latin America and the Caribbean [ECLAC] 2011, table 2.1).

This is potentially a problem because natural resource prices fluctuate, and narrowly concentrated export economies are highly exposed to those fluctuations. South American countries have benefited in the past decade from the impact of China's economic growth and its enormous need for agricultural and mineral imports. A slowdown in China's growth could cause prices to fall, hurting the very same countries that have benefited so much from the increase of the past decade. Not knowing the price you will receive for your exports makes it more difficult to engage in meaningful long-term planning and budgeting for governmental investment and programs.

True, history is full of examples of successful export-led economies, including Japan in the 1950s, 1960s, and 1970s and Korea and China today. In Latin America, Chile and Mexico are the extreme cases. Chile has a traditional reliance on copper exports to finance growth, and Mexico has a dominant trade partnership with the United States. Germany's exports have jumped from one-third to one-half of its total output (see Figure 3.2), but as part of the European Union, Germany's trade has a different composition from the exports of a Latin American country or the exports of China, Korea, and Japan. Intra-Europe trade is more like trade among regions within a large country such as the United States, Brazil, or Mexico.

I use just a few countries to illustrate the role that exports play in countries' total output. The percentage of GDP coming from exports increased in the 2000s and reached 23 percent in 2011 for Latin America as a whole. Keep in mind that there is a world of difference between the composition of exports in high-exporting countries such as Korea and Germany versus high-exporting countries such as Chile and Peru. In Korea and Germany, exports consist mainly of manufactured goods and business services, whereas the South American countries' exports are

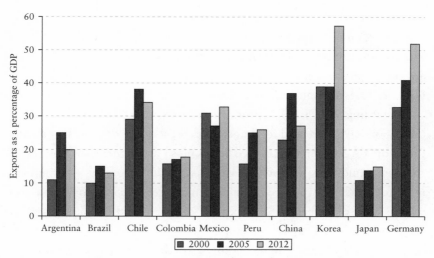

FIGURE 3.2 *Exports as a percentage of gross domestic product, 2000–2012*
Source: World Bank, World Development Indicators (database).

mainly minerals (copper in Chile; minerals and fishmeal in Peru). Even in Mexico, exports are mainly products assembled for US firms taking advantage of lower-cost labor south of the border. Again, this means that very few of the profits from these exports make their way into the hands of ordinary Latin Americans. These basic, raw material exports do not lend themselves to the creation of a shared society because only a few "share" in the gains.

That is why it is so important that Latin America diversify its exports and substitute for its imports products that it can produce competitively in Latin American markets. The good news is that even as the main trend has been to concentrate exports because of the growing China market, there has been a gradual shift of exports to regional partners and some shift toward more sophisticated manufactured exports.

These small bright spots in the diversification of Latin American exports toward more sophisticated products that are more employment intensive and, particularly, more human capital intensive need to be expanded more rapidly. The primary commodities boom should be considered a windfall, and the fruits of this windfall need to be invested in new and more sustainable economic development opportunities.

Latin America is not the ideal place for developing manufactured exports because its labor is not nearly as cheap or as highly productive relative to wage levels as labor in South Asia, Southeast Asia, and China. Yet, there are many opportunities for gaining value-added through processing agricultural products and minerals and then exporting these processed products.

According to ECLAC,[3] Latin American exports to other countries in the region have increased to almost 20 percent of the total, which means that more diverse exports (United States plus Latin American region) still represent almost 60 percent of all exports. Medium- and high-technology manufactured exports have also slowly increased as a fraction of exports to Europe (25 percent of total exports in 2009) and to Latin America (40 percent of total exports in 2009).

The best way to sustain economic growth in the future, however, is to build up domestic markets for domestically produced manufactured goods, business services, wholesale and retail trade, construction, and education and health services. And the best way to increase domestic markets is by fostering an economic development process that increases incomes at the bottom somewhat faster than it increases incomes at the top of the income distribution.

So at the end of the day, today's export boom needs to be translated into growth of domestic markets. When that happens, Latin America will have to depend less on high commodity prices for its well-being. It is in the long-term interest of Latin America's business sectors to ensure that this happens.

REFORMING FISCAL POLICY FOR INVESTING IN THE POOR AND PROMOTING GROWTH

Good fiscal policy—government tax and spending policies—not only promotes macroeconomic stability and growth, but it is also a powerful tool for directly reducing poverty and inequality.[4] Governments around the world have raised and spent funds to invest in the poor and to indirectly redistribute income, with the goal of improving welfare and constructing more prosperous and equal societies. In many countries these efforts have been remarkably successful.

Not all aspects of fiscal policy have the same impact on the poor, of course. Yet, fiscal policy can play a major role in redistributing wealth. Governments that raise sufficient funds and spend them effectively on investments that benefit the poor can significantly reduce poverty and inequality.[5]

Investments such as health care, early childhood education, improved primary and secondary education, job training programs, irrigation systems and other improvements that enhance the productivity of poor farmers, increased access to communications systems, and improved sanitation all contribute to increasing the poor's productive capacity. Transfers, such as old-age pensions, unemployment insurance, and conditional cash transfers reduce the probability that poor families will reproduce their poverty and the social costs of poverty into the next generations.

Unfortunately, fiscal policy in Latin America does not have a good record of investing in the poor or redistributing income through transfers. Governments have seldom generated high levels of public revenues. Tax systems have generally been neutral or regressive, failing to shift the revenue burden to rich households. The services provided by government spending have often been of low quality, particularly those going to low-income families. And government investment and spending programs have tended to benefit middle- and upper-income groups more than the poor. The combination of inadequate revenues, low-quality services, and poor targeting has helped explain why poverty has declined so slowly and why inequality has remained extraordinarily high. The Latin American state has not done a good job of investing in the poor to improve their standard of living.

Figure 3.3 compares the impact of two fundamental tools of fiscal policy—taxes and transfers (e.g., pensions, unemployment insurance, and conditional cash transfers)—on inequality in Latin America and Europe. Before considering the effect of direct taxes and transfers, note that Europe has rates of pretax and pretransfer inequality not terribly different from those in Latin America. After taxes and transfers, however, inequality drops significantly in Europe (10 to 15 percentage points in the Gini index) but only slightly in Latin America.

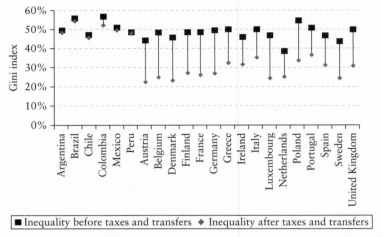

FIGURE 3.3 *Redistributive impact of taxes and transfers, by change in Gini index, 2008*

Source: OECD (2008, fig. 4.1).

Government Revenues Are Low in Relation to OECD Standards

Government revenues average 25 percent of GDP in Latin America (central government tax revenues represent 19 percent of GDP according to OECD/ECLAC/CIAT 2012, table 7.1), compared with 34 percent of GDP in OECD (Organisation for Economic Co-operation and Development) countries. Taxes, the most important component of revenues in most countries, are significantly lower than would be expected given Latin America's level of development. Argentina and Brazil are notable exceptions, with tax revenues in excess of 30 percent of GDP—which many economists believe is an overestimate of true revenues in those countries (OECD/ECLAC/CIAT 2012).

Why is Latin American tax revenue low? The problem does not appear to be low tax rates. Latin America's statutory tax rates for personal and corporate income taxes are only slightly lower than in other parts of the world. VAT rates, which are an important source of revenue in Latin America, are close to international norms. Together, they should provide adequate revenues.

A more serious problem is that many taxes are simply not collected. Latin America collects a relatively small portion of the taxes that its nominal rates would imply. The shortfall appears to be due largely to a failure to collect personal income taxes. In the OECD countries, personal income tax collections constitute over 9 percent of GDP, compared to just over 1 percent in Latin America. Personal income taxes make up 25 percent of total tax revenues in OECD countries, versus just 4 percent in Latin America. Effective tax rates (i.e., based on actual collections) for the richest 10 percent of Latin American households average just 8 percent, compared with nearly 40 percent in the United States.

Collections are low mainly for two reasons. First, tax evasion is high in most countries. Estimates of personal and corporate income-tax evasion often reach 40 percent or more. This is because government agencies responsible for collecting taxes tend to be weak, lacking the power and the resources necessary to enforce the law. Few countries even measure tax evasion or effectively penalize offenders. Furthermore, citizens tend to perceive tax collection as unfair and do not believe that the government will make good use of the taxes they pay. Also, because the combined tax burden facing corporations (corporate income taxes, the VAT, and payroll taxes) is among the highest in the world, many small businesses opt to remain in the shadow economy. Roughly 40 percent of Latin American economies are informal (a rate exceeded only by Sub-Saharan Africa), operating outside the laws established to govern economic activity. The second reason is that, under the fiscal code, there is a proliferation of deductions and other legal loopholes for evading taxes.

Tax Systems in Latin America Tend to Be Neutral or Regressive in Terms of Income Distribution

The major part of the revenue burden falls on poor and middle-income households. This is because an unusually high proportion of revenues in Latin America comes from indirect taxes, such as payroll taxes or the VAT, which are usually regressive, while a relatively low proportion comes from direct taxes (e.g., personal and corporate income taxes), which are almost always progressive. Roughly 40 percent of Latin America's revenues come from indirect taxes, versus 26 percent in OECD countries. When direct and indirect taxes are combined, the poorest fifth of the population often pay a larger percentage of their income in taxes than do the richest fifth.

Government Spending Favors the Rich

By properly spending the revenues they raise, governments can reduce poverty and inequality in at least two ways: by providing services (primarily education and health care) that build human capital among the poor and by transferring income (primarily via pensions, unemployment insurance, conditional cash transfers, or school feeding programs) so wealth is redistributed directly to the poor. Unfortunately, in Latin America, neither of these is implemented in sufficient measure to be effective, for the following reasons.

1. On balance, more benefits go to the richest fifth of the population, and the poorest fifth receive less than their share.
2. Public services that might enhance opportunities for the poor, such as education, are often too low in quality to have a significant impact.
3. Pension programs, by far the largest part of public spending on transfers, overwhelmingly benefit the richest fifth of the population.
4. Programs that clearly reduce poverty and inequality, such as conditional cash transfers, account for a relatively small proportion of social spending.

This combination of inadequate funding, low quality, and poor targeting has led most experts to conclude that fiscal policy is either neutral or regressive in Latin America, thereby failing to address the political problem of profound inequality in pretax incomes and wealth.

CONDITIONAL CASH TRANSFERS AND THE FIGHT AGAINST POVERTY

Programs that work to directly reduce poverty have a key role to play in achieving our vision of an inclusive, shared society. Social safety nets ensure that the worst deprivations associated with poverty—hunger, insecurity, lack of access to health care systems, disruption of schooling—are reduced. The next generation is always seen as the hope for the future, but as I point out in Chapter 4, in many developing countries children are the main victims of poverty. Often, the market does not provide the right incentives to help the poor emerge from poverty in the long term; for the chronically poor, immediate concerns tend to outweigh long-term investments, including those in the human capital of their children.

Children are the ones taken out of school to work or care for younger siblings, or they go to school with sick bodies or empty stomachs. As discussed in the section on poverty, children are disproportionately represented among the income poor. This immediate lack of the basic requirements for leading a healthy, productive life has serious residual effects for these children throughout their lives—and for society as it confronts a further generation that does not have the means or capacity to pull itself up from below the poverty line.

With hope placed in future generations but reality to contend with now, conditional cash transfers (CCTs) were designed to remedy the dual short- and long-term nature of poverty. CCTs address this double-edged sword by fulfilling immediate consumption needs through the cash transfer, while the conditions attached to the transfer, such as the requirement to keep children in school, help poor households to build the human capital (health and education) needed to ensure that the next generation has better prospects for escaping the poverty trap.[6]

During my presidency, inspired by what I had seen of CCT programs in Mexico and Brazil, I initiated a CCT program in Peru called Juntos. It was designed to reach the very poorest Peruvians. It was not an easy task to identify this group accurately, but we did manage to do so and began transferring the equivalent of US$30 per month to about 37,000 households in 110 districts. To continue to receive the monthly cash transfers, families had to make sure their children regularly attended school (85 percent attendance rates) and that children and pregnant mothers got regular health (including prenatal and postnatal) checkups and vaccinations at clinics in their districts. The administrations that followed mine have expanded the program so that now more than 500,000 households get this supplement.

I am very proud of initiating Juntos. CCTs are a Latin American innovation and one of the main reasons income inequality has declined in countries such as Mexico, Brazil, and Peru. After having been proven successful—by achieving many of their goals of not only encouraging poor households to comply with the conditions but also helping to reduce the poverty gap—these programs have spread to almost every Latin American country and some Caribbean countries. In the past decade, CCT programs have become the main weapon for fighting poverty in Latin America. They now reach more than 22 million families in 17 Latin American countries (including the Caribbean).

The idea behind these programs is that direct monetary transfers to families can change the ability of families to access education and health care and other basic services. While the amount of cash transferred in CCT programs is not enough to pull a family out of poverty, it can significantly reduce the depth and severity of poverty, thus allowing poor households to think beyond daily consumption needs and invest in their human capital. The main goal is to break the cycle of intergenerational poverty by improving the opportunities and capabilities of children living in poverty, and evidence shows they are working to reduce poverty, increase school attendance, and improve the health of the poor, particularly children. The long-term effects of reducing the reproduction of poverty could be very significant in our efforts to achieve a shared society.

Evaluating the Effects of CCT Programs

Most CCT programs include evaluation elements in their design, which allows for the collection and analysis of new data to assess their effectiveness and to give us a better picture of what is really happening in terms of poverty and social services. Since their inception, the academic debate among development economists and public health and education experts regarding CCT programs has been mainly about their social and economic outcomes. Further, policy makers have been aware of the need for ongoing impact evaluation of the social programs implemented by governments. Economic and social evaluations of CCT programs generally have been very positive. They suggest that the programs contribute significantly to alleviating poverty in the short term, but the jury is still out on their contributions in the medium and longer terms.

The Oportunidades (originally Progresa) program in Mexico, which gives cash and in-kind transfers every two months to mothers with children in grades 3 to 6, was found to have a strong positive impact, thanks to the conditions attached, on school enrollment/attendance and health status.[7] Bolsa Escola (changed to Bolsa Família) in Brazil, another program considered to be very successful, transferred monthly payments to poor households with children aged 6 to 15 as long as they were enrolled in grades 1 through 8 and had at least an 85 percent school attendance rate. The transfers were conferred to the female head of the household, similar to the system of Oportunidades. Bolsa Escola was also found to have a significant impact on school attendance.[8]

A careful World Bank study[9] shows that the program I began— Juntos— reduced the poverty gap by 5 percent in Peru in just a few years. This study also shows that the Mexico and Honduras CCT programs led to smaller reductions in the poverty gap, and the Colombia and Nicaragua programs had much larger impacts of 7 and 9 percent reduction, respectively, in the poverty gap. This same study shows that Juntos had positive impacts on the use of health care services by children under age 5 and by pregnant mothers, although it fell far short of the program's goal of universal use of health care facilities by recipients. Juntos participants also increased food consumption significantly.

The positive effects of CCTs can also aid whole communities, even if everyone is not receiving the transfer directly. As the poorer households are able to augment their consumption due to the added monetary income, they will spend more in their communities and thus be increasing the welfare of the community as a whole. So CCTs boost the economic security of the poor household but also help to build economic opportunity in their larger community.

Social protection measures, like CCTs, can help insulate both individuals and economies from shocks and crises. During the last global recession, the countries in Latin America that had already implemented social safety net programs were partly insulated from the shock of the economic crisis. For instance, the Oportunidades program is cited as having largely stemmed a greater increase in poverty in Mexico that might have resulted during the recession from the tight economic relationship that country has with the United States.

During the recent recession, a number of Latin American countries tried to take additional measures to protect the poor and indigent from falling further into poverty. Argentina expanded welfare payments to 3.5 million children through its Universal Child Allowance (Asignación Universal por Hijo). Some countries, including Mexico and Brazil, expanded their CCT program coverage, and in others, like Chile and El Salvador, temporary supplementary income programs were undertaken to support individuals in the poorest urban municipalities.[10]

Some have pointed out that a potential downside of CCT programs is that political parties in power use them to "buy" votes from the poor. Allegations have been made of partisan bias in CCT allocation and electoral manipulation. There seems to be little empirical evidence for these charges. However, the media and much public debate tend to portray the creation of CCTs simply as another way for politicians to reward their followers, to establish political patronage ties with the program beneficiaries, or to buy votes. My view is that there is nothing wrong with rewarding political parties that implement effective social programs with one's vote. The important thing is that CCTs be awarded objectively with mechanisms to ensure independent, transparent, and nonpartisan oversight of the allocation process (e.g., through the office of the comptroller-general or similar authority).

The dilemma in Latin American democracies is that, given past experiences, the quality of democracy is judged more by the capacity of the state to deliver results to private interests, such as higher profits for companies or subsidies to certain groups, than by the generation of public services, such as potable water, health care, and quality education.

ACCESS TO MICROFINANCE AND ENABLING DEVELOPMENT IN POOR POPULATIONS

Another great success in the struggle to empower Latin America's poor economically is the growth of microfinance. Microfinance makes small loans available to low-income entrepreneurs to promote economic development in marginal communities worldwide. These micro-loan programs in Latin America have much to be proud of. However, in the Microcredit Summit's count of the 124 million very low-income people with microloans in 2011, 110 million were in Asia and only about 3 million were in Latin America. So 45 percent of the very poor in Asia had accessed microfinance compared to 9 percent of the very poor in Latin America.

When asked about his strategy to create the Grameen Bank in Bangladesh, Nobel Prize winner Muhammad Yunus responded:

I did not have a strategy; I just kept doing what was next. But when I look back, my strategy was, whatever banks did, I did the opposite. If banks lent to the rich, I lent to the poor. If banks lent to men, I lent to women. If banks made large loans, I made small ones. If banks required collateral, my loans were collateral-free. If banks required a lot of paperwork, my loans were illiterate-friendly. If you had to go to the bank, my bank went to the village. Yes, that was my strategy. Whatever banks did, I did the opposite.[11]

This statement recognizes a basic truth about the commercial banking system and its failure to serve the poor. It also reminds us that microfinance would never have existed if the rules of banking had not been broken. Nonetheless, when we turn to our central bank governors, our superintendents of banks, our finance ministers and ministers of the economy, and our aid agency specialists and ask them to build and regulate microfinance, we cannot figure out why the results look so much like mini–commercial banks and why they still miss the very poor. Just as Muhammad Yunus broke the rules of banking, there are "microfinanciers" today who are breaking the rules of microfinance to create new breakthroughs.

When microfinance leaders in Latin America were asked for their top choices for plenary and workshop topics for the 2009 Latin America Caribbean Microcredit Summit that I attended, the most popular choice was "Breaking the Rules of Microfinance to End Poverty: Innovations from Around the World." One of the innovators presenting at the Summit was Ingrid Munro of Jamii Bora in Kenya. Jamii Bora's innovation could provide important lessons for the most intractable problems in Latin America. Jamii Bora, which means "good families," has grown from lending money to 50 women beggars ten years ago in one of the worst slums of Nairobi to serving more than 200,000 members today.

Munro did not stop at providing microcredit to help the poorest slum dwellers. Jamii Bora built a town with decent housing and business space for entrepreneurs because, as Munro observed, "Every poor person's dream is to move out of the slums, not to patch up the slums." Over 2,000 families moved out of the slums and into the newly created

Kaputiei town. For the same monthly mortgage they had paid for their one-room shacks, each family now lives in a home with two bedrooms, a bathroom, a kitchen, and a living room. But "sub-sub-prime lending" works because in order to qualify for a mortgage, the residents must have successfully repaid three micro–business loans. Another of Munro's breakthroughs and secrets to success is that the Jamii Bora consists entirely of former members, previously destitute themselves.

Microfinance leaders working in Latin America have proposed the creation of a regulatory framework that (1) allows microfinance institutions to accept and on-lend deposits and (2) does not require an ownership structure that pushes the microfinance institutions (MFIs) away from reaching the poor. The push for allowing MFIs to take savings came from ACCIÓN, Deutsche Bank, BRAC, COPEME, Global Partnerships, and others. This is something that Professor Yunus has encouraged for years. Rick Beckett of Global Partnerships made the following observation about both points:

MFIs need to access saving to serve the needs of borrowers, lower their cost of capital, and remain competitive and sustainable. Many regulatory structures in Latin America presume or require private equity ownership of regulated financial institutions and thereby limit or complicate efforts by a mission-driven NGO to become regulated, access savings, and maintain full ownership control without introducing owners into the equation whose motivations are more economic in nature [and less focused on social returns]. In each country, there could be a regulatory classification that encourages nonprofit ownership of a regulated entity with full access to savings, provided the MFI maintains sound financial ratios and performance [so that deposit holders are protected].[12]

DEMOCRACY AND DECENT WORK

What is decent work? It is work that gives people the opportunity to earn enough for themselves and their families to escape poverty, not just temporarily but permanently. . . . The concept is not limited to the income component. A decent job provides social security and ensures protection by labor laws, and a voice at work through freely chosen workers' organizations. It gives the job a human face and makes sure that people can work in dignity and freedom.[13]

Productive employment and decent work for all, at the economy-wide as well as the household level, is an end goal and also part of the process of sustainable development.[14] Among the fundamental changes brought about by development is a transformation of the structure of production and employment. As development takes hold, manufacturing and service sectors grow and more formal employment relations increase, although informal work typically remains significant in small-scale services and commerce well into the development process. At the household level, a secure and fairly remunerated job is not only the best path to escape poverty, but it can also transform poor people's lives. The assurance of a more stable and predictable income stream for at least one of its members provides a household with some ability to plan for the future, to support investment in schooling for the children, and to access health and credit services, even for other members of the household to start and grow a business.

A country that is not able to provide enough decent work opportunities for its working-age population, especially young women and men, is at risk of slipping into social dislocation, which can be politically destabilizing, lead to increased crime and violence, and become a threat to security and peace within and among nations. I discuss this further in Chapter 7 when I address the extent and complexity of organized crime in the region.

There is an emerging consensus on the centrality of decent work to sustainable development. In 2013, the UN secretary-general's report to the General Assembly, "A Life of Dignity for All: Accelerating Progress towards the Millennium Development Goals and Advancing the United Nations Development Agenda beyond 2015,"[15] states that a post-2015 agenda should include emphasizing inclusive growth, decent employment, and social protection, among others. Productive employment and decent jobs should be central in the new agenda. It should be recalled that this was overlooked in the original Millennium Development Goals (MDGs) and was only introduced as a late arrival in 2007. Furthermore, the first results of the extensive UN-led reflections and consultations on post-2015 development goals (published at the beginning of the September 2013 General Assembly) indicate that job creation is seen as a pressing need and a top priority in almost all countries.[16]

Labor markets in Latin America are characterized by more limited formal employment opportunities than in developed countries, relatively low salaries, frequently poor working conditions, and the lack of labor market institutions to organize constructive dialogue around labor market issues. Because most people in the world today hold governments responsible for economic and social progress, these factors tend to undermine Latin Americans' faith in democracy as a political system that will improve their quality of life.

A major contributor to poverty in developed countries is unemployment. Although unemployment plays a much smaller role in "permanent poverty" in Latin America, it is still important. Globally, unemployment has risen by about 30 million since the onset of the crisis to a total of nearly 200 million. These figures tend to underestimate the problem, however, as falling employment participation rates suggest that a further 30 million have given up the frustrating search for work. Beyond the sheer number of additional jobs needed, the quality of jobs requires urgent attention. Around 900 million working women and men are employed but not able to earn enough from their work to lift themselves and their families above the $2/day poverty line.[17]

Figure 3.4 shows the official unemployment rates by Latin American country over the past 20 years. They vary from very high and rising rates up to the early 2000s in Colombia, Argentina, Uruguay, and Venezuela, to low and falling rates in Bolivia and Mexico. But many of these differences are the result of how unemployment is reported. For example, because Mexico does not pay unemployment insurance, there is little reason for Mexicans who are unemployed to report that they have lost their jobs. Instead, they swell the ranks of those who work at the lower tier of the informal labor market.

Nevertheless, the movement of unemployment rates over time within a country does measure changes in labor market conditions. Almost all countries had lower unemployment after 2002, when Latin American economies began to attain higher rates of economic growth. Overall,

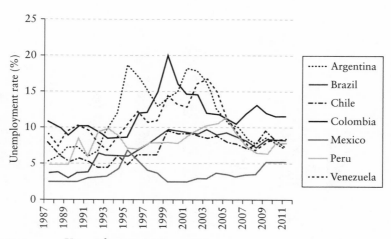

FIGURE 3.4 *Unemployment rate, 1987–2011*

Source: World Bank, World Development Indicators (database).

unemployment rates in the region rose from 5.5 percent in the late 1980s to 6.5 percent in the mid-1990s, and to 9.4 percent in 1999 as commodity prices fell in global markets (World Bank Indicators 2008). With rising commodity prices after 2004, the unemployment rate began to drop sharply. This drop suggests that Latin American unemployment, as elsewhere, depends on economic growth rates, and growth rates in many Latin American countries still depend heavily on world commodity prices. Lower unemployment definitely contributes to lower poverty as well.

The path to inclusive, equitable, and sustainable development must be anchored in decent jobs. Countries that achieved major job creation and poverty alleviation addressed the structural factor underlying poverty and underemployment. Again, policies included extensive social protection with active support for the diversification of their economies, inclusive access to finance, and employment-friendly macroeconomic policies that fostered both investment and consumption.

Informal Labor Markets

That said, one of the major barriers to protecting Latin Americans from falling into abject poverty, even if they have work, is that such a high percentage of the economically active population are in the informal

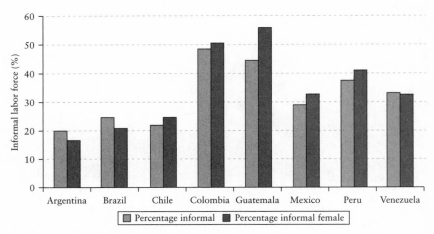

FIGURE 3.5 *Informal labor force, 2012*

Source: ILO, ILOSTAT Database (Total Employment, by Status in Employment) (2014).
Note: Informal labor market defined as "own account workers" plus "contributing family workers"
(http://www.ilo.org/ilostat).

sector. The informal sector may be defined in several different ways. The
International Labour Office defines it as "own account workers" plus
"contributing family workers." Under that definition, of the 262 million
economically active Latin Americans in 2012, about one-third worked in
the informal labor market (Figure 3.5), and another 6 to 7 percent were
unemployed. Thus, only about 60 percent of Latin Americans were employed for wages on a part-time or full-time basis.

Other definitions set the figure for Latin Americans in informal employment even higher. For example, Ribe, Robalino, and Walker (2012,
fig. 2.7) define informal labor as unskilled salaried workers in small firms
plus the self-employed. By that definition, the average proportion of informal labor in Latin America was 47 percent in 2007. Chile had the lowest
level of informality at 37 percent, and Bolivia the highest with 75 percent.

Whatever the definition, much of the informal labor market offers relatively low-income work, and many formal-sector employees may work as
informal workers during economic downturns because many Latin American countries have no unemployment insurance. Effectively, employment
in the lower tiers of the informal labor market and being unemployed from
a low-income job both translate into poverty. Thus, work in the formal

and informal labor market is governed in part by economic cycles: a part of the workforce moves in and out of formal employment, depending on the availability of jobs and the value of wages after taxes in the formal labor market (since income is not usually taxed in informal markets).

High levels of informality in the economy are also often correlated with inequality of incomes and power, and this is also the case in Latin America. High levels of informality make it difficult to create a socially inclusive economy because you cannot enforce livable wage requirements or regulate against discrimination, maltreatment of workers, or poor working conditions. Since 2000, over 50 percent of Latin America's and the Caribbean's workforces are employed in the informal sector.

Informality does not only affect those who are informally employed. A large informal sector results in wages in the formal sector being kept lower by the reserve army of underemployed informal-sector workers. Most of the Latin American poor are working poor: people who are employed but, despite working, cannot earn enough money to move their households out of poverty.

Informality also affects the region's ability to provide extensive social insurance systems. While formal workers do often enjoy packages of social benefits with their formal employment contracts, informal workers have limited access to any kind of social insurance system—whether income protection, pensions, or health. Most countries in the region operate social insurance systems that are based on the Bismarck model, in which employers and workers make mandatory contributions. Because such a large percentage of the employed population work in the informal and agricultural sectors, it is incredibly difficult to enforce this kind of social security program.

On the positive side, informality has been declining in the region. In seven out of the nine countries where informality can be measured consistently over time, informality has decreased since 2000 (Ribe, Robalino, and Walker 2012). This is partly because the region has seen an increase in larger, more formal firms in the 2000s, and there is evidence to suggest that part of the reason for the decline in informality is the movement of workers from small, informal firms to become formal employees at larger corporations. Furthermore, a significant fact to emerge from the recent

World Bank report is that an improvement in wages plays a fundamental role in the decrease in income inequality that Latin America has seen over the past few years.

Other core elements of success in fighting informal jobs include stable and sound government institutions committed to the rule of law, human rights, property rights, and a conducive environment for starting and growing businesses. Labor market policies and institutions such as minimum wages and employment protection legislation are key ingredients for ensuring that the benefits of development are widely distributed and workers' rights are protected.[18]

Resolving the Nexus between Informality and Low Wages: Women, Youth, and Children

If we are going to create sufficient numbers of decent jobs and increase real wages in Latin America, the number one priority for the region is to continue to generate economic growth. Yet, that is a necessary but not sufficient condition. In addition, the rate of population growth needs to continue to fall, the reservation wage (the lowest wage at which individuals are willing to work) of those in informal labor markets has to be pushed up through policies that improve the earnings capacity of the marginally self-employed, wage discrimination against women must be reduced sharply, and a strong, forward-looking labor movement, suited to the conditions of the twenty-first-century global economy, needs to emerge in the region.

Generating more income for the urban self-employed requires a rather different strategy than generating decent jobs in the formal labor market. There have been a number of studies of informal labor markets in Latin America, and they suggest that, at least for the higher tiers of this labor market, a significant constraint in generating more income is a lack of credit. As I discussed earlier, the informal labor market includes most low-income Latin Americans. More credit could provide increased income and possibly the expansion of employment to include nonfamily members. Of course, one of the main issues for Latin American governments in helping to expand informal labor markets is whether to tax owners of small businesses—that is, to "formalize" them. To what degree would taxing this income constrain further expansion?

Many of the poorest Latin Americans live in rural areas and are self-employed as subsistence farmers. In the Andean countries and Central America, a high fraction of rural subsistence farmers are indigenous peoples. The rural self-employed population also work part-time or seasonally as low-paid labor, either in industrial agriculture, construction, or informal labor markets in nearby towns and cities. This rural, but also part-time urban, workforce could be helped economically with a sustained effort to improve rural life (namely, access to public services and eradication of poverty) in Latin America.

Many of the poor are also women. To generate decent work for women, a government effort is needed to reduce discrimination against women in labor markets. Much progress has already been made on this issue in Latin America, but more is required. Women represent 40 percent of the region's economically active population, and in some countries they have higher levels of education than men but earn only 70 percent of the wages paid to men of similar age and education. In informal labor markets, women play a significant role but tend to have less access to capital than men.[19] Thus, reducing gender-based earnings discrimination and gender discrimination in access to capital for small business (informal labor market) investment is part and parcel of ensuring that the most capable individuals get to work in jobs where they can maximize their productivity.

In many developing countries young people have to find some work, as social protection systems do not yet offer cash support to the unemployed.[20] Informal work is frequently the only option, which means long hours of low pay and no access to legal protection against unacceptable working conditions. In absolute numbers, global youth unemployment is estimated to stand at 73.4 million in 2013, an increase of 3.5 million since 2007. Youth unemployment rates tend to be around two to three times higher than the total unemployment rate. Young people continue to be almost three times more likely than adults to be unemployed, and the upward trend in global unemployment continues to hit them strongly. The OECD has warned that this would be the first generation in recorded history that will live in worse social conditions than their parents. In addition, more young women and men are neither working nor participating in education or training—the so-called NEETs.[21] In Latin America and the Caribbean, the NEETs rate was estimated at 19.8 percent in 2008.[22]

The irregular nature of employment among youth and the tendency to leave education early are more prominent features in developing economies. Many young people are so frustrated that they have given up looking for work. Our future human capital is thus being eroded, and frustration is mounting.[23]

Human capital is key to any stable, prosperous society, yet employers maintain that most workers do not have the behavioral and cognitive skills needed for today's economy. On the other hand, young workers feel disillusioned in trying to improve their skills and enhance their chances of competing because there are so few jobs available. Long-term unemployment and a patent lack of opportunities for youth may in turn lead to social unrest and political instability.

Furthermore, vulnerable populations can be targets for recruitment by radical groups, gangs, or other criminal organizations in the short term. In its *World Development Report 2013*, the World Bank warned that jobs are essential to social cohesion. Jobs not only convey a greater sense of dignity and belonging in society, but they also encourage voice and participation.[24] The motivation to join gangs for unemployed and underemployed young men is not merely economic necessity; it often also stems from the need to compensate for the lack of trust, support, and social ties that exclusion from productive opportunities brings about.[25]

Perhaps the most important scarring is in terms of the current youth generation's distrust in the socioeconomic and political systems. Unemployment and frustration make young people particularly vulnerable to exploitation in many different ways, ranging from not being paid or receiving the working conditions they have a right to expect based on national labor legislation to more sinister forms of exploitation like forced labor through unregulated labor migration schemes and trafficking.[26]

To tackle problems relating to the quality of employment for young people, it is necessary to ensure that labor laws, minimum wage regulations, and social security provisions are fully complied with. Other options include short-term skill training and reskilling programs, improving employment services and job-matching activities, job subsidies, public works programs, microfinance schemes, and the promotion of small businesses, especially those run by young entrepreneurs.[27]

A disputed area in the decent work discussion is how to deal with working children. When children work, they not only earn very low wages, but they are unlikely to attend school every day; if they do, they are likely not to do as well as when they do not have to work.[28] However, poor families often rely on their children's income to survive. In order to reduce child labor, it is therefore necessary to improve the family's financial conditions and to increase the incentive to send children to school. Figure 3.6 shows the extent of child labor in Latin America. Boys between 7 and 14 years old are much more likely to work than girls, at least in the wage labor force. Countries with large indigenous populations, such as Bolivia, Peru, Guatemala, and Paraguay, have a much higher fraction of children working.

As discussed, conditional cash transfers with a schooling condition attached both help supplement families' incomes and reduce the incentive for families to withhold their children from school to send them out to earn money. This decreases child labor, and it also provides an incentive and opportunity for families to have their children continue on to higher levels of schooling and therefore have access to better jobs.

With declining population growth rates and the expectation that the increase in women's labor force participation should peak in the next 15

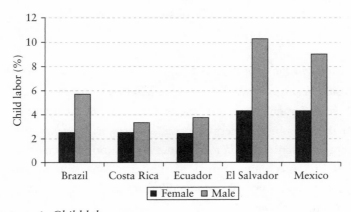

FIGURE 3.6 *Child labor, 2011*

Source: World Bank, World Development Indicators (database).

to 20 years (provided that government policies overcome gender barriers in labor markets), labor supply in the region should begin to stabilize relatively soon. Sustaining economic growth in conditions of limited labor force growth means that governments must immediately start emphasizing the following types of policies that could help raise labor productivity significantly in the next decade:

- Contribute to raising average levels of education among less educated groups in the region—for example, marginal urban, rural, and indigenous.
- Increase the quality of education across all groups.
- Use conditional income transfers to improve pupils' school attendance and preventive health measures in low-income populations.
- Make microcredit available for investment in small, self-owned urban businesses; local energy production; and improved and sustainable food production.
- Improve the quality of labor relations in workplaces with the goal of increasing worker productivity, job mobility, working conditions, and wages.

Finally, it is worth noting that developed-country labor unions are pressuring for fair labor practices in Latin America as an integral part of free trade agreements. Latin American governments can use this pressure to make constructive improvements in their country's workplaces, including work and salary conditions—improvements that increase productivity as well as costs.

Synergy: Investing in Jobs That Are Both Decent and Green

Green and decent jobs are jobs that contribute to preserving and restoring the environment in traditional sectors such as manufacturing and construction or in new, emerging green sectors such as renewable energy and energy efficiency. Green jobs reduce consumption of energy and raw materials, limit greenhouse emissions, minimize waste and pollution, protect and restore ecosystems, and enable enterprises and communities to adapt to climate change.[29]

The concept of green jobs promotes employment that is environmentally friendly, provides decent work opportunities, and aims at achieving societies that are socially inclusive. The concept of green jobs has proven to be very useful, particularly for developing countries faced with the need to address social and environmental challenges at the same time.[30]

In 2012, a joint report released by the International Labour Organization (ILO), the United Nations Environment Programme (UNEP), the International Organization of Employers (IOE), and the International Trade Union Confederation (ITUC) concluded that 15 to 60 million additional jobs are possible. From the supply side, there is also a need to expand the production of green goods. In a recent study, major companies in Europe were asked, "What is the reason for offering green products and services?" The highest share of responses (48 percent) fell into the category "because of customer demand," showing that the market for environmentally friendly products is providing for new growth models.[31]

While outcomes are, of course, country specific, the report argues not only that this potential for jobs creation exists in developed countries, but that emerging and developing countries can also benefit significantly from such a transition. In Chapter 1, I pointed out all of the natural advantages our region has in this regard. It is entirely up to us whether we take or miss this opportunity.[32]

Therefore, Latin America has to increase its green investments. According to the ILO/UNEP/IOE/ITUC report cited above, OECD countries account for the bulk of global renewables investments (almost 82 percent in 2006, of which the European Union and the United States together accounted for 74.1 percent), compared with 7.5 percent for China, 4.3 percent for India, 3.1 percent for Latin America, and 3.5 for all other developing countries.[33]

To ensure the transition from the prevailing economic model to more resource-efficient, socially and environmentally sustainable economies, a comprehensive policy approach is needed. This approach must recognize the relevance of human capital development through investment in green and decent jobs and deliver the right mix of policies, including providing an effective combination of incentives structures and support to facilitate the greening of the economy. This can include environmental tax reform—in particular an eco-tax that shifts the burden to resource use and pollution and away from labor. Part of the revenues from the tax could be used for greening education, skills, and research and development. It can also involve ensuring that investments in greening human capital and employment, decent work, and social inclusion are at the core of any sustainable development strategy.[34]

SUMMING UP

This chapter highlights the next steps Latin America must take to achieve sustainable and inclusive development. I point out that diversifying our regional exports is crucial. We need to inject value-added into our products. I also discuss the need to create decent jobs, the process of expanding conditional cash transfers, microfinance, and green jobs. Chapter 4 focuses on the heterogeneity of Latin American political systems within an overall trend toward inclusive and sustained development in and through democracy. While the region has, overall, achieved a democratic system, there are still several outliers engaging in what is called "competitive authoritarianism."

CHAPTER 4

The Quality of Democracy in Latin America

AS FAR AS I AM CONCERNED, democracy—deep democracy, in which all citizens are convinced that they are full participants in the political process—is a necessary precondition for my vision of a shared society. For me, this is a fundamental premise of building inclusiveness in Latin America. That is why it is important to understand where we stand in the process of developing our democracies. I feel that even with today's unusually encouraging scenario, our democracies are both fragile and far from the level of inclusiveness—in both political and economic terms—required to achieve the "deep democracy" associated with highly developed societies.

Our democracies are fragile because in most Latin American countries they have not been sustained for long periods of time. They have been subject to military takeovers and periods of populist authoritarianism, and these "political habits" continue to hang over our current electorally democratic regimes. Any vision of deepening democracy and a shared society has to consider these alternatives as distinct threats, precisely because today's democracies in Latin America are not "deep"; indeed, many are highly corrupt and skewed in favor of the rich and already powerful, and thus are regarded by many Latin Americans with great suspicion. Yet, that said, these same Latin Americans consider democracy the ideal form of government and one that they value. In this chapter, I assess the Latin American democracy landscape as a basis for understanding how best to move forward against the threats and toward the ideal that such a vast majority of our citizens crave.

SOME HISTORY

You do not have to be a political archeologist to document the origins of democracy in Latin America. Democracy in our region is a relatively recent development. Latin America's early-nineteenth-century independence movements—inspired by the struggle for self-determination in the United States and France—shook the region from south of the Rio Grande to Patagonia. These were the first steps toward liberty that various groups, hardwired into the social strata of Spanish and Portuguese colonial societies, only achieved gradually and in stages. The first beneficiaries of the new freedoms of independence were criollos—a social class comprising the locally born people of pure Spanish ancestry. Then came the blacks, freed from slavery, at various times in the nineteenth century (as in the United States) and, later still, rights for indigenous peoples, still a point of tension today. Unlike in the United States, democracy in Latin America was often interrupted by military coups and dictatorships. Civil rights in Latin America, including the right to vote but also the right to freedom of association and freedom of expression, have not been a constant historical feature of the region and have been granted to various stakeholders in fits and starts.

Rather than full democracies, what we have had in Latin America are proto-democracies—irregular and imperfect systems that only granted democratic rights to those who paid taxes, low as they may have been. The origin of political parties in the region is not associated with European institutionalism, which arose from the appearance of the first parliaments and clustering of social groups or sectors within them, but rather with responses to specific historical situations resulting from ideological debates, antagonistic struggles, or crises marked by violence.[1]

Our countries were initially governed by powerful groups linked to the military. It was somewhat natural that power was configured around guns. Independence in Latin America was a process of struggle and wars led by military men. Once their mission was accomplished, victorious military leaders assumed the responsibility for the construction and conduct of our nascent republics. It was not easy. State building in our region went hand in hand with the configuration of new borders. There were many wars between us to define the territorial limits of our newly liberated countries. Instead of creating a united (or even federated) Latin American region, we fought to divide it among ourselves, usually creating artificial national borders that had little to do with cultural or historical differences between the people living in each of the new nations. In the midst of the wars for independence in which each country raised its flag, anthem, and national identity, we were also igniting the democratic imagination—a far-off dream for many in that stage of independence, and even in the later republican era. The ideal of a "Patria Grande" has always been present in politicians' speeches, but it has always been negated by actions.

This recent democracy in the region as we know it now comes as part of what Samuel Huntington has called the third wave of democratization worldwide. According to Huntington, the first wave of democratization includes the American and French revolutions. The second wave was after World War II when the Allies promoted the establishment of democratic institutions in West Germany, Italy, Austria, and Japan. During the same period, in our region Uruguay and Brazil had established democratic governments, and Costa Rica then returned to democracy in the late 1950s. Argentina, Colombia, Peru, and Venezuela, however, had military governments during this time. For this reason, we say that, in general, Latin America only fully entered a period of democratization during the third wave. The third wave occurred after 1974, beginning with the fall of the 30-year Salazar dictatorship in Portugal, when authoritarian regimes were replaced by democratically elected leaders in approximately 30 countries in Europe, Asia, and Latin America.[2]

Thus, Latin America began its "Democratic Spring" just over 30 years ago. It is only since the late 1970s and early 1980s that we can say the region is democratic as defined by Schumpeter, Huntington, and others' minimalist theory of democracy: a system of government that is born and reborn in the voting booth. In 1977, only Costa Rica and Venezuela could be considered democratic countries. The remaining 16 countries were ruled by military or civilian dictatorships of various stripes.[3] As noted recently by the president of the Inter-American Development Bank, Luis Alberto Moreno, "It seems incredible, but just 30 years ago, only a third of the 18 countries in the region were governed democratically."[4]

Huge progress has been made. Almost every country in Latin America today enjoys some form of democracy. Elections take place regularly; we now have relative separation of powers, vigorous freedom of expression (although with lingering shadows of repression in some countries), and open trade policies that increasingly integrate us into the world economy. The challenge facing us now is one of creating a higher-quality democracy, building on the institutional and political practices that have been established.

Four decades ago, civil rights were virtually absent in the region. In that long period, authoritarianism was the hallmark of governments in this part of the world. Latin America was a region where presidents came to power to stay for as many years as they controlled the military, regardless of civil liberties. Somoza, Stroessner, Pinochet, Odria, and Velasco are names that date back to a time when the word *democracy* simply did not exist in the region. The achievement of democracy in Latin America was the result of a long process of maturation of social forces that lay dormant in our countries for many decades and finally bloomed in the late 1970s. Between 1977 and 1994, 15 of 16 countries that were considered undemocratic in Latin America embraced democracy. The exception was, and remains, Cuba.[5]

This is not to say that democracy had never existed in the region, but democracy has been intermittent. Between the 1960s and the 1970s, there was a surge of military coups in Latin America. These autocratic governments supported an "inward facing" economic development known as the import substitution model.[6] Import substitution industrialization (ISI) is when a nation isolates itself from trade and tries to industrialize using only its domestic market as an engine. The policy was partially successful but was costly and ran out of steam in the economic turbulence of the 1970s. Argentina, Brazil, Chile, Uruguay, and Peru are examples of this period when debt grew and foreign capital largely was driven away from the region. When the United States' monetary policy raised real interest rates worldwide to stop its own inflation in the early 1980s, Latin American economies and the ISI development model collapsed. As the effects of the collapse worsened living conditions for many, the working classes in the region began organizing protest movements that demanded freedom and civil rights, together with changes of regimes.

The transition to full democracy did not follow the same path in every country. Each country's story has its nuances and peculiarities. The vote—one of the requisite elements of a true democracy—was not granted to everyone at the same time. Different social classes each had to fight for their right. In Peru, for example, women could not vote in local elections until the 1950s. The illiterate could only vote after the Constitution of 1979 was ratified. The elections themselves have improved and became more transparent and reliable over time. About the same time the literacy requirement was dropped in Peru, Mexico was undergoing a process of opening up channels for more competitive political elections. Slowly but surely, the certainty of winning that candidates of the Partido Revolucionario Institucional (PRI) had held was challenged, until in 2000 the party experienced its first electoral defeat after 71 years in power.[7]

These fluctuations in the longer trend toward democracy have made us a region with only a recent memory of democracy. But we also have great hope that this will not be a barrier to deepening and strengthening the ability of the system to deliver tangible democratic benefits. We have seen that the system can work in the region, but it has not always delivered the measurable results we hoped for, especially for our poorest groups. We will talk about this more in Chapter 9 when we discuss strengthening the state capacity needed for this delivery system to function.

Not everyone agrees that being able to deliver concrete and tangible results to the population is necessarily the goal of a democratic system. There are theorists who say that democracy is simply an election mechanism, a system of control and power that favors civil liberties, a regime where the law prevails, and that these things do not necessarily ensure a successful government or the solution to all the problems of society.

This may be a valid argument in academia, but in the real world, where people's lives and livelihoods are at stake, it is imperative that we make democracy deliver concrete results to people. In addition to the moral imperative of having a government that is *by* and *for* the people, if we do not deliver results, there is always the possibility that the neglected masses will rise against the democratic states themselves and undermine social stability—or worse, rise up in their dissatisfaction and actually bring an end to the constitutional order, the rule of law, and even to democratic governance itself. At a minimum, we should be able to expect that our democracies represent all citizens relatively well. In other words, democratic governments should recognize and guarantee basic civil rights for all (i.e., life, liberty, property) and should try to channel and address the demands of the people. This is what makes a democratic government legitimate.[8]

ELECTORAL DEMOCRACY AND POLITICAL HETEROGENEITY

What is not in doubt is that the region has, by and large, instituted electoral democracies. Other than Cuba, all governments are now considered electoral democracies. What are still under debate are the variants, quality, and depth of those democracies when you look beyond simply holding elections. In its report *Freedom in the World 2012*, Freedom House measured the range of freedom and civil rights in 195 countries and produced a ranking of whether countries were more or less democratic according to these variables. They found that in Latin America, only Chile, Costa Rica, and Uruguay had developed democracies that provided their citizens with rights nearly equivalent to those found in democratic nations in Europe, Canada, and the United States. Brazil, the Dominican Republic, Panama, Colombia, El Salvador, Mexico, and Peru were considered slightly lower-level democracies that had reliable electoral systems, peaceful transition between political parties, and a separation of powers between the different branches of government. Nicaragua and Venezuela were rated lowest, with the least depth of democracy and fewest freedoms and civil rights in the region.[9]

In Larry Diamond's words, while most of the countries in the region have achieved the status of electoral democracies, only a few can be considered liberal democracies.[10] I understand liberal democracy, following Diamond's definition, as a "thick" conception of democracy (in contrast to the "thin" minimalist conception presented above). On this thick side, a political system should be considered a liberal democracy only when it ensures the following attributes:

- Substantial individual freedom of belief, opinion, discussion, speech, publication, broadcast, assembly, demonstration, petition, and the Internet

- Freedom of ethnic, religious, racial, and other minority groups (as well as historically excluded majorities) to practice their religion and culture and to participate equally in political and social life
- The right of all adult citizens to vote and to run for office (if they meet certain minimum age and competency requirements)
- Genuine openness and competition in the electoral arena
- Legal equality of all citizens under a rule of law
- An independent judiciary to neutrally and consistently apply the law and protect individual and groups rights
- Thus, due process of law and freedom of individuals from torture, terror, and unjustified detention, exile, or interference in their personal lives—by the state or nonstate actors
- Institutional checks on the power of elected officials, by an independent legislature, court system, and other autonomous agencies
- Real pluralism in sources of information and forms of organization independent of the state, and thus a vibrant "civil society"
- Control over the military and state security apparatus[11]

The recent history of Latin America is characterized by "political heterogeneity"[12] across countries. In 2010, the center-right governments of presidents-elect Sebastian Piñera and Juan Manuel Santos were voted into power in Chile and Colombia, respectively. In Brazil, the center-left Dilma Rousseff won the vote. The same happened in Chile with Michelle Bachelet in 2014. The 2011 elections saw Ollanta Humala in Peru win with a center-left rhetoric that was more moderate than the one he voiced in 2006, and his enacted policies are even more moderate than his rhetoric. In Guatemala the center-right Otto Perez Molina won, whereas in Argentina a center-left Cristina Kirchner took the elections. In Ecuador a "socialist of the 21st century," Rafael Correa, was reelected in the first round of voting. In Venezuela, in a disputed and very close election held to replace Hugo Chavez, Nicolas Maduro, Chavez's vice-president with similar socialist views, was apparently elected. Clearly there is not a regional conformity in political leanings, which seems to symbolize the triumph of democracy in the region.

What we need to do now is deepen the democracies we have established. This requires extending democratic rights to everyone in our societies: every individual has the right to participate in the political process, be protected under a rule of law that is fair and equitable, and live within social and economic systems that ensure fair and equal access to information. For political scientists such as Guillermo O'Donnell, Larry Diamond, Juan Linz, and Seymour Martin Lipset, this kind of democracy is a system of governance that ensures meaningful and extensive competition among individuals and organized groups (especially political parties) for all effective positions of power in government through regular, free, and fair elections that do not include the use of force or exclude any social groups. This kind of democracy guarantees a certain level of civil and political liberties, including freedom of expression, freedom of the press, freedom to form and join organizations, and the integrity of political competition and participation.[13]

DEMOCRACY IN THE REGION AND ITS QUALITY

According to Latinobarómetro (2013), support for democracy, on average, fell in the region in 2010–2013 from 61 percent to 56 percent after four years of steady increases.[14] While democracy is now overwhelmingly considered the preferred system of government, the recent decrease is disappointing considering that more than half of Latin Americans lived under military rule less than a generation ago. Additionally, only 8 percent of adult Latin Americans consider that there is full democracy in their country, while a majority of them believe that democracy faces important problems (46 percent)[15] or that it is not really a democracy (9 percent).

But perhaps the results reflect how each individual country has its own characteristics and interpretations of what democracy is: Latin America is diverse. It is not just a single homogeneous geographical area. The results could also be interpreted as a claim lodged by citizens against a state that is not, in their estimation, delivering what they would expect a fair democracy to deliver. Now that Latin Americans have become used to "basic" democracy, they have begun to expect more of it, and they are not content with how their current systems are working. Democracy brings greater demand for a quality, "deepened" democracy, and this is reflected in the polls. We must try to ensure that these results create a demand for strengthening the system and not weakening it.

By any standards, democracy in Latin America is still the system that Latin Americans prefer above any other system of government. Except for 3 of the 18 countries in the sample (Guatemala, Mexico, and Bolivia), citizens indicated they felt democracy is preferable to any other form of government. The warning is that a very large proportion of the population do not seem entirely satisfied with the quality of democracy we have.

One of the underlying reasons for this dissatisfaction is probably because our democratic governments are either failing to deliver results (i.e., access to basic services like health, education, and infrastructure) or are doing so at an unacceptably slow pace. There are whole communities in Latin America that have waited 40 years to have access to potable drinking water or electricity. Can we expect someone who has not seen an improvement in his or her quality of life on these basic matters to give democracy a favorable review?

THREAT 1: WHAT ABOUT THE SPECTER OF A MILITARY COUP?

Fortunately, what does seem to have disappeared from the horizon in the region is the interruption of democracy via the classic military coup. The call to the barracks that was characteristic of the regime change pendulum in Latin America seems to have been safely eradicated with the advance of what could be called civic consciousness. This is reinforced by a more interconnected world in which military coups are increasingly considered an unacceptable form of regime change. The Inter-American Democratic Charter, adopted by the Organization of American States in 2001, is a direct expression of the new illegitimacy that nondemocratic forms of government have in the region. The charter states that "the peoples of Latin America have a right to democracy, and their governments have an obligation to protect and defend it" (http://oas.org/charter/docs/resolution1_en_p4.htm).

However, it may surprise some that, even with such a high level of approval for democracy, many citizens would support a military regime in extreme situations of "high crime" or "corruption." The Latinobarómetro report (2011) found that in Peru, 55 percent of respondents in 2010 felt a military coup might be justified in the case of a corrupted democratic process.[16] The study found evidence that a perception of poor economic performance under the incumbent government increased the degree of support for military takeovers. Popular support for democratic transition was also weakened by a lack of tangible results or a mishandling of a crisis situation.

The most recent situation regarding the exercise of military power against a democratically elected government was in Honduras in 2009, when a group of soldiers forcibly relocated the sitting president out of the country, a move that was widely discussed and explained later as an act required by the civil authority. The military action was condemned by the Organization of American States (OAS), but ultimately it was shown that both the legislative and judicial branches adhered to the constitution and laws of the country.[17] Other than this use of military force, the region does not seem in danger of falling back on military coups.

According to Latinobarómetro (2011), military rule in Latin America is rejected by the majority of people in at least 13 of the 18 countries. In total, 66 percent of Latin Americans report they would not under any circumstances accept a military government, an increase of three percentage points compared to the same survey a year earlier. Yet, this figure has its own nuances in each country. In Paraguay (52 percent), Mexico (53 percent), and Peru (54 percent), the population appears divided about rejecting the military, while Guatemala is the only country in the region where less than a majority—40 percent—say they would reject a military government (meaning 60 percent would accept!).[18]

THREAT 2: COMPETITIVE AUTHORITARIANISM VERSUS DEMOCRACY

I said earlier that the region is not a homogeneous bloc but rather is made up of unique, individual countries characterized by similarities and differences. With the exception of Cuba, all of them are electoral democracies and have relatively open economies. In some countries, electoral systems are characterized by regular, transparent, competitive elections, but in others, also with elements of representative democracy, democratic mechanisms are manipulated by the government to extend its reach so it can change the rules of the game and concentrate power, restrict freedom of expression, and have full control over the management of the economy.

Various studies of these countries describe the political system in the latter group of countries as one of "competitive authoritarianism,"[19] that is, systems that are legitimized through the results of electoral competition in which opposition groups exist, although there are not generalized conditions of equal competition in elections for all political groups. Levitsky and Way affirm that while competitive authoritarian regimes fall short of democracy, they also fall short of full-scale authoritarianism.[20] In competitive authoritarianism, violations of the minimum criteria of modern democratic regimes are both frequent enough and serious enough to create an uneven playing field between government and opposition. Although elections are regularly held and are generally free of massive fraud, incumbents usually abuse state resources, deny the opposition adequate media coverage, harass opposition candidates and their supporters, and in some cases manipulate electoral results. Journalists, opposition politicians, and other government critics may be spied on, threatened, harassed, or arrested. Members of the opposition may be jailed, exiled, or—less frequently—even assaulted or murdered. However, although incumbents in competitive authoritarian regimes may routinely manipulate formal democratic rules, they are unable to eliminate them or reduce them to a mere façade. Rather than openly violating democratic rules, incumbents are more likely to use bribery, co-option, and more subtle forms of persecution, such as the use of tax authorities, compliant judiciaries, and other state agencies to legally harass, persecute, or extort cooperative behavior from critics.[21]

In other words, the result is a minimalist democracy in which the political leader, once elected, adopts rather authoritarian forms of behavior, such as changing the constitution, politicizing the judiciary, restricting freedom of expression, or using up public resources in an unsustainable manner. For instance, some elected leaders distort government programs to further their electoral ends; this is particularly true of programs with large amounts of resources, such as education, health services, and conditional cash transfers. This neopopulist conduct ultimately undermines democracy because it transforms efforts to develop the creative capacities of the poor into programs that reproduce political power, usually convincing the poor to be dependent on the state without resolving any of the underlying structures of their dependency. This kind of pseudo-populist system was tested very well in my country in the 1990s with then president Fujimori. It has since been refined in other countries in the region.

Why is there support for such pseudo-populist, less "democratic" systems? It is clear that Latin Americans support democracy over any other form of government, but we still want to see results. This is reflected in a general dissatisfaction among Latin Americans with the lack of progress in democracy—namely, about 70 percent of the population believe that democracy in their country is not moving forward or has gotten worse.[22]

If we look a little closer at the data, we find that one of the prime reasons for the discontent is crime, followed by unemployment, according to Latinobarómetro (2011 and 2013). Corruption is considered another serious issue; 48 percent of Latin Americans feel that democracy has not curbed the advance of corruption, 33 percent believe it should do more to ensure social justice, and 31 percent think democracy has not done enough to increase citizen participation or improve government transparency mechanisms.[23]

Even in the best interpretation of the data there is clearly dissatisfaction in Latin America about the tangible results of democracy thus far. Yet, in countries with restricted democracies or competitive authoritarianism, such as Ecuador, Argentina, and Venezuela, people seem largely satisfied with the kind of democracy they have. Despite their *apetito reeleccionista* (craving to be reelected),[24] Correa has a high and rising approval rating (73 percent in 2013), Kirchner has fallen substantially (from 57 percent to 43 percent in 2011–2013) but still maintains substantial satisfaction, and Maduro's government is supported by almost half (47 percent) of Venezuelans.[25]

Socioeconomic status and level of education are frequently pointed to by studies as factors in people's support for democracy. Some of these studies conclude that certain segments of society are more vulnerable than others to supporting undemocratic alternatives: as Carrión and Zárate state, "The poor in particular seem to lead this group of 'fickle friends of democracy,' as they have been seen at the head of protests against democratic governments during times of economic crisis."[26]

Regarding the education factor, the Latinobarómetro study referred to above found that "age and education are the most important determinants of support for democracy. This result is consistent with our studies of democracy in the Americas and once again reinforces the idea that education is one of the most effective ways to build a political culture of support for democracy."[27]

Przeworski's studies[28] also found a cause-and-effect relationship between economic progress (which includes income distribution and social mobility) and democracy, in the sense that "underdevelopment, slow economic growth, and gross inequalities in income distribution affect the consolidation of democracy" and also that "democracies in poorer countries are more likely to perish when they experience economic crises than when their economies grow."[29]

The less educated masses and poor are the numerical majority. They are much more pragmatic in their desires, and they expect immediate results. In this respect they are more vulnerable to populist government policies that distort the concept of a democracy that delivers results. These governments have strong subsidy policies, based on their own resources: commodities, which currently command an excellent price in the international market but are not renewable. This allows them to allocate large budgets to emergency programs or social assistance, which by their nature should be temporary, but in the hands of populist governments end up becoming permanent. The policy of giving someone a fish rather than teaching her to fish is unsustainable in the long term.

Populism is a form of government that uses confrontation as a management tool on the one hand and cooperation-submission on the other. The former works against those who oppose the regime, and the second works with all partners and, in turn, has two aspects: clientelism that is targeted at the poorest and most vulnerable, and perks that favor the middle and business classes.[30] When there is no quality education, entrepreneurship and freedom cannot grow; when democracy is not inclusive and effective, it is fertile ground for growing competitive-authoritarian regimes. Therefore, the defense of human rights should not be understood only as an opposition to extreme abuses, such as governments using violence against their citizens. Rather, it is also about how to quiet the noises of empty stomachs and broken dreams. It is about how a democratic state can ensure a decent life for all children born into our societies.

INSTITUTIONAL TRUST AND PERSONAL TRUST

Interpersonal trust is the key to understanding the strength of the social fabric on which democratic institutions must stand. What is still under discussion is whether this interpersonal trust is a product of a greater civic culture that improves the quality of democratic institutions or whether, on the contrary, it is the quality of democratic institutions that develops a deeper civic culture and institutional trust. Either way, the fact is that Latin Americans are still far from our European counterparts and the United States on the issues of interpersonal trust or trust in our institutions and democratic system. In Europe, trust indicators reach 70 percent, while in Latin America they sit at only 22 percent. In Peru, the confidence level is even lower: 18 percent.[31]

In addition, we are still a region that does not fully trust the institutions undergirding our societies. Figure 4.1 shows the trend in institutional trust for seven institutions in Latin America, from 1996 to 2011. The Church was historically one of the most trusted institutions in the region, but it has suffered a tremendous blow in recent years. Confidence in the Church as an institution has fallen from 76 percent in 1996 to 64 percent in 2011. Political parties are another institution in the region that cannot seem to engender high levels of trust—perhaps for the reasons we have pointed to here, including the lack of actions that will result in medium- and long-term benefits for the majority of people living in Latin America.

There is also a paradox in the region with regard to political parties and their relationship with the strengthening of our democratic systems. A common phrase in political theory is that "there can be no democracy without political parties." On the one hand, 58 percent of Latin Americans claim to be aware that political parties are one of the essential parts of any democracy. This awareness increased two percentage points between 2010 and 2011. But it is one thing to say it and another thing to practice it. Political parties are at the bottom of the ratings in assessments of

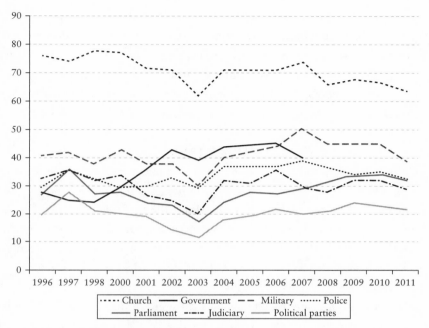

FIGURE 4.1 *Institutional trust, 1996–2011*

Source: Graph prepared by the author based on Latinobarómetro (2011).

citizens' confidence in institutions. In 1996, 20 percent of Latinobarómetro interviewees said they had some trust in political parties. In 1997, the figure reached its highest point of 28 percent of the interviewees expressing trust in these institutions. In contrast, political parties hit bottom with 11 percent in 2003, and according to the latest Latinobarómetro publication on this issue (2011), political parties scored 22 percent.

In other words, we Latin Americans are aware that political parties are essential to democracy, but we do not have confidence in them and therefore we do not tend to participate in political organizations. When people were asked which of the following things you should not fail to do if you want to be considered a citizen, only 14 percent responded "participate in a political party" (Latinobarómetro 2011). Nevertheless, Latin America continues the effort to strengthen its party structures and has tested a series of electoral reforms, including internal-to-party elections of candidates and increased transparency of fundraising and financial reporting.

Latin Americans have little confidence in the police, the judiciary, and the legislature, and this holds true regardless of any increase or decrease in economic growth. I especially want to emphasize here the general decline in confidence in institutions no matter how we measure it. As reported in Latinobarómetro, "We are facing a widespread disenchantment of the population as a whole about all of the major institutions in our society."[32]

MOVING FORWARD

Without dwelling too much on the types of democracy we have in the region, what the Latinobarómetro study indicates is that most Latin Americans want governments that are working for both the majorities and minorities in our countries. We Latin Americans want to see governments working to better distribute income, and we also want our governments to be increasing the size of the pie.[33] In other words, we want a functioning democracy that delivers results.

In this sense, democracy takes on a different dimension. Rather than just being a system of government, the idea of a democracy acquires a practical dimension as an organizing mechanism for more efficient economic development but also more equal social distribution.

Citizens . . . judge its [democracy's] virtues from the perspective of their experience of contact with its institutions or their impact on their own lives. In a context of low educational levels and information that is politicized by partisan media, they judge democracy on what they experience and have experienced in their daily lives. A citizen who is or has been in a situation of social or economic exclusion and for whom institutions such as political parties and parliament have done little will attach a low value to these institutions. In this first generation of citizens exposed to it, democracy tends to be judged by its results.[34]

In his quite optimistic view about the future of Latin America, Luis Alberto Moreno notes, "The experience of the last decades in the region has also shown that the democratic system, beyond ensuring the effective realization of civil rights, is the best framework to establish open, inclusive, and cooperative societies."[35]

Latin Americans today have greater awareness of our civil and social rights, and at the same time, we differentiate between economic and social guarantees. In other words, more people believe it is better to guarantee rights such as freedom of religion (76 percent), choice of profession (70 percent), free participation in politics (66 percent), or freedom of expression (59 percent), and fewer believe it is essential to ensure rights such as guaranteeing equal opportunities for employment (36 percent), access to social security (36 percent), or a fair distribution of wealth (31 percent).[36]

However, there is evidence of progress from our years of economic discipline and sustained growth: 150 million Latin Americans have moved into the middle class in the past decade.[37] The World Bank defines *middle class* as households that face a low probability of falling into poverty. In Latin America, it means households earning approximately between $10 and $50 per person per day on a PPP-adjusted basis.[38] There is also a perception that distributive justice seems to have improved, although the change in perception (and the change in reality) is modest. Latinobarómetro reports, "On examining the justice of income distribution, we find that in 2013, for the first time since measurement of this indicator began in 2001, 25 percent of Latin Americans consider it "fair." Between 2001 and 2007, this figure increased by ten points, from 11 percent to 21 percent.[39]

An even more dynamic change is observed in access to the most common technology available to the poor: the cell phone. Seventy-eight percent of the population now have a mobile telephone device in Latin America, and the percentage continues to increase. If we measure the potential for social mobility by access to education, that, too, has increased. According to the Economic Commission for Latin America and the Caribbean (ECLAC), those in the labor force with secondary education increased from 20 percent to 35 percent, while the number of those with higher education has more than doubled, from 7 percent to 18 percent.

The business climate has also steadily improved. The "Latin American Economic Climate" indicator—developed by the private economic research center Getulio Vargas Foundation (FGV) of Brazil and the University of Munich—stood at 5.5 points in January, which is 5.2 points above October 2013 and 5 points above January 2012.[40] A similar trend can be seen in the "Doing Business" report published by the World Bank, which reveals there has been progress in the region in terms of investment climate. But the report also suggests that policy makers seeking to strengthen the private sector need to pay attention not only to macroeconomic factors but also to the quality of the laws, regulations, and institutional arrangements governing daily economic life.[41]

Specialized media such as *The Economist* and others have highlighted the positive progress in the business climate as well as the advance of democracy in the region: "The democracy index, calculated in 2010 by the Economist Intelligence Unit for 167 countries, placed Latin America and the Caribbean in the best levels, just after North America and Western Europe. This indicator focuses on five general categories: electoral process and pluralism, civil liberties, government functionality, participation, and political culture."[42]

I am not going to focus on them all here, but I do want to point out that these issues will be underlying the discussion throughout this book. Economic growth in and of itself is not the goal; the goal is how to take advantage of the growth to make sure the benefits reach those most in need. That is, how do we transform this period of economic growth into a time of providing better opportunities for all? Quality education, health services, and infrastructure are crucial to this discussion and the basis on which we can build more trust in government and a sense of inclusion in the decision-making process.

Better distribution of quality public services is key to becoming a shared society. As I state repeatedly, when those at the bottom and the middle feel that the "public" in the public sector is serving them, they believe that democracy is more than just symbolic. Beyond better distribution of services, however, deepened democracy requires increasing political participation at every level of government and developing trust in the political institutions serving this participating public. Below I discuss the problems of public corruption and violence that destroy that trust and generate cynicism and fear of participating in the political process. Beyond the issue of economic distribution, deepening democracy in our region demands directly taking on such underlying institutional problems.

SUMMING UP

The purpose of this chapter is to introduce the reader to the heterogeneity of Latin America's political systems. Whereas most of our countries enjoy a democratic system, there are important differences among them. Their quality varies tremendously from one country to another. I identified three main types of political regimes: liberal democracies, electoral democracies, and competitive authoritarianism.

In Chapter 5, I focus on the challenges that poverty and inequality pose for development. As I mentioned in Chapter 1, increasing economic and social equality is one of the three fundamental propositions of my view of progress. In other words, Chapter 5 addresses an indispensable condition that Latin America must meet if it is to make the leap forward to inclusive growth and sustainable development by 2050.

CHAPTER 5

Eradicating Poverty, Reducing Inequality, and Promoting Sustainable Development

I HAVE SPELLED OUT a vision for a highly developed Latin America in 2050. To achieve that vision, I believe Latin America needs to be much more equitable and more socially inclusive. Steady, long-term economic growth is clearly important to these objectives; however, economic growth is not the end but rather the *means* to development. Development is synonymous with improvements in people's well-being, not simply improvements in a nation's gross domestic product. Money does not have an intrinsic value. The value of money is in what it can purchase, and what it is used to purchase—for example, access to health care, schooling, food, and housing—can improve personal welfare and shape the nature of society. If we want to have a shared society—if we want to have healthy societies, healthy economies, and healthy democracies—we need to use our money to invest in the minds and well-being of all our people.

Until relatively recently, many development theorists and policy makers seemed to focus on economic growth without considering whether it was the kind of growth that improved people's quality of life. During the 1980s and 1990s, the development theory in vogue was neoliberalism, which promoted, among other things, free markets and secure property rights. It also advanced the "trickle-down" hypothesis, which claims that any economic growth, even when it benefits only a small, already well-off group of families at the top of the income pyramid and is initially hard on the poor, is good for the entire society because the wealth will trickle down to the "bottom" as the wealthy spend what they have earned. In this framework, inequality was not regarded as essentially bad but simply as a step along the way to greater economic progress.

These ideas still hold sway in policy circles, but they have been widely criticized. First, while economic growth is an essential part of addressing poverty, economic growth is not sufficient to reduce poverty. The real question is, who receives the benefits of economic growth? In part, this depends on levels of inequality. Inequality and poverty are intricately related, and it turns out that initial levels of inequality have been shown to have a dual effect on poverty. They may slow economic growth (making the benefits "pot" smaller than it could be), while also reducing the portion or share of the economic growth that poorer people receive (Birdsall and Londoño 1997; Wodon and Yitzhaki 2002). This connection with poverty means that inequality should be particularly important to all policy makers and leaders who are interested in reducing national or global levels of poverty. So reducing poverty and inequality can also be a means to achieving the more traditional measure of development: economic growth.

Second, focusing on economic growth as a single development goal ignores what people actually care about: the quality of life. In the 1990s, we began to realize that while many countries were successful in terms of their rate of economic growth, they still had large proportions of citizens who lived in poverty or did not have access to basic services. Economic growth was not improving well-being the way it was meant to. The recognition that economic growth was a means to, and not just an ultimate goal of, development seemed to have been forgotten. Economists and development theorists began to consider ideas of development beyond the world of economics and to explore how they could define development differently—not just in terms of an abstract "income per capita" but rather in terms of human "capabilities" and freedoms.

Amartya Sen, a Nobel Prize–winning economist, is the best-known proponent of the human capability perspective on development.[1] His writings advanced the "development as freedom" concept that identifies key opportunities people must access to develop the capabilities they need to be able to freely choose their own life path. He makes the case that education and health care, as well as political and economic participation, are "constituent" freedoms, meaning they are essential in their own right (not just as a means to increasing economic growth). They are needed "to realize human potential in a broader sense" (Sen 2001; Watkins 2000). The United Nations Development Programme (UNDP) defines this as "people's effective freedom to choose between options they consider valuable and have reason to value" (UNDP 2010, 17).

The fundamental lesson for those of us who are leaders is that if governments are meant to help enable their citizens to live productive and fulfilling lives, they should focus on ensuring access to these constituent freedoms instead of just trusting that economic growth will automatically provide them. Sen himself defines the goal as "advancing the richness of human life, rather than the richness of the economy in which human beings live, which is only a part [of human experience]."[2] This is aligned closely with our vision of a shared society.

WHY DO WE CARE ABOUT INEQUALITY?

Income inequality is starkly on the rise across the world. According to Oxfam, almost half the world's wealth is owned by 1 percent of the population, while the bottom half of the world's population owns the same amount as the richest 85 individuals in the world. Since 1980, the richest 1 percent have increased their share of income in 24 out of 26 countries for which data are available.[3] This worrisome situation applies to developed and developing countries. In the United States, the share of income taken by the top 1 percent has more than doubled since the 1980s, returning to where it was on the eve of the Great Depression. Since 2009, the richest 1 percent have captured 95 percent of all income gains, while the bottom 90 percent have gotten poorer. The International Labour Organization affirms that labor's share of income has fallen over the past two decades in 26 out of 30 advanced economies—even though labor productivity has risen.

There is no doubt that inequality is one of the most entrenched scourges of our age. Inequality is highlighted in this chapter because inequality and poverty are intricately related and because inequality is also directly related to well-being. If we do not address issues of inequality, it is much more difficult to address poverty. A country that has eliminated poverty but remains highly unequal will not be a shared society and will continue to experience social unrest.

As mentioned, high initial levels of inequality can slow economic growth and reduce the share of the economic growth that poorer people receive. These effects have been attributed to a variety of factors, ranging from inequality established during the colonial era to government ineffectiveness to inequalities in access to social services. While many maintain that inequality affects only the poor, we believe inequality hampers the achievement and well-being of even the most privileged—thereby putting a cap on a society's potential in a broad set of economic and social domains.

Wilkinson and Pickett (2011) call developed countries with high levels of inequality (such as the United States) societies that have achieved material success but social failure. How or why this is the case can be seen in the research of Neckerman and Torche (2007) and Wilkinson and Pickett (2011), who explore the consequences of inequality in a society. Their list of social ills either caused or exacerbated by inequality comprises a surprising number of diverse problems, including:

- Poorer health—increased obesity, heart disease, and so on, and decreased life expectancy
- Decreased educational performance, particularly of poorer children
- Increased crime, especially violent crime and homicides, and increased incarceration for all types of crime
- Increased mental illness and negative effects on individuals' sense of psychological well-being
- An increased proportion of teenage births, infant mortality, and lower overall children's well-being
- Decreased social mobility or "equality of opportunity" (individuals are more likely to remain in the income stratum of their parents)
- Diminished levels of trust in, and connectedness with, fellow citizens

What is striking about the evidence presented by Wilkinson and Pickett and Neckerman and Torche is that these effects are found in *all* strata of society. For example, while poor children do much better educationally in more equal countries, the wealthiest children in more equal countries also do better than the wealthiest children in unequal countries.

The societal effects of inequality suggest that, ultimately, inequality contributes to the slow breakdown of community, and thus society, through increased alienation from fellow citizens, increased segregation, decreased social mobility, and increased frustration, anger, and psychological angst regarding a social and political system that does not seem to serve the interests of the majority. If Latin America is going to make its leap forward to becoming a socially inclusive society, we must tackle inequality head on.

WHERE IS LATIN AMERICA IN TERMS OF INEQUALITY?

Over the past two decades, Latin America has made progress in terms of reducing income inequality. The standard way to measure inequality is with the Gini coefficient. The Gini coefficient calculates how equally or unequally a population's income is distributed. It can range from 0, which represents everyone having an equal share of wealth, to 1, which represents one person having all the wealth. The closer to 1 a population is, the closer it is to perfect *in*equality.

The average Gini coefficient for the region has decreased from 0.5311 in 2000 to 0.4933 in 2010,[4] and in almost all Latin America countries, the Gini coefficient in 2010 was lower than it was in 2000 and, in fact, lower than it has been for 30 years. It is one of the only regions that has decreased inequality (as measured by the Gini and by the distribution of income by deciles) since 2000.

However, Latin America is still the *most unequal* region in the world in terms of income inequality. It is promising that some progress has been made in terms of decreasing inequality, but inequality among and within countries remains very high. On average, the top 10 percent of income earners in the region received 38 percent of the income in 2012, down from 43 percent in 2002; the bottom 40 percent received 12 percent of the income, up from 10 percent in 2002. Table 5.1 shows the distribution of income by deciles in different countries in the early 2000s and in 2011–2012. The important point to note is that the bottom 40 percent of income earners still earned only 12 percent of all income. In my country, Peru, the bottom 40 percent of income earners increased their share somewhat more, but only from 11 to 13 percent in 12 years of very rapid growth.

Measuring inequality in terms of income (as the Gini coefficient or the decile distribution does) probably underestimates the extent of the inequality with respect to what we really care about—access to opportunities or the development of capabilities—because it does not include differential access to basic services, wealth, and social capital (such as

TABLE 5.1 *Percentage change in share of national income,*
2000–2002 to 2011–2012

Country/years	Bottom 40 percent of income earners	Middle 40 percent of income earners	Top 20 percent of income earners	Top 10 percent of income earners
Bolivia				
2000	6.2	26.0	67.6	52.0
2011	12.2	36.8	51.2	34.0
Brazil				
2001	7.2	25.2	67.8	52.8
2012	9.8	29.6	60.8	46.2
Chile				
2000	10.2	28.4	61.4	46.2
2011	12.4	30.2	57.4	42.2
Colombia				
2000	10.2	28.4	61.4	46.2
2012	10.6	31.4	57.8	41.8
Costa Rica				
2000	12.6	35.6	52.0	35.2
2012	11.6	33.2	55.2	38.2
Ecuador				
2000	10.2	29.0	60.8	45.4
2012	13.2	34.6	52.0	35.6
Mexico				
2000	10.6	30.6	59.0	43.2
2012	12.8	32.2	54.8	39.4
Peru				
2001	10.8	32.6	56.6	40.6
2012	13.4	36.6	49.6	33.4
Venezuela				
2000	12.8	36.0	51.4	34.4
2012	15.6	38.2	46.0	29.6
Latin America[a]				
2002	10.1	30.9	59.0	43.0
2012	12.2	33.5	54.3	38.2

Source: Economic Commission for Latin America and the Caribbean, CEPALSTAT, Social Indicators,
Income Distribution.
[a]Simple average.

social networks that can help with finding work). It is likely that an inequality measure that took these factors into account would find inequality even higher than it appears in the Gini coefficient, particularly because wealth is distributed much more unequally than income almost everywhere in the world.

To get a sense of the negative impact inequality has on well-being, let's take a look at the UNDP's Human Development Index (HDI; see Table 5.2). When adjusted for inequality, the HDI show significant change in the levels of human development in each region. Whereas Latin America scores 0.73 on the HDI overall, once inequality is incorporated, this falls to 0.54—a loss of 26 percent!

My point is that high levels of inequality negatively affect well-being, cohesion, and inclusion. Though some of the structural sources of inequality may be difficult to address in the short term, if we do not put together a plan to tackle inequality, it will be nearly impossible to be successful in combating our other challenges discussed below. And it will be nearly impossible—even if we maintain high economic growth rates with these levels of inequality—to achieve our 2050 vision of an inclusive, shared society.

Apart from being high, inequality in Latin America has been persistent and associated with low mobility. First, let's look at the persistence of inequality: the most unequal countries in the early 2000s were also the most unequal in 2010. In the *Regional Human Development Report for Latin America and the Caribbean 2010*, UNDP found a high correlation between the level of education of one generation and the next, which was within the range of 0.37 and 0.61, while the US coefficient was 0.21.[5] These results indicate that in 16 Latin American countries, the level of education of a generation influences the next one more than twice as much as it would in the United States. The probability that a person reaches at most the educational level of his or her parents is higher in Latin America and the Caribbean than in other high-income countries. As mentioned above, education is a determinant of a person's income, so the above statistics point to a close correlation between intergenerational income and persistent inequality.[6]

Second, low mobility has been due to resistance to any effort to eradicate poverty. There has been no equitable growth in Latin America and

TABLE 5.2 *Human Development Index, by world regions, 2012*

Region	Human Development Index (HDI)	Inequality-adjusted HDI (IHDI)		Inequality-adjusted life expectancy index		Inequality-adjusted education index		Inequality-adjusted income index	
	Value	Value	Loss (%)	Value	Loss (%)	Value	Loss (%)	Value	Loss (%)
Arab states	0.652	0.486	25.4	0.669	16.7	0.320	39.6	0.538	17.5
East Asia and the Pacific	0.683	0.537	21.3	0.711	14.2	0.480	21.9	0.455	27.2
Europe and Central Asia	0.771	0.672	12.9	0.716	11.7	0.713	10.5	0.594	16.3
Latin America and the Caribbean	0.741	0.550	25.7	0.744	13.4	0.532	23.0	0.421	38.5
South Asia	0.558	0.395	29.1	0.531	27.0	0.267	42.0	0.436	15.9
Sub-Saharan Africa	0.475	0.309	35.0	0.335	39.0	0.285	35.3	0.308	30.4
World	0.694	0.532	23.3	0.638	19.0	0.453	27.0	0.522	23.5

Source: UNDP (2013).

the Caribbean. Growth has been concentrated at the top of the population pyramid. This characteristic can be represented by relating the Gini index to GDP per capita. Milanovic and Muñoz de Bustillo[7] found that these two factors are independent, concluding that the income received as a result of economic growth has not been redistributed to the poor. Inequalities in education also play an important role in mobility in the region. In short, inequality in Latin America and the Caribbean has been persistent and accompanied by low mobility among the population, making it difficult to fight, especially when public spending on primary education has been regressive. According to the World Bank, expenditure in the region per student in primary education fell from 12.6 percent of GDP per capita in 2000 to 12.4 percent in 2008.[8]

WHY DO WE CARE ABOUT POVERTY?

Closely related to inequality is the issue of poverty. The effects of poverty go well beyond a lack of money. The actual experience of poverty is devastating to people's health, psychological sense of well-being, and life opportunities. In his paper "When Deprivation and Differences Do Matter: Multidimensionality of Poverty in Latin America and the Caribbean," Enrique Vásquez questioned to what extent one-dimensional indicators of poverty such as monetary poverty are able to reflect people's deprivation and welfare. He calls for an urgent change of perspective toward a more complete picture of the problems faced by the poor.[9]

In this sense, poverty can be viewed in terms of vulnerability and insecurity—an individual's or household's ability to absorb unanticipated economic shocks like theft, illness, loss of a job, and so on. When you are poor, even a small, unanticipated shock can send your household over the edge into extreme hardship. You constantly live on the brink, and the stress from this aspect alone has serious long-term implications for the health of poor individuals and, ultimately, for our societies.

I believe that the eradication of poverty should be the first and most important goal of any democratic government. It is already a primary social concern of the world's multilateral institutions like the UNDP and the World Bank. This is why, in our vision for Latin America, we argue that poverty must be eradicated by 2050.

WHAT IS POVERTY?

While this may sound like a question with an obvious "right" answer, there is actually a lot of disagreement about how best to measure poverty. Historically, poverty has been measured using either income or expenditure. Some organizations use the poverty lines of $2 and $1.25 for poverty and extreme poverty, respectively, while others use $4 and $2.50. This is also called monetary poverty.

This measure of how much an individual earns per day is still widely used, but a growing number of organizations, economists, governments, and activists have rejected it as the best measure of "real" poverty. This is because the income/expenditure account of poverty probably underestimates the extent, depth, drama, and deprivation of poverty, which are affected by much more than just income. For example, the Oxford Poverty and Human Development Initiative (OPHI 2013) found that poor people themselves describe poverty and ill-being as encompassing far more than just money. For them, it includes poor health and nutrition, a lack of adequate sanitation and clean water, social exclusion, low education, bad housing conditions, violence, shame, disempowerment, and more. These conditions are correlated with income but may continue even as income rises if society does not simultaneously focus on them as associated conditions.

It is clear that the effects of poverty are multidimensional and compound one another. They are not just about low income, just as development cannot be measured by economic growth alone. Vásquez highlighted the importance of a multidimensional indicator for Latin America because it would allow for a more complete analysis of the deprivations of people in different dimensions and for a resolution of the paradox between growth and conflict in the region.

To address this gap between what we have been measuring and what we know to be true about the actually lived experience of poverty, new approaches to measuring poverty have been developed. These include the Human Development Index (HDI), the Multidimensional Poverty Index (MPI), the Human Opportunity Index (HOI), and the Happy Planet Index (HPI), among others. Instead of using the flawed income-only measure to assess levels of poverty, we need to look at a number of dimensions that better reflect the real experience of poverty.

I draw on the Multidimensional Poverty Index (MPI)[10] for our reflections on poverty in this book. It is well aligned with the sense of the multifaceted nature of poverty I wish to capture when I discuss this issue. The MPI takes into account a number of factors, including health, education, and living standards, which can be seen in Table 5.3. Across the ten indicators used to measure deprivation, if a family is considered deprived in more than one-third of the indicators, then it is considered MPI poor.

Globally, around 1.7 billion people in the 109 countries included in the MPI analysis live in multidimensional poverty. This indicates that about

TABLE 5.3 *Multidimensional Poverty Index indicators used to measure deprivation*

Dimension	Indicator	Deprived if . . .	Relative weight
Education	Years of schooling	No household member has completed five years of schooling.	0.167
	Child school attendance	Any school-aged child is not attending school in years 1 to 8.	0.167
Health	Mortality	Any child has died in the family.	0.167
	Nutrition	Any adult or child for whom there is nutritional information is malnourished.	0.167
Standard of living	Electricity	The household has no electricity.	0.056
	Sanitation	The household's sanitation facility is not improved (according to the MDG guidelines), or it is improved but shared with other households.	0.056
	Water	The household does not have access to clean drinking water (according to the MDG guidelines) or clean water is more than 30 minutes walking distance from the home.	0.056
	Floor	The household has dirt, sand, or dung flooring.	0.056
	Cooking fuel	The household cooks with dung, wood, or charcoal.	0.056
	Assets	The household does not own more than one radio, TV, telephone, bike, motorbike, or refrigerator, and does not own a car or a truck.	0.056

Source: Alkire and Santos (2010, 17).
Note: "MDG" stands for Millennium Development Goals.

one-third of the population live in "acute" poverty in those countries. This exceeds the estimated 1.3 billion people there who live on $1.25/day or less (considered "extreme" poverty by the World Bank's income measures), but it is below the share who live on $2/day or less. According to Sabina Alkire and Maria Emma Santos (2010), the differences between the measures can be attributed to the fact that the MPI measures the deprivations people experience directly, rather than using monetary poverty as a proxy.

As might be expected, then, different measures of poverty give slightly different perspectives on the situation. The benefit of the MPI, as opposed to using only monetary poverty indicators, is that interventions can be targeted directly to the deprivations a certain population is actually experiencing. For instance, despite being "equally poor," it could be the case that one country's population is deprived of access to basic services but has access to health care, while in another country the situation is reversed. The programs and policies needed for attacking poverty in those two countries would be radically different. Using the MPI rather than income allows policy makers to target interventions directly where they are needed.

In Latin America, the Mexican government was the first country to adopt the MPI as its measure of poverty; other countries' governments have expressed interest. I expect that all countries will eventually adopt a measure similar to this one.

WHAT ARE THE LEVELS OF POVERTY IN LATIN AMERICA?

Using traditional measures of low wages, absolute levels of poverty have declined substantially in Latin America over the last decade. Between 1992 and 2011, extreme poverty (under US$2.50/day) in the region has fallen from 27.5 percent to 12.6 percent and poverty (under US$4/day) has fallen from 44.5 percent to 35.8 percent of the population. Table 5.4 shows how that differs across the major regions of Latin America.

Poverty is not equally distributed across the Latin American region. Central American and Andean countries have much higher percentages of their population living in poverty than the Southern Cone countries

TABLE 5.4 *Poverty rates in Latin America, by region, 1992–2011*

Region	US$2.50/day poverty line					US$4.00/day poverty line				
	1992	1998	2003	2011	Change 1992–2011	1992	1998	2003	2011	Change 1992–2011
Extended Southern Cone										
Poverty (percent)	30.5	22.3	24.7	10.7	–19.7	46.7	37.3	40.6	21.5	–25.2
Number of poor (millions)	63.8	51.1	60.5	28.6	–35.2	97.8	85.3	99.2	57.3	–40.6
Andean region										
Poverty (percent)	26.5	25.3	29.4	12.2	–14.3	43.8	42.5	48.9	25.8	–18.0
Number of poor (millions)	25.3	27.1	34.2	15.8	–9.5	41.9	45.6	56.8	33.4	–8.5
Central America										
Poverty (percent)	23.1	27.2	21.4	16.1	–7.0	41.3	45.3	38.6	32.7	–8.7
Number of poor (millions)	28.7	37.5	31.6	26.2	–2.4	51.3	62.5	57.0	53.1	1.9
Latin America										
Poverty (percent)	27.5	24.4	24.8	12.6	–14.8	44.5	40.8	41.9	25.8	–18.8
Number of poor (millions)	117.7	115.4	126.2	70.6	–47.1	190.9	193.3	212.8	143.8	–47.1

Source: CEDLA, SEDLAC (Base de Datos Socioeconómicos para América Latina y el Caribe) (2013), http://sedlac.econo.unlp.edu.ar/esp/estadisticas-detalle.php?idE=17.

of Argentina, Chile, and Uruguay. The extended Southern Cone includes Brazil and Paraguay, and their poverty rates are much higher.

Some nuances also exist. For example, going back to the definitions of Table 5.4, the percentage of poor in Guatemala is lower than in Honduras, but a higher proportion of Guatemala's poor are living under conditions of severe deprivation—meaning they are deprived in terms of more than half of the MPI indicators (Alkire, Conconi, and Roche 2013).

Policy-wise, this more nuanced analysis is more useful. It shows where each country could get the most "bang for its buck" in terms of MPI poverty interventions. For instance, in Uruguay, 96 percent of its relatively low levels of poverty come from lack of access to education, while in Peru, 60.6 percent of the relatively high levels of poverty come from not having access to basic living standards. We look at all of these aspects of poverty in more depth for the region as a whole in Chapter 8.

The MPI has been calculated for 18 countries in Latin America and the Caribbean.[11] According to the findings, Latin America was the second-least-poor region worldwide in 2010, with an MPI of 0.048 (see Figure 5.1). According to this methodology, 51 million poor people, or 10.4 percent of the population, resided in this region. However, these data

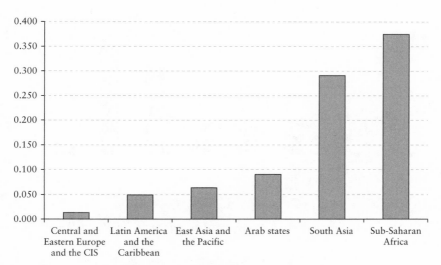

FIGURE 5.1 *Multidimensional Poverty Index, 2010*

Source: Alkire and Santos (2010, 46).

were highly variable among countries, ranging from 1.6 percent of poor people in Uruguay to 57 percent in Haiti. However, there were differences between subregions because poverty was higher in the Andean and Central American countries and relatively lower in the Southern Cone. Education and living standards were the prevalent problems of Latin America and the Caribbean in 2010, and they accounted for 39.04 percent and averaged 35.57 percent of the MPI in 2010, respectively. Therefore, changes in access to and quality of education and basic services can definitively contribute (and in that order of importance) to the multidimensional poverty reduction in Latin America and the Caribbean. In conclusion, the MPI is a useful tool that can better guide policy decision makers to determine which deprivation to prioritize when solving the problem of poverty.

What is the difference between multidimensional and monetary poverty? The figure for the multidimensional poor population in Latin America and the Caribbean (10.40 percent) was among the values obtained using the monetary poverty threshold of PPP$1.25 (7.40 percent) and PPP$2.00 (15 percent). Figure 5.2 shows the divergences between the two method-

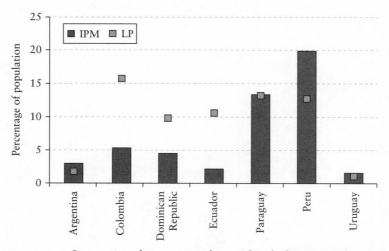

FIGURE 5.2 *Comparison between incidence of multidimensional poverty and monetary poverty (US$2.00 PPP)*

Source: UNDP (2011) and World Bank, World Development Indicators (database) (2012).
Note: Multidimensional poverty data correspond to 2011, while the monetary poverty data are for 2012. It is assumed that there were no significant variations in the level of poverty between 2011 and 2012.

ologies for a group of countries in the region. It can be observed that in some cases multidimensional poverty is greater than monetary poverty, while in others it is the opposite. According to Alkire and Foster (2011), these divergences appear because multidimensional poverty measures deprivations directly as opposed to monetary poverty. People may obtain different results when converting their income to reduce deprivation in other dimensions (e.g., differences in education spending). In summary, each method measures something in particular and uses certain variables despite using the same sources of information, such as household surveys respective to each country.

WHO ARE THE POOR?

Gender and Ethnic Disparities

Latin America is an incredibly diverse region in terms of ethnicity and culture. Over 400 different ethnic groups live in Latin America and the Caribbean. This brings a wealth of experiences and perspectives into our societies. We are rich in our diversity.

However, historic disparities and residual discrimination mean that inequality is not equally distributed in our region. Still today, within the high levels of inequality in Latin America, clear divisions along geographic, ethnic, and gender lines persist. Each of these three aspects is correlated with inequities in earnings, and they are also interrelated and mutually reinforcing.

Geographically, people living in rural areas tend to be poorer than those in urban areas. Table 5.5 shows the difference between urban and rural poverty in Latin America and the Caribbean according to the income measure of poverty as reported by the Economic Commission for Latin America and the Caribbean.

Many of the poorest Latin Americans are self-employed as subsistence farmers in the rural areas. This rural/urban difference is complicated by the fact that across Central America and in many of the Andean countries, the majority of rural subsistence farmers are indigenous. Even outside subsistence farming, the gaps between rural indigenous workers and rural white workers are larger than in urban areas (Ñopo 2012).

TABLE 5.5 *Percentage of population living below the poverty and extreme poverty lines, by urban and rural areas*

Year	Poverty			Extreme poverty		
	Total	Total urban area	Total rural area	Total	Total urban area	Total rural area
1990	48.4	41.4	65.2	22.6	15.3	40.1
2005	39.7	34.0	59.8	15.4	10.3	33.3
2010	31.0	25.5	52.4	12.1	7.6	29.5
2011	29.4	24.2	49.8	11.5	7.2	28.8

Source: ECLAC, Statistics and Economic Projections Division, Social Statistics Unit, based on special tabulations of the respective country's household survey data.
Note: Data as of December 6, 2012. Estimates are based on the following countries: Argentina, Bolivia, Brazil, Chile, Colombia, Costa Rica, Dominican Republic, Ecuador, El Salvador, Guatemala, Haiti, Honduras, Mexico, Nicaragua, Panama, Paraguay, Peru, Uruguay, and Venezuela.

There are also considerable earnings gaps between men and women. Economically active women have more years of schooling than working men, but they earn at least 10 percent less than their male counterparts (Ñopo 2012). They are also underrepresented at the managerial position levels. While there are clear gender differences across economic sectors (e.g., men tend to work in construction and agriculture, while women dominate the social and personal services sectors), evidence suggests this is not the source of the gender earnings gap (Ñopo 2012). Interestingly, although women across the region earn, on average, less than men at all ages and at every level of education and in all types of employment, it is only in rural areas where women earn at levels comparable to men.

Unequal gender pay is often taken for granted as "simply the way things are" in the region. "Hierarchical segregation—the fact that managers tend to be men (white) and subordinates women (minorities)—is commonly accepted as the norm in the region's labor markets" (Ñopo 2012, 5).

However, this is not how things *should* be. To achieve our socially inclusive society, we need to address each and every one of these aspects simultaneously in a coordinated and consistent manner. All people, regardless of gender, race, ethnicity, language, or birthplace, should be given the opportunity to be productive, welcome members of our society. All people should be given fair and equal pay for their work, regardless of whether they are men or women and regardless of the shape of their nose or the color of their skin.

Child Poverty

Along with the gender/ethnic disparities, it is important to discuss the serious issue of child poverty in Latin America. Children do not get a second chance at receiving a healthy start in life, and they rarely get another opportunity to access quality basic education. This means that childhood poverty almost guarantees the intergenerational transmission of poverty and inequality.

If today's children do not have the opportunity to develop their minds and bodies, they will grow to be adults who have limited opportunities. Their *capabilities*, according to Sen's definition of the word, are stunted because of factors outside their control. In terms of reducing intergenerational poverty in the long term, perhaps what needs to concern us most is the welfare and well-being of children today.

A recent ECLAC and UNICEF study used a multidimensional framework (similar to the MPI) to measure child poverty in Latin America. Factors such as nutrition, access to drinking water, quality of housing, and school attendance were included in the study. Using these metrics, nearly half (45 percent) of all children living in Latin America are affected by at least one "moderate to severe deprivation" (UNICEF/ECLAC 2010). This means that right now over 80 million Latin American children's opportunities to develop to their full potential are being compromised.

Of course, Latin America is as diverse in this aspect as it is in others. The study finds that some countries, like Chile, Costa Rica, and Uruguay, have less than 25 percent of their children living in poverty, while others, like Bolivia, El Salvador, Guatemala, Honduras, and Peru, have over 66 percent of children living in poverty. Figure 5.3 shows the distribution of child poverty across the region.

Overall, progress has been made in reducing poverty, but it is still unequal progress and has not yet created the kind of inclusive society I envision for our region. Certain groups are still more likely than others to live in poverty, and millions of our children are struggling with basic necessities.

Yes, we have to ensure that average income per capita keeps rising and that the fruits of economic growth are distributed more equally, because

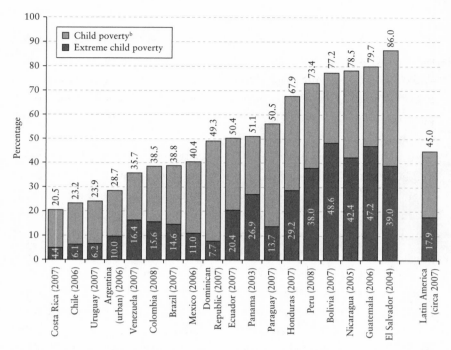

FIGURE 5.3   *Children in extreme poverty and total poverty*ᵃ

Source: ECLAC, on the basis of special tabulations from household surveys from the respective countries.
ᵃChildren aged 0 to 17.
ᵇIncludes extremely poor children.

both growth and distribution are keys to the reduction of poverty. Yet, the additional challenge is that we cannot work on poverty and inequality solely through macroeconomic policy. The issues surrounding an inclusive society are intricately related to social dimensions of well-being, such as health, education, and security, which are not necessarily just related to average income per capita. In a later chapter, I will argue that these aspects need our focused attention. It is important how much people earn, but available health, education, and security services not only improve earning capacity but directly improve people's everyday sense of well-being.

SUMMING UP

There is no doubt inequality is one of the most entrenched scourges of our region. Inequality and poverty are intertwined. If we do not address issues of inequality, it is much more difficult to address poverty. A country that has eliminated poverty but remains highly unequal will not be a shared society and will continue to experience social unrest. This chapter examines the situation of inequality and poverty in Latin America and presents the results of several measures of these phenomena in the region. I firmly believe that "monetary poverty measures" are insufficient. We need a multidimensional approach to poverty, such as the one I introduced above. As mentioned, high initial levels of inequality can slow economic growth and reduce the share of the economic growth that poorer people receive.

Chapter 6 focuses on the challenges and next steps needed to achieve environmentally sustainable economic growth in Latin America. I highlight the need for greater sustainability in the extraction of renewable and nonrenewable resources and the importance of minimizing the region's urban footprint on the environment.

Embracing Sustainable Development

IN THE DESCRIPTION of my vision for Latin America, I point out that our region has been blessed with bountiful natural resources. I also feel we might have been cursed by this bounty, depending on how you look at it. The cursed part comes in because our easy access to commodity revenues through natural resource extraction has allowed us to ignore the need to invest in our people. It has also lulled us into ignoring the environmental impact of our economic growth. Because we "needed" the revenues and did not create other ways of generating them, we have allowed our rain forests to be cut down, our water supplies to be threatened by mining, and our ecological balance to be damaged by petroleum extraction. A truly shared society is not concerned solely with economic gains: we have to remember that we are also going to share our world with our children and grandchildren. We have the opportunity to shift our mind-set and our investments to ensure that we develop sustainably. We still have the ability to choose how and when we extract resources wisely, and we must always be aware that economic growth that precludes a healthy future for our children is not true growth.

Environmental degradation in Latin America is driven by several interconnected and multidimensional forces, including international trade, demographic growth, rapid urbanization, climate change, and a nascent institutional framework unable to fully address a wide range of environmental issues. While complex, it is clear that restoring and maintaining our environmental resources could become a major source of sustainable development in Latin America. We just have to decide to do it.

In the last 50 years, the population in our region has more than doubled, to 595 million. Its urban population has increased dramatically, from 49 percent to 79 percent of the total population. These two forces combined have exerted increased pressure on the environment. For example, the demand for water in Latin America increased by 76 percent in just two decades, average electricity consumption quadrupled, and solid waste production more than doubled. Also, expansion of slums and their high density has placed their inhabitants in a situation of vulnerability and environmental risk with regard to climate change. Climate change, combined with the strain humans place on the environment, means that floods, landslides, droughts, colder winters, and drier summers are becoming more and more common. The poor suffer most from these environmental changes because they have fewer means with which to withstand them.

However, the extractive nature of our economies affords perhaps a stronger explanation of the strain on our natural resources and the degradation of our ecosystems, which threaten future economic growth and environmental sustainability. Latin America has enormous quantities of natural resources. As mentioned earlier in this book, we have 23 percent of the world's oil reserves, 50 percent of its copper reserves, 47 percent of its silver reserves, 18 percent of its gold reserves, and 37 percent of the world's renewable internal freshwater sources.

It is not surprising, then, that primary goods such as minerals, hydrocarbons, agriculture, livestock, forestry, and fishery account for 73 percent of the region's exports. Of these, the extraction of minerals and hydrocarbons, such as oil and gas, is particularly damaging to the environment because it contributes to deforestation, land erosion, and pollution, and threatens the health and natural environments of local communities. Furthermore, the recent boom of commodity exports of energy, metals, and food has increased pressure on the environment. The technology in use today means that extracting or producing these commodities requires large amounts of energy and water resources.

Although our region consists of only 15 percent of the earth's surface, Latin America is home to 20 percent of the ecoregions in the world.[1] The World Wildlife Fund has identified a group of 238 ecoregions considered priority areas for global conservation. Fifty-three of them—nearly a quarter—are located in Latin America. In addition, Bolivia, Brazil, Colombia, Ecuador, Mexico, Peru, and Venezuela are included among the 17 "megadiverse" nations in the world. "Megadiversity" is based not only on the total number of species in a country but also on the degree to which each organism is unique to that country. Together, the 17 megadiversity countries contain, amazingly, over 70 percent of the earth's species!

We have one of the most ecologically diverse regions on the planet because of its high concentration of mammal, bird, reptile, amphibian, insect, and plant species. However, our biodiversity is quickly dwindling. The region has 5 of the 20 countries with the highest number of endangered species of fauna, and 7 of the 20 countries with the highest number of endangered plant species. The results of our past approach to development make it clear that if we do not act now and take assertive measures to protect the environment, we run the risk of causing it irreparable damage and losing our biodiversity.

New developments in agricultural practices also contribute to environmental degradation. Latin America has a farming area of around 720 million hectares and the potential to become the agricultural hub of the world. The growing international demand for meat (beef, pork, poultry) has led to the expansion of grasslands—often at the expense of forest area. This has put additional pressure on the production of grain for animal feed. All this, combined with the expansion of the biodiesel sector and the growing use of cereals, sugar, oilseed, and vegetable oils to produce fossil fuel substitutes, is pushing the agricultural frontier into wilderness areas. As a result, our region has one of the highest rates of deforestation and habitat loss in the world. We have about one-quarter of the world's forest area, but by the year 2000, 64 percent of global forest loss took place in Latin America. To this we need to add soil and water pollution from the use of agrochemicals, loss of soil quality from monocultures, desertification, and the intensive use of water resources for irrigation. We are particularly concerned with the high water consumption of soybean plants, which constitute one of our main exports to China and—as a cash crop—have increased phenomenally in the past 15 years, particularly in Argentina and Brazil.

On a positive note, Latin America is not ranked among the major polluters of the earth's atmosphere: we are responsible for only 12 percent of global greenhouse emissions. But we are very vulnerable to the effects of global warming through the increased intensity and frequency of hurricanes, precipitation, floods and droughts, changes in temperature levels, melting of glaciers, and rising sea levels. Recent environmental catastrophes have led to governments in the region introducing a wide range of environmental legislation. Our problem is thus not the absence of norms and regulations. Rather, it lies in our institutional inability to enforce the laws we have already passed. The implementation of environmental policy has been particularly weak when confronted with financial and trade incentives that run contrary to sustainability initiatives. We are often allowing private profits to prevail over environmental protection, sustainable development, and the wider public good.

ACHIEVING ENVIRONMENTALLY SUSTAINABLE ECONOMIC GROWTH

Of course, I am not the only one who has noticed that we need to shift our focus. The region has already been making moves to address these environmental challenges. It has already begun to take steps to introduce more sustainable policies in its agriculture, livestock, fishing, forestry, mining, oil extraction, and urban sectors. However, Latin America still needs to adopt a more sustainable growth model capable of generating prosperity, while protecting the environment and the rights to clean water and sustainable habitat of its local communities. The question is: How do we do this?

Sustainable Agricultural Production

Around 30 percent of the land in Latin America is suited for agriculture. Currently, the largest foreign markets are China (soy), followed by the United States (fruit, sugar, and flowers), and the European Union (fruits and oilseeds). Argentina and Brazil are the two countries with the highest percentage of territory devoted to agricultural production. However, other countries such as Bolivia, Chile, Ecuador, and Paraguay have agricultural growth rates higher than the regional average.

Estimates project a bright outlook for the agriculture sector in Latin America. This can be explained in part by the rising prices of agricultural products. By 2050, there will be more than 9 billion people living on the planet, 70 percent of whom will live in urban areas. More people on the planet means more food will be consumed, so more food will need to be produced, and that food will have to be better distributed to the people who need it. At the same time, income levels in developing countries are expected to rise, which will also result in greater food consumption, especially of products with greater value-added and higher animal protein content. Meat consumption is expected to increase from 27.4 kilograms to 52 kilograms per person annually by 2050, and this growth is expected to produce a 50 percent increase in the demand of cereals for animal feed. Finally, growth in the biofuels sector will tend to expand the production of agricultural products. It is estimated that by 2020, 13 percent of grains, 15 percent of vegetable oils, and 30 percent of sugar production will be devoted to biofuels. The growing demand for agricultural products provides significant opportunities for agricultural and agro-industry development in our region.

Latin America can still expand its agricultural frontier, but its ability to do so will be limited by water and land constraints. This means that in order to meet the increasing demand for food and raw materials, our region will need to use its current land and water resources more efficiently, improve its productivity, and invest in research and development to introduce sustainable practices and diversify its production.

The bottom line is that Latin America needs an effective plan to meet the opportunities and challenges associated with a sustained increase in the demand for agricultural products. The instability and uncertainty of agricultural prices make decision making difficult for long-term horizons. This increases the costs of accessing food and makes it difficult to determine the costs of inputs and raw materials for sectors such as livestock and agro-industry, which discourages medium- and long-term investment decisions. It is necessary to understand the causes of price volatility in agricultural products so we can make better investment and production decisions with that information to design countercyclical policies that buffer external shocks and prevent food security crises. Our governments must strengthen their capacity to establish and endow agriculture agencies specializing in the monitoring, assessment, and analysis of market, production, and financial risks. Our governments need to have effective policy departments in charge of designing sustainable agriculture policies.

The region's investment in agricultural research and technology institutes should be redoubled in order to build upon the existing comparative advantage in agricultural products and to diversify production into agro-industry goods with greater value-added. This underscores the importance of creating incentives for agricultural research to identify new market niches. Latin America is the cradle of agricultural biodiversity, so our governments should take concrete measures to protect the diversity of seeds and species. We must build upon this advantage and protect our production against the danger of succumbing to genetically modified monocultures, which threaten the region's agricultural diversity and the quality of its soil.

Public and private investment in research and technology is essential for tailoring best practices to local realities, as well as promoting technology transfer and igniting innovation. Research and technology transfers should be differentiated by large-, medium-, and small-scale farmers in order to address their specific needs and challenges, while protecting the environment. Research should provide the information, knowledge, and tools necessary to increase productivity and spur innovation at each of these levels of agricultural production. Our research centers must also continue to monitor climate change with the objective of developing policies that can adapt agricultural production to new long-term climatic conditions, mitigate short-term shocks, and reduce the impact of agriculture on environmental degradation. This involves tighter controls and regulations on the use of water resources and pesticides that are harmful to the environment.

To increase productivity and competitiveness in the agricultural sector, we must work to increase the quantity and quality of our products in a sustainable way. Increasing quantity does not mean expanding our agricultural frontier. This "strategy" threatens the environment and fosters degradation. Instead, we must focus on producing more by using current available resources more efficiently. For example, controlled irrigation systems allow for a more sustainable use of water resources. Improved infrastructure allows for quicker delivery of products to national and international markets. In addition, competitive markets are demanding higher quality in agricultural products. This includes improvements in the products' appearance, durability, and nutritional properties. The opportunity is there for Latin America to become a leading supplier of high-quality agricultural products, rich in nutritional value. As I mentioned before, improvements in the quantity and quality of our agricultural products will require greater investment in research, technology, and innovative production techniques.

One way to tackle this problem is for our governments to pay attention to food security from a landownership perspective. Although international investment in agriculture can be positive, governments must have clear policies regarding optimum levels of foreign ownership of agricultural land. Given the expected increase in future demand for agricultural products, along with great volatility in food prices, governments must take preemptive steps to analyze their position on foreign ownership of agricultural land and design policies and regulations to protect national food security. It is estimated that foreigners own 10 percent of the land in Argentina and 20 to 30 percent in Uruguay. Brazil, Argentina, and Chile have begun to address this issue in their public policy–making spheres by setting limits on the amount of land that foreign investors and national companies with foreign capital can acquire. As pressures for landownership increase, more countries in the region will have to develop policies that meet their food security needs.

Sustainable Livestock Production

The growing global demand for meat and milk products offers promising opportunities for Latin America's livestock sector. It is expected that by 2030, livestock will represent 48 percent of agricultural products in the region. With the exception of beef, other types of meat such as poultry, pork, and lamb are expected to experience long-term growth. By 2019, the region will provide 17.4 percent of the world's meat supply. Similarly, by 2020, Latin America will increase its share of exported milk from 25 to 45 percent of its total milk production. But to be sustainable, this growth must address issues related to appropriate water management, carbon emissions, protection of biodiversity, and quality of soils.

In addition, the expansion of highly profitable crops has tended to push small-scale livestock farmers onto lower-quality land. This has made small farmers more vulnerable to external climate shocks. Government support is needed to provide training and access to tools and resources to improve the productivity of degraded soils, livestock feeding practices, and the safety and quality of products. Designing and implementing policies that target small-scale family farmers can improve environmental sustainability by introducing practices that mitigate environmental damage and adapt to new climate conditions.

Our governments must put in place policies to improve the livelihood of rural households, decreasing poverty and food insecurity. With the use of research and technology we can contribute to the recovery of pastures and degraded lands by introducing species more resilient to droughts and adverse climatic conditions. To this must be added the introduction of strategies for more efficient water management and protection of river basins. This process should also include extending lines of credit to small-scale farmers so they can have access to the tools necessary to improve productivity and management of water, waste, and land resources.

Human capital development is essential. Accreditation of training institutions can enable the transfer of knowledge to promote sustainability, increase productivity, and pursue business opportunities. Our governments must improve the delivery of information services such as weather information, pricing, and trends in the livestock market. With more accurate and reliable information, farmers can lower risk when making investment decisions and seek new market opportunities.

As a region we must continue to strengthen our early-warning systems and monitoring of disease outbreaks. More can be done to provide technical assistance to small-scale farmers to reinforce sanitary practices as well as access to veterinary services. We need the political will and determination to implement such measures in order to reduce the risk of animal disease outbreaks and their subsequent impact on the health of our communities.

Sustainable Fisheries and Aquaculture

Aquaculture is a food sector with one of the highest rates of growth globally. Again, here is a major opportunity for Latin America's exports and production for internal consumption. The average fish intake of our population is 9 to 11 kilograms per person per year, which is 35 to 45 percent lower than the international average. The nascent stage of aquaculture offers room for growth, especially considering that commercial fishing has reached its catch limit. Strategies can still be implemented to make even traditional fishing more sustainable in our region.

South America continues to be the regional leader in commercial fishing and aquaculture with 86 percent of wild catches and 84 percent of aquaculture facilities. Chile and Peru are among the ten major fishing countries in the world. Some popular export products include pelagic fish, anchovy, jack mackerel, sardines, Spanish mackerel, and giant squid. Further, Chile, Brazil, Colombia, Ecuador, and Mexico accounted for 83 percent of all aquaculture production in the region.

Back in the 1950s, aquaculture was used by Latin America's small-scale farmers to supply local communities with mollusks and freshwater fish. But with time, aquaculture in our region has turned to an export model specializing in high-value products such as salmon, white leg shrimp, freshwater fish, and mollusks. Currently, the aquaculture sector is dominated by large and highly competitive companies using technology-intensive production. This trend has left behind small-scale aquacultures and artisanal fishermen, who depend on intermediaries to commercialize their products and provide them with inputs such as the fishmeal they use to feed farm-raised fish.

Yet, the main factor affecting the sustainability of fisheries and aqua-cultures may be a weak regulatory framework and lax enforcement of laws and regulations. This includes failure to enforce fishing bans, site permits, and imports of disease-free genetic material. We must work actively to introduce clear regulations and enforcement procedures to protect mangrove areas from the unregulated expansion of aquacultures and prevent the salinization of inland soil. Our governments must also address regulations related to water and wastewater management in or-der to prevent contamination of the ocean and freshwater resources from aquaculture practices.

As in traditional land agriculture, greater investment in research and technology is needed to improve fishing and farming practices and to in-crease productivity. We need studies to identify opportunities to diversify production toward native species and prevent the loss of diversity of fish stock, mollusks, and crustacean species. We need to provide technical assistance to subsistence farmers to introduce sustainable aquacultures, which hold the potential to diversify their sources of income and dietary intake. We need to develop clear and effective sanitary procedures to prevent and mitigate the outbreak of diseases affecting the health of our local communities.

The introduction and development of information communication technologies (ICTs) can be effective tools in providing adequate and timely information on supply, demand, and prices in fish markets. This strategy can help empower artisan fishermen and small-scale fish farmers, providing them with better tools to make more informed investment and production decisions. I welcome initiatives such as the Aquaculture Network of the Americas, which was established in 2010 with the purpose of facilitating the exchange of information among countries. Collaboration among our countries is essential for sharing best practices and promoting technology and innovative strategies.

Sustainable Forest Management

The combination of global deforestation and forest degradation is the second major cause of CO_2 emissions in the world after emissions coming from the energy sector; CO_2 has been identified as a major cause of global warming. Latin America has 23.6 percent of all the world's forests, and forests cover 47.4 percent of the region's territory. We produce 15 percent of the world's round wood, 15 percent of its firewood, 11.6 percent of its sawn wood, and 14 percent of its board production. Since the 1990s, the production of wood as a percentage of GDP has increased steadily.

Thus, one of the major environmental concerns in our region is sustaining our vast forests. While forests are one of the main ways to control CO_2 emissions, because trees and plants absorb CO_2, deforestation as an industry produces more carbon emission than the transportation sector. As a region we clearly need to adopt sustainable forestry strategies to avoid deforestation and the uncontrolled expansion of agriculture into forest areas to help lower carbon emissions, preserve soil quality and biodiversity, prevent landslides, and reduce the intensity of floods.

There are a number of international best practices we could draw upon to improve our sustainable forest management, forest rehabilitation, reforestation, and afforestation. For instance, the United Nations Programme on Reducing Emissions from Deforestation and Forest Degradation (UN-REDD) offers a financial incentive for developing countries to reduce carbon emissions by preventing deforestation and forest degradation. Once carbon is traded in international markets like any other commodity, our region will benefit tremendously by deriving value from the carbon stored in our forests. The REDD+ market has the potential to reach $30 billion per year, and these resources could assist environmental conservation and rural development in the region. The transfer of resources from polluting countries to countries preserving carbon resources such as ours will allow us to establish a more sustainable development model than the current one based on the extraction of nonrenewable resources.

We have begun taking steps in this direction. In Brazil, for example, landowners have the rights to the carbon stored in their land. In Costa Rica, the government signs contracts with private landowners to maintain carbon underground in exchange for the right to trade carbon in the future. This opens an interesting policy debate where most of the remaining countries in the region will need to make decisions regarding who owns carbon rights and who can trade them. Here I must emphasize the importance of respecting the rights of indigenous and local communities that depend on the forests for subsistence. In the end, governments must ensure that the proceeds generated from carbon trading make it back to the local communities. We must respect indigenous and local communities' rights to free and prior consent because a sustainable and long-term partnership will require the engagement of all actors involved.

Along similar lines, our region has been a pioneer in the adoption of a market-based approach of payments for environmental services. For example, Costa Rica established a National Forestry Financing Fund to issue certificates to landowners in exchange for forest conservation efforts. Using contributions from the private sector, the fund issues these certificates to finance the program of payments for environmental services.[2] Latin America was also the first region to establish a system of payments for river basin services to improve the management of water resources. Several countries have begun taking concrete steps in the preservation of biodiversity and forest areas. For example, Brazil introduced a National Climate Plan to reduce illegal deforestation and created an Amazon Fund to promote reforestation and enforcement of environmental laws and regulations.

As I mentioned earlier, the inclusion and involvement of rural communities in the management of forest resources are essential for achieving environmental sustainability in the region. Indigenous groups in numerous countries have been leading this approach, where they blend traditional knowledge with forest management strategies. Devolving forest management to the local level has opened the door to new opportunities such as ecotourism, green employment, and small to medium-sized forestry enterprises that market organic and sustainably grown forest products, while preventing the illegal logging of forests.

This strategy serves a twofold purpose. It protects the environment and prevents carbon emissions associated with deforestation. It also empowers rural communities to earn a more sustainable livelihood. We must act as enablers so that indigenous communities can receive training to strengthen sustainable practices in farming and employment of forest resources for subsistence, and to prepare the communities for the challenges associated with forestry management.

But let us not fool ourselves. Sustainable forestry requires a strong institutional and enforcement framework. Clear guidelines must be developed to define what constitutes a legal or illegal activity. Logging companies should operate under concrete regulations stipulating sustainable use of soils as well as reforestation and forestation activities. Environmental preservation requires clear procedures regarding landownership rights related to future carbon trading and establishing protected areas in the form of national parks and reserves. Strong governance and rule of law are necessary to monitor the management of forest areas and the compliance with regulations to prosecute and punish activities that endanger the environment, wildlife, and livelihood of local communities. Finally, it requires strategic plans to both prevent deforestation and rehabilitate degraded soils.

Information Communication Technologies for Sustainable Development

In terms of technology, our region continues to lag behind the most developed nations. I like to look at this challenge as a tremendous opportunity. Bridging the technology gap will allow our economies and societies to reap great benefits. The introduction of ICTs in our region presents a great opportunity to improve sustainability, productivity, transparency, and the inclusion of our rural populations.

If implemented well, ICTs can enhance the sustainable development of the agriculture, livestock, fishery, and forestry sectors. ICTs also provide an opportunity to develop the monitoring of sustainable practices in the extraction of nonrenewable resources. A sustainability study conducted by ECLAC in 2009 shows us some of the direct benefits of introducing ICTs:

- Improvements in the monitoring and forecasting of sowing, harvesting, and production processes
- Reduction in the risks associated with climate change, price volatility, spread of cross-border plants, and animal diseases
- Establishment of small-scale family enterprises
- Greater ease in processing transactions and developing of innovations
- Improvement of employment opportunities in the rural sector and social inclusion

But what exactly are ICTs? ICTs can be hardware, software, or networks used to collect, store, process, transmit, and present information. This can take the form of voice, data, text, or images. It involves the dissemination of information related to products, services, and institutional frameworks, as well as market operators, suppliers, manufacturers, consumers, public agencies, research institutions, and regulators. ICTs have the potential to facilitate the social inclusion of rural areas and disadvantaged populations because they can break historical, economic, social, and geographical patterns of isolation.

However, it is true that a sound telecommunications infrastructure is a necessary precondition for the mass adoption and utilization of ICTs. We need to improve access to mobile telephony with adequate reception and broadband in remote rural settings, improve connectivity, and enhance public access to the Internet. We need to increase the availability of financing mechanisms for communities and individuals in rural areas to access these technologies. We also need to instruct communities in the use of ICTs and in their application and benefits. Mere access to ICTs will not improve people's lives unless communities can discern tangible benefits from their implementation. This means that we must invest resources in training our communities. To be clear, we must redouble our efforts to improve access to ICTS and enhance mass digital literacy training and financing mechanisms. Continuous and sustained work on this front will allow us to start bridging our technological divide.

In rural Latin America, the most common use of ICTs involves land telephone lines, followed by mobile telephones. As mentioned earlier, access to mobile telephony is more restricted in rural areas than in urban settings. We must change this because ICTs can empower rural dwellers by giving them access to the information and knowledge they have been deprived of for so long. A simple text message can deliver real-time market prices, demand and supply trends, and severe-weather alerts. Access to information empowers rural farmers against abuses from intermediaries, strengthens their bargaining power, and allows them to make more informed decisions.

Other types of ICTs involve cutting-edge technologies such as precision agriculture and traceability mechanisms. Precision agriculture (PA) is concentrated in large-scale farming of wheat, maize, soy, and sunflower crops in Brazil and Argentina. To a lesser extent, other countries have also introduced PA in the production of tropical fruit, coffee, flowers, and higher-value-added products such as wine. Uruguay has been the leader in the use of traceability technology in the livestock sector. In 2006, it introduced a mandatory animal identification system, and since 2010, it requires all animals to be registered with the National Information and Registry System. Traceability technology includes radio frequency identification devices, electronic readers, and wireless data transmission networks. The introduction of PAs and traceability devices comes as a response to increasing demands from export markets for higher quality and health standards.

Great opportunities lie ahead in terms of the benefits that can be derived from a more comprehensive implementation of ICTs to improve productivity and competitiveness, increase transparency in the dissemination of market information, and mitigate external climate shocks by providing timely warnings and forecasts. In my opinion, there is no doubt that we must board this train, but to do so, we need to invest heavily to improve our current infrastructure and connectivity networks.

GREATER SUSTAINABILITY IN THE EXTRACTION OF NONRENEWABLE RESOURCES

Since colonial times, mining has been one of the region's most polluting activities and one of the most harmful to the health of local populations. Mining generates large amounts of polluting waste and has devastating effects on the water, soil, and forests. The trouble is that Latin America is the region with the greatest capital investment in the mining sector. Some of the key minerals extracted include copper, coal, gold, silver, and construction materials such as sand and cement. Since 2000, investment in this sector has increased by 400 percent.

In Peru, foreign investment in the mining sector has increased by 1,000 percent in the last decade. Not surprisingly, mining activities in my country have had a devastating effect on groundwater quality, which is affecting the health of our local communities. However, Peru is not alone. Between 1975 and 2002, gold mining in the Brazilian Amazon produced around 2,000 tons of gold. Rising gold prices meant big revenues for Brazil. But gold mining released close to 3,000 tons of mercury into the natural environment. Mercury pollution in the water affects fish and local communities that depend on rivers for their subsistence, causing severe health and environmental problems.

Here is another example: Latin America has about 23 percent of the world's oil reserves but accounts for around 8.3 percent of world consumption. Oil drilling has high environmental costs such as the irreversible transformation of land and marine ecosystems, as well as harmful health and biodiversity consequences related to oil spills. Despite its high environmental damage, countries such as Venezuela, Brazil, Mexico, and Ecuador are highly dependent on the exploitation of oil reserves.

Up to now, the environmental costs of mineral and oil extraction have been borne by our local communities. However, numerous countries in the region have begun to take concrete steps to strengthen the institutional framework regulating mining and oil extraction. Although imperfect, there are mechanisms that can be put in place to introduce sustainable practices and environmental protection.

Many governments in our region included *prior consultation* provisions in their national constitutions in the 1990s, but only in recent years have they started to enforce them in practice. Common application of the law includes requiring companies to conduct assessments on the environmental and social impact of concessions that have already been approved. This has created intrinsic conflicts between indigenous communities, governments, and the private companies. The implementation of the Indigenous and Tribal Peoples Convention (ILO 169) has been subject to competing interpretations and disagreement on issues such as whether communities have veto power over unfeasible projects, how much time is given to communities to review assessments, the extent of the consultation process, and the role of national and subnational governments. Our governments, along with indigenous and environmental groups, must continue to make progress toward establishing an institutional framework that protects and enforces free, prior, and informed consent.

To do so we must promote public discussions to develop a better understanding of the consultative process and seek a national consensus on the extent of the consultations. Consultations should be an ongoing process from the beginning to the end of extraction projects. This means breaking the consultation process into different stages. The first stage is the initial assessment and consultation of the project's environmental and social impacts with a clear time frame so projects can be approved or rejected within a specified period. This would help minimize delays and uncertainty for investors, while protecting the rights of the communities.

The second stage would consist of ongoing consultations during the implementation of activities to add flexibility and adaptability. The third stage would involve posttermination assessments to ensure that companies have complied with cleanup and environmental rehabilitation procedures. To this I would like to add that the scope of consultations should be expanded to include neighboring communities beyond the impact zone of extractive projects, which can also be affected by environmental degradation. This is necessary to ensure long-term environmental sustainability.

Finally, we must work toward strengthening national and subnational governments' participation in the consultation process to ensure that the law is being enforced and to verify the validity of the environmental and social impact assessments. The engagement and participation of civil society and nongovernmental organizations are essential for demanding greater accountability from both governments and extractive corporations. In addition to making the process more consultative, in Chapter 9, I also present some new ways of thinking about how to better distribute the economic benefits of mining as part of achieving a more shared society.

There appears to be a general consensus on the need to rethink ways in which the mining and oil companies can be better integrated into the rest of the economy. As part of that integration, companies should be required to generate greater positive spillover effects in terms of employment, technology transfers, and improvements in productivity, competitiveness, and sustainability. If managed well, taxes, along with royalty payments from mining and oil extraction, could help spark innovation and more sustainable growth models. For example, Chile has been effective in establishing an Innovation Fund for Competitiveness administered by the Ministry of Economy. The fund uses mining revenue to support investment in technical education, research, and development, and to provide capital for entrepreneurial initiatives. The government of Colombia has also adopted a similar strategy allocating 10 percent of royalty payments to national research and development programs, aiming to increase diversification and sustainability.

Similarly, in 2010, the Ecuadorian government introduced the Yasuní-ITT Initiative, which is an innovative approach to oil extraction. The Yasuní National Park is located in the Ecuadorian Amazon and is the most biodiverse region in the world. But the IIT oil fields inside the park hold 20 percent of the country's oil reserves. Instead of extracting these oil resources, the government has introduced the Yasuní-ITT Initiative to keep the oil underground in order to preserve the environment and contribute to the fight against global warming by preventing the emission of 407 million metric tons of CO_2. The initiative also guarantees the voluntary isolation of the Tagaeri and Taromenane indigenous communities. In exchange for keeping the oil and carbon underground, the government asks the international community to contribute 50 percent of the revenue the country forgoes by not extracting its oil. An international trust fund managed by the UNDP has been established to handle contributions from governments, multilateral agencies, corporations, NGOs, and individuals around the world. The fund will be used to invest in renewable energy, education, and health. This strategy provides an example of an innovative approach to preserving the environment and the local indigenous communities living in the park, fighting global warming, and starting the economic diversification process distinct from the extraction of nonrenewable resources. Our region needs more innovative approaches such as those adopted by Chile, Colombia, and Ecuador to pave the way toward a more sustainable development.

One of the main challenges ahead is ensuring that resources reach the local communities where mining and extraction take place. This involves improving the capacity of the local civil service through training and the provision of technical assistance in the management of resources and the design and implementation of projects. A disproportionate share of resources transferred to subnational governments ends up invested in provincial capitals, leaving rural areas unattended and lacking in infrastructure. The end result is that rural communities remain impoverished and lacking access to basic services such as education, health, and sanitation. We see this happening even today in my own Peru. In 2012, the province of Huari received $53 million in revenue from mining extraction in the Altamina mine. But the people living in San Marcos, the closest town to the mine, still lack basic services such as potable water. This example is not unique to Peru. It is a fate suffered by many rural communities throughout the region. This calls for a drastic improvement in governance at the national and subnational levels, as well as the inclusion of provisions in the contracts and leasing agreements with mining and oil companies to implement greater corporate responsibility.

The aim is for corporations and subnational governments to be directly accountable for improvements in the livelihood of local communities living close to mining and extractive zones. For example, many mining companies in Chile, Colombia, and Peru have begun investing in local enterprises and microcredit to empower local communities. Evidence shows that companies that sign international conventions and agreements on human rights and good governance protocols demonstrate a greater commitment to corporate responsibility practices. They are more likely to give back to local communities and protect the environment. As citizens we must demand that governments do business only with corporations that exhibit a good history of corporate responsibility and care for local communities and the environment.

Finally, we face the challenge and responsibility of strengthening environmental government agencies. We must address gaps in the laws and regulations governing environmental protection in order to give ministries the authority to enforce environmental rules and regulations. Currently, most environmental ministries have no power to enforce the law, which leaves them toothless in the face of irregularities and abuses. These agencies need to strengthen their institutional capacity, their research and technology departments, and their monitoring, assessment, and evaluation mechanisms.

The way the industry currently works, the negative environmental impact of mining and oil extraction is an unavoidable reality. However, effective action by environmental ministries and agencies can play a crucial role in protecting the environment and mitigating negative environmental and social consequences—and maybe even force the industry to innovate in its extraction methods to make them less impactful. Government action includes holding mining and oil companies responsible for extensive investment in the rehabilitation of the land once activities have been terminated. Environmental agencies need to hold companies responsible for minimizing their environmental footprint while in operation, reducing their electricity and water consumption, investing in renewable sources of energy, and minimizing air, water, and land pollution. Thus, we must strengthen the institutional framework in the region to make crystal clear to companies prior to investing that they will be held accountable for their actions. Only then will the region be able to head toward a more sustainable growth and development model.

MINIMIZING THE REGION'S URBAN
FOOTPRINT ON THE ENVIRONMENT

Latin America is one of the world's most urbanized regions. It has a rapid rate of motorization (vehicle ownership per capita per 1,000 people), high levels of urban sprawl, and an increasing exposure to natural disasters in coastal areas. As the region's economy continues to grow and the demand for urban infrastructure increases, it will confront ever-increasing environmental challenges. The sustainability of Latin America's economic growth and our ability to create a shared society will depend on our governments' ability to protect our natural resource endowment. Fortunately, since the 1992 Rio Summit, Latin America has been at the forefront of green innovation.

- Many countries in our region have introduced densification subsidies to attract people to city centers and to revitalize these areas. This has helped reduce the cost of transportation and provision of services in many cities. Reducing urban sprawl is beneficial because it makes it easier and less costly to provide basic services to urban populations. Between 2001 and 2008, solid waste services were extended to more than 63 million people, increasing collection coverage rates from 81 to 93 percent of the urban population in the region.

- Although Latin America has the highest rate of growth in motorization—a 4.5 percent increase in automobile ownership per year—it has been a pioneer in the development and implementation of mass transit systems. The innovative introduction of Bus Rapid Transit (BRT) systems throughout the region has been a key tool in improving public transportation, lowering congestion, and reducing carbon dioxide emissions.

- Our region has a significant potential for generating renewable energy because it has wide availability of hydroelectric, geothermal, wind, and biomass resources. Currently, our energy generation is split between thermal and hydroelectric production. Latin America holds 22 percent of the world's hydroelectric potential. Not surprisingly, the region has invested actively in low-carbon electricity generation, which doubled between 1990 and 2009. Hydroelectric power remains the most important source of electricity, followed by natural gas, which in the same period has expanded from 10 to 21 percent of total energy consumption. Interestingly, the use of oil and biodiesel for electricity production has declined in importance. Electricity generation in Latin America has a lower carbon footprint than in any other region in the world. For this reason we must continue to build upon our comparative advantage in the generation of renewable energy, which will help us pave the way toward more sustainable development and a prosperous future.

To close our discussion of sustainable development in the region, I would like to underscore the fact that Latin America has a great potential to achieve environmental sustainability. It is within our reach, but we must act now. We need to invest actively in research and development, in telecommunication infrastructure, in the adoption of new technologies to bridge our technological divide, and in building a stronger national and subnational state capacity to strengthen our institutional and regulatory frameworks.

SUMMING UP

This chapter pinpoints the challenges and measures required to attain sustainable development in the region. If we do not take this challenge seriously, we may miss our opportunity to build a sustainable future. If we do not act now, we will lose our unparalleled biodiversity. We will deplete our finite mineral and oil reserves. We will cause irreparable damage to our water and land resources. If we do not act now, we will jeopardize our future economic growth and the livelihood of our population. But I am confident, because of the four factors that I introduced at the beginning of this book, that Latin America can and will continue down the road it has begun to travel, which will lead us to a brighter future of sustainable growth and shared prosperity.

Chapter 7 focuses on the necessity to strengthen Latin America's institutions—to advance the rule of law, the fight against corruption, and the promotion of citizen security. In particular, I refer to the role of the state in fighting social insecurity, the relevance of victimization, fear and perception of insecurity by Latin Americans, the direct and indirect impact of narcotrafficking, gangs, and crime.

CHAPTER 7

Deepening the Quality of Latin America's Institutions

DESPITE SOME EXCEPTIONS to the rule, weak institutions have been a major hindrance to Latin America's economic and social development. I am convinced that strengthening them is crucial to achieving my vision of a truly shared society by 2050. When I talk about *institutions*, I refer to formal rules such as constitutions and legal systems, as well as informal norms and habits. Institutional quality matters because it provides the framework necessary for state policies and reforms to be carried out effectively and for sustained economic and social development to take place. Institutions are an integral component of the state's capacity to deliver concrete and measurable results.

The weak institutional environment in our region translates into a low enforcement of rules, de facto discretion over their implementation, and short institutional durability. Formal rules in Latin America tend to change along with shifts in political power. As Harvard professor Steven Levitsky's work on Latin American politics shows us, this generates "high uncertainty and short time horizons, as actors cannot reliably use formal rules to guide their expectations about others' behavior." Uncertainty weakens the rule of law, which in turn hinders state capacity and the protection of citizens' civil and human rights. Weak institutions prevent the effective implementation of policies. The inconsistent interpretation and enforcement of the law leads to acts of corruption and illicit activities. In my opinion, the issues that derive from weak institutions are serious and numerous.

Shifts in our institutional environment have tended to come in waves in response to specific historical factors affecting most countries in the region. Work conducted by Eduardo Lora shows us that in the first of the most recent waves, institutions changed in response to the 1980s debt crisis and the implementation of the Brady Plan.[1] Significant reforms were introduced in economic policy–making institutions in charge of monetary and fiscal policy. These included norms and regulations applied to the operation of central banks, finance ministries, and budgeting agencies. Between 1988 and 1996, 12 central banks were reformed by law or by constitutional change, giving them greater autonomy. As I discussed in earlier chapters, central banks are more independent than ever before, and governments have a greater capacity to manage their budgets. Regardless of their political inclination, a large number of governments in our region have chosen to pursue prudent macroeconomic management during the past two decades.

Our region has also made progress in reforming regulatory agencies. According to a study conducted by Kaufmann, Kraay, and Mastruzzi, Latin America has a regulatory framework for economic activity comparable to that of East Asian countries and not too distant from that of developed nations. Although the response to the financial crisis of the 1980s and 1990s varied among countries, in general it led to processes that strengthened the regulatory framework for economic activity. In the same period, developed nations underwent a process of financial deregulation. This is one of the main reasons why the region fared better in managing the effects of the 2008 global financial crisis. Thus, in my experience, some of the most effective institutional reforms in Latin America have been those associated with economic activity—perhaps because after the crises of the early 1980s, this was the area of regulation that seemed in most urgent need of reform.

The wave of democratization also produced reforms in political institutions. Out of the 18 Latin American countries, 14 reformed their presidential election rules. First, the number of countries that use a simple majority system has decreased, while the number of two-round runoff systems has risen. All countries have moved in the direction of increasing the legitimacy of presidential elections. Second, 15 of the 18 countries have laws that permit presidential reelection. Third, the average presidential term was decreased from an average of 5 years to 4.7 years, with the exception of Bolivia, where the term was increased. Finally, presidential and legislative elections are no longer held simultaneously.

Although many of these reforms are positive, the frequency with which they change has been high. This shows us that political rules are not yet firmly rooted and that our region is still in the process of solidifying its democracies. Not surprisingly, we have seen how elections rules changed in Bolivia in 2013, which will allow President Morales to run for a third consecutive term. My point is not that any change is necessarily good or bad but that we must be careful to include checks and balances when reforming our political institutions. Changes can been positive, but we should be wary of reforms that weaken the democratic alternation of power because this can easily lead to a decrease in the quality of democracy.

The second wave of reforms took place in the mid-1980s, introducing changes to the judicial system. The aim of the reforms was to strengthen the judicial branch and improve the administration of justice. There were three main types of reforms: to the law, to the implementation of the law, and to the oversight of external agencies and branches. In this process most countries reformed and simplified their criminal codes to facilitate access to justice by larger segments of the population. In an attempt to ease and speed up processes in overburdened judicial systems, laws were passed to introduce alternative dispute settlement mechanisms. However, the scope of other important reforms turned out to be quite narrow and perhaps insufficient. This includes improvements in the operation of courts, police, and judicial agencies, as well as attempts to strengthen the administration of courts, the creation of specialized judicial agencies, the training of judges, and the use of technology to increase efficiency.

Reform outcomes are diverse and vary from country to country. Costa Rica has been effective in the appointment of judges based on merit and credentials, while Brazil has introduced a high-remuneration scheme to its judicial system. But, the way I see it, most countries in our region have been unable to establish true judicial independence from the executive branch. While laws have been passed, enforcement of the laws remains weak. Much work remains to be done in terms of reducing political interference in the appointment of magistrates and judges. We must continue to work to increase judiciary budgets, improve salaries, and create specialized oversight bodies. Not surprisingly, people's confidence in the judiciary system remains low. In subsequent sections I discuss in greater detail the negative consequences that a weak judiciary has for the rule of law, corruption, insecurity, and illicit activities such as trafficking in narcotics. The implications are serious because they have a profound effect on the quality of democracy in our region.

Returning to the third wave of reforms, the early 1990s brought a series of tax reforms throughout the region. Faced with budgetary constraints, due to decreased revenue from tariffs after trade liberalization, our governments resorted to other, indirect taxes to fill the revenue gap. Instead of building sustainable tax foundations, many Latin American governments prioritized the simplicity of value-added taxes over more progressive direct forms of taxation. The consequences of this poor institutional design are still felt today. As I noted in Chapter 4, the poor and most vulnerable groups in our societies suffer the most because taxation fails to act as a mechanism of redistribution. Regressive taxes such as VATs increase inequality because they tax consumption, not income or wealth. Because the poor consume a higher fraction of their income than do the wealthy, sales taxes tend to fall more heavily on Latin America's lower-income groups, although not necessarily on the lowest-income groups (who may buy little in formal markets).

Thus, our region is in dire need of introducing progressive taxes and reformulating the social contract between the state and its people. Given our history of low government accountability and state capacity to deliver public services effectively, informal norms put a low value on citizens' sense of responsibility to pay taxes. Deepening democracy therefore requires shifting people's informal norms and habits by improving the state's capacity to deliver concrete and measurable results. In this regard, direct taxation is an essential tool for increasing citizens' participation in holding governments accountable for their actions. As Larry Diamond notes (and as I discussed in Chapter 4), democracy is designed to make governments accountable to the people they serve because they are also beholden to them for government revenues. Only if we ensure this dependency of the government on its people and achieve increased accountability to taxpayers will the region be truly able to achieve higher levels of shared development.

Between 1993 and 2004, Latin American pension systems underwent significant reforms in 11 of the 18 countries. Bolivia, the Dominican Republic, El Salvador, Mexico, and Nicaragua followed the Chilean model in the introduction of fully funded pension systems. Fully funded systems are managed by the private sector, and the pension depends solely on the amount saved by the contributor. According to their proponents, such systems aim to increase social security coverage and efficiency and to reduce the fiscal burden on the central government. But we know that recessions and high fees greatly increase the vulnerability of pension holders.

On the other hand, Colombia and Peru adopted a more flexible approach in which workers had the option of choosing the system they preferred. Argentina, Costa Rica, Ecuador, and Uruguay opted for a mix of public system and fully funded systems. Not surprisingly, the results of many such pension reforms have not been as favorable as their proponents promised. The population covered by these plans has decreased from 46 percent to 26 percent of total population. High administrative costs and low pension guarantees led many workers to opt out of these systems. The problem is that these pension systems failed to provide social safety nets to the great majority of the population working in the informal sector. In my eyes, pension systems will remain flawed until we are able to cover workers in both the formal and informal sectors.

Until the 1980s, all countries except for Argentina and Brazil were politically, administratively, and fiscally centralized. The return to democracy started a process of decentralization, which persists until today. For example, average subnational public spending increased from 13.1 percent in 1985 to 17.3 percent in 1996 to 19.3 percent in 2004. The decentralization of the election of mayors has been followed by the decentralization of the election of other intermediate levels of government. This also spurred the institutional reform of subnational responsibilities. Until the mid-1990s, this included subnational provision of basic infrastructure services such as trash collection, road maintenance, and urban works in local communities. By 1996, these responsibilities were extended to nutrition, hospital management, and potable water, which require greater organization and administration. In terms of tax collection, Argentina, Brazil, and Colombia have been the most effective in decentralizing local taxes. Brazil is the only country in the region with subnational value-added taxes, which account for 24 percent of the country's tax revenue.

During my presidential term, I was able to introduce one of the most significant institutional reforms in the history of Peru: its decentralization process. Today Peru is divided into local and regional governments and a central government, each with its set of stipulated rights and responsibilities. However, one of the main barriers to decentralization has been the mismatch between subnational mandates and their actual capacity to deliver results. Part of our learning process has been to recognize the limitations that come with decentralizing at subnational levels and to provide technical assistance to increase the capacity of local governments.

Since the mid-1990s, many countries faced problems related to subnational overborrowing, generating fiscal imbalances at the national level. This led to reforms of subnational fiscal institutions to limit borrowing and increase spending accountability. Most recently, some countries in the region have made headway in the introduction of automatic and electronic transactions to facilitate transparency and efficiency in the transfer of funds to subnational governments. As we can see, decentralization in Latin America is an ongoing process that needs to develop and improve.

Reform efforts have also targeted laws for greater access to information and dissemination of budgets and fiscal statements since the mid-1990s. Twelve countries have introduced laws to increase transparency, but only five of them have fully internalized transparency into the operations of their government apparatus. In the sections that follow, I analyze transparency in more detail, especially as regards the rule of law and the fight against corruption.

Although a wide array of institutional reforms have taken place in the last decades, a note of caution is called for. Institutional reform in the region has been characterized by abrupt, frequent, and radical change. Discretion over the enforcement of rules and regulations is still selective at many levels, and not all citizens are treated equally under the law. Our recent democratic history shows us that the cost of institutional replacement is low and the uncertainty produced by that is high. This is bad because it strengthens informal social norms that enable citizens to circumvent the law. Uncertainty increases public distrust and increases the risk of conducting business, all of which negatively affect growth and development.

Experience shows us that strengthening institutions requires the involvement of formal and informal power holders. Together they can generate gradual but deep-rooted reforms based on consensus and joint collaboration, rather than the arbitrary imposition of laws and regulations by those in power. Institutions based on consensus and debate tend to be more durable than those imposed by decrees. Consensus among opposing parties presupposes the introduction of checks and balances to curb abuses of power. Similarly, the unbundling and incomplete adoption of reforms has hindered their durability and legitimacy. Often, for reforms to succeed, they must be introduced in bundles in order to provide additional safeguards and more sustainability.

Latin America must continue down the path of strengthening its institutions in order to deepen democracy and increase its legitimacy in the eyes of its citizens. Institutional reforms are often more complex, uncertain, and harder to implement than economic reforms because they involve a wide range of actors, with their own sets of interests, and are thus dependent on the political process. I look at this in more depth in Chapter 9 when I discuss state capacity to deliver. Policy makers must place a strong emphasis on generating continuity and deepening the observance of formal norms and regulations so they can override informal norms and habits.

STRENGTHENING THE RULE OF LAW

Deepening democracy in Latin America is threatened not only by weak institutions but by a weak rule of law as well. Guillermo O'Donnell has argued that "the rule of law is among the essential pillars upon which any high-quality democracy rests." An effective rule of law protects political rights and civil liberties, provides accountability to preserve equality of the law among all citizens, and prevents abuses from the power of the state. Following O'Donnell's work, the rule of law must be understood as a moving target. As society changes, so do the struggles for new rights and the reinterpretation of old rights.

Political and civil rights include the rights of voting and joining a political party, engaging in a contract, having freedom of speech, not suffering violence, and receiving fair treatment from the government. An effective rule of law establishes a balance between citizens' rights and responsibilities.

Similarly, an effective rule of law includes certain key characteristics. First, laws and the lawmaking process must be proactive, open, clear, and stable. Second, the judiciary system must remain independent. Third, hearings must be fair, open, and free of influence. Fourth, courts must be easily accessible and must maintain power of oversight to ensure compliance with the law. Finally, crime-preventing agencies should not have impunity to act beyond the law.

In our region, Costa Rica and Uruguay stand out as two notable examples of functional, strong, and independent legal systems. Both countries have an established legal system servicing their entire territories, reaching citizens across income levels, and offering citizens political and civil rights. Unfortunately, to varying degrees, the rule of law remains weak in almost every other country in our region.

Latin Americans of all stripes have a long tradition of ignoring the law. Informal social norms generate strong incentives to bypass the law rather than comply with it. This has historically benefited powerful stakeholders, as their political and economic position has granted them a level of impunity from the official sanctions that would otherwise come from evading compliance with regulations and duties, such as paying taxes, protecting worker rights, and enforcing environmental protection laws. Enforcement of the law has often been lax in regard to those in power but stronger in regard to the disadvantaged. This asymmetry has helped foster inequality in our region. It is the poor who feel the full force of the bureaucracy when requesting legal documents or simply going to a hospital or police station. Evidence shows that all citizens are not treated equally before the law. This is one of the main challenges ahead as the region strives to improve the rule of law, decrease inequality, and deepen democracy.

An effective rule of law is one in which the legal system functions effectively across its entire territory. This also means that laws are applied equally to all individuals irrespective of income level or position in society and that laws are enacted to prohibit and punish discrimination against the poor, women, foreigners, and minorities. One area of concern in our region is the way in which the legal system treats indigenous communities, as well as the insufficient recognition of indigenous rights and cultures in national constitutions. To this I must add the need to revise our laws and regulations so they do not continue to discriminate against women and minorities.

Furthermore, an effective rule of law is one in which the judiciary is free of influence from political pressures and private interests. The judiciary in Latin America is "too distant, cumbersome, expensive, and slow for the underprivileged to often even attempt to access it. And if they do manage to obtain judicial access, not surprisingly the evidence available points to severe discriminations."[2] In contrast, a strong rule of law allows any citizen to report abuses from his or her landlord or the police, with the certainty that the process will be fair and expeditious. Our judicial institutions remain weak and in need of further reform to gain independence from political influence and to ensure that the poor and illiterate have access to courts and legal counsel.

The rule of law also requires the police and armed forces to respect individuals' rights and to provide fair treatment to detainees without violating basic rules and procedures. Although progress has been made in this area, much work remains to be done to improve prison conditions and provide prompt trials to those detained. As I argue in the next section, police reform continues to be a pending task in the fight against corruption and in eradicating informal norms regarding bribes and illicit activities.

THE FIGHT AGAINST CORRUPTION

The prevalence of corruption is one of the main factors hindering Latin America's full economic and social development because it threatens institutions and the rule of law, and it weakens the state's capacity to deliver concrete and measurable results. Corruption is generally recognized as the use of public power for private gain. It takes numerous forms, and its impacts are manifold.

To begin with, corruption is not just another "tax." Unlike a tax, corruption entails secrecy, uncertainty, and arbitrariness. Corruption is illegal and must be kept secret, which creates further inefficiencies in resource allocation to avoid detection and punishment. Corruption agreements are not enforceable in court, which leads to a greater element of uncertainty and unpredictability than licit activities. In addition to this, bribes tend to be arbitrary and unpredictable. Unlike a tax, corruption payments do not contribute to public revenue but benefit private parties instead. Thus, corruption is more distortionary than a tax.

There is also evidence that corruption has a negative effect on growth. A well-known study conducted by Paulo Mauro shows that corruption lowers total investment, thereby reducing GDP growth. Corruption reduces the efficiency of investment by diverting resources to less productive areas and less efficient firms. In addition, evidence shows that corruption has a stronger negative effect on growth than taxation. This is in part due to higher transaction costs caused by the uncertainty and secrecy surrounding bribes and because corrupt agreements are not enforceable by law.

Evidence also underscores the detrimental effect of corruption on the provision of public education and health services. The prospects of illicit revenue derived from infrastructure projects tend to result in lower investment in health and education. Similarly, corruption tends to siphon resources away from existing education and health budgets, as well as other areas of public investment. At a micro level, corruption decreases access to education and health by reducing their quality and increasing their costs. This disproportionately affects the poor, who might need to pay bribes for services that should otherwise be free of charge.

Despite some progress in the fight against corruption, it continues to be a major problem in our region. The latest Transparency International report shows that, with the exception of Chile and Uruguay, Latin American countries rank high in the 2013 Corruption Perceptions Index. This can be observed in Figure 7.1. At the bottom, Chile's and Uruguay's rankings are comparable to those of developed nations. At the top, Nicaragua, Honduras, Paraguay, and Venezuela show evidence of rampant corruption.

Corruption tends to be higher in countries with lower levels of economic and human development, lower levels of education, weak institutions and rule of law, limited political competition, relatively large state influence in the economy, lack of judicial independence, low civil service wages, low levels of interpersonal trust, and large natural resource endowments. Not surprisingly, the countries with stronger institutions and rule of law, such as Chile and Uruguay, have the lowest levels of corruption in our region.

I am convinced that fighting corruption is essential for true economic and social development. Our governments must curb corruption in order to regain citizens' trust in the political system and to deepen democracy.

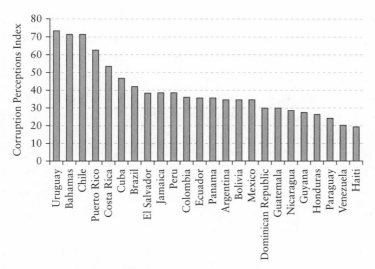

FIGURE 7.1 *Corruption Perceptions Index, 2013*
Source: Transparency International, 2013 Corruption Perceptions Index.

Luckily, mechanisms do exist to help us in the fight against corruption. One is horizontal accountability. On paper, most developing countries have anticorruption bodies and audit agencies, but they rarely serve the purpose of controlling corruption and preventing abuses of power. As argued by Larry Diamond, "Integrity and transparency in government are best achieved when state agencies of horizontal accountability interlock and overlap in systemic fashion."[3] The beauty of horizontal accountability lies in overlapping authority, so that if one agency fails to detect or deter an illicit act of corruption, another agency will most likely catch it.

Horizontal accountability does not work in isolation. For example, "if an audit agency uncovers fraud, a countercorruption commission imposes civil penalties for it, and an ombudsman stands to investigate and report if any piece in the process breaks down or needs assistance."[4] Horizontal accountability requires the effective cooperation of numerous agencies. Interlocking authority makes processes reinforcing. It increases the barriers to corruption because it creates many layers of oversight that make it difficult for an act of corruption to remain hidden.

Latin America is not short on laws penalizing corruption or the misuse of public funds. What is missing, however, is the effective enforcement of these laws. For this reason, I argue that special attention must be devoted to laws regulating conflict of interest and laws that require the disclosure of finances by public officials and their families. All public officials should be made to declare their assets before taking office and every year while in office. It is essential for this information to be publicly available so the media and civil society can scrutinize it in order to demand greater accountability.

To increase transparency, citizens must have the legal right to request and receive public information, including public procurement processes, budgets, fiscal spending, and contracts. Once accessed, this information gains value when it is published publicly or online, facilitating scrutiny from the media and civil society.

But the fight against corruption is not possible without effective anticorruption agencies. Such agencies are in charge of monitoring and auditing public officials and public institutions in order to detect and deter illicit activities. Their work must be comprehensive, with random audits carried out on a regular basis, so the threat of detection is credible. Similarly, all government bureaus, agencies, and ministries should have their accounts audited and their performance evaluated regularly. In order to add redundancy to the system of horizontal accountability, governments should have in place offices for general auditors to conduct random audits and evaluations. Presidential systems of government also require congressional oversight committees to create checks and balances on executive power and thus to strengthen horizontal accountability. These committees usually investigate waste, fraud, and abuse of power in the executive branch.

It is important to have an ombudsman's office to receive and investigate the public's complaints concerning acts of corruption and abuse of power. This channel provides another venue for catching acts that escaped the notice of other agencies or scrutinizing anticorruption commissions themselves. Here I would like to emphasize the fact that all public officials, including those working in anticorruption agencies, must be subject to audits and evaluations.

Staff working on anticorruption commissions must be well remunerated in order to increase incentives for effective work. These bodies need to be well equipped with technical skills and technological tools, such as accountants, detectives, specialized lawyers, computer specialists, and the technology necessary to collect and analyze data and conduct audits.

For anticorruption commissions to be effective, they must be supported by an efficient legal system capable of imposing actual sanctions and punishment. Similarly, credibility relies on an independent judiciary free of political influence. If government officials are to be audited and tried for their wrongdoings, it is crucial for the judiciary system to have the means to punish offenders regardless of their position in government or economic status in society.

Horizontal accountability also depends on vertical accountability, which involves fair and competitive elections. Vertical accountability rests on the premise that citizens use their vote to reward or punish candidates based on their past actions and accomplishments. According to this premise, politicians engaged in corruption scandals should be punished by voters, who will shift their votes to better and more qualified candidates. But for elections to accomplish this mission, they must be fair and competitive. Thus, electoral commissions are essential to guarantee that no fraud or vote buying takes place during elections. As with the judiciary system, it is imperative for electoral commissions to remain independent from the influence of incumbent officials or the ruling party.

Not surprisingly, it is often argued that transparency is the best disinfectant against corruption. The region must therefore continue to increase transparency in the dissemination of public information such as procurement processes, contracts, budgets, and financial statements, as well as statements of public officials' assets before assuming office and while in office. But transparency is only effective if anticorruption commissions work hand in hand with the media, nongovernmental organizations, and civil society to increase scrutiny over public information. Thus, an independent and free press, along with an active civil society and a vigilant citizenry, are essential pieces in the fight against corruption. For democracy to take deeper root, institutions and the rule of law must be strengthened, and citizens must be empowered with true civil rights.

SOCIAL INSECURITY: LATIN AMERICA'S MOST PRESSING CONCERN

Besides being the most unequal region in the world, Latin America is also the most violent region not currently at war. This statement tells us once again of the serious challenges confronting the region and why we must act now if we want to deepen democracy and generate sustainable development. In other words, Latin American countries will not be able meet these goals by 2050 if they cannot provide citizen security. According to a recently published report by the United Nations Development Programme (UNDP), *citizen security* can be defined as the condition of living free of fear and free of want. This concept encompasses a large variety of threats: natural disasters, wars, community conflicts, food insecurity, and crime. Regardless of the level of development of each country, these threats affect people's rights and opportunities for human development with different intensities. Therefore, human security entails the protection and effective exercise of core human rights, including the right to life, to physical and material integrity, and to a decent standard of living. Without any doubt, human security is one of the biggest concerns of Latin Americans.

According to the 2012 Latinobarómetro report on social insecurity, Latin America has 9 percent of the world's population, but it is home to 27 percent of the world's homicides and 10 out of the 20 countries with the highest homicide rates. For the second consecutive time, the report finds that the main issue concerning Latin Americans is no longer poverty or economic crisis; instead, for the average Latin American, insecurity, violence, and gangs are at the top of his or her list of concerns. In 2013, 24 percent of Latin Americans considered that crime was the most important issue for the region; they ranked unemployment as the second most important (16 percent).

Although actual violence varies from country to country, the perception of high insecurity is a common denominator throughout the region. This is not surprising given that insecurity and violence derive from the existence of weak state institutions, a weak rule of law, and high levels of corruption, which leave citizens with a sense of defenselessness against violation of their rights, person, and property.

The perception of violence appears to be greatest in Guatemala, followed by El Salvador and Brazil. Conversely, the countries that perceive themselves as least violent are Uruguay and Ecuador. There appears to be an informal legitimization of violence as a means of solving interpersonal, family, and social issues. This relates back to the perception in the eyes of our citizens of weak state capacity to enforce laws and administer justice.

According to a UNDP report (2013), five out of ten Latin Americans perceive that security in their country has deteriorated: up to 65 percent stopped going out at night due to insecurity, and 13 percent reported having felt the need to move to another place for fear of becoming victims of crime. Figure 7.2 shows what its citizens consider the main threats to security in the region.

Today, Latin America is facing a paradox. Although the economies in the region have shown an annual average growth of 4.2 percent during the past ten years and have significantly reduced poverty and unemployment levels (UNDP 2013), rates of violence and crime are still high. The explanation for the growth in crime and violence is multidimensional, according to the UNDP. The first dimension is the economic-structural situation, including low-quality jobs and insufficient social mobility,

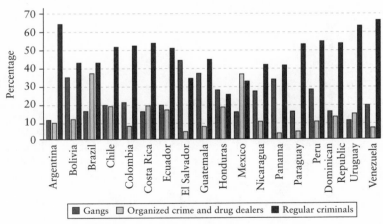

FIGURE 7.2 *Main threat to security according to citizens, 2012*

Source: UNDP (2013).
Note: These responses refer to the following question: "I will mention some groups and I will ask you to indicate which one represents the greatest threat to your safety." Other groups that were included in this question were police or military personnel, family members, and neighbors.

which in the context of consumer-driven economic growth has generated "aspirational crimes." Second is the social dimension, reflecting structural changes in families, including a significant increase in single-parent households, dropout rates, and accelerated urban growth that erodes the social fabric. The third dimension comprises crime drivers such as weapons, alcohol, and drugs. Finally, the fourth dimension is the lack of capacity of the state—police forces, judges, prosecutors, and prisons—to adequately address security challenges.[5]

One of the objective indicators used to measure violence is the rate of homicides. As Figure 7.3 shows, Honduras and El Salvador have the highest homicide rates, followed by Venezuela in third place. Three of the five countries with the highest rates of homicide in the world are in Latin America. Currently, Central America has a higher annual death rate than occurred during the civil wars of the 1980s and early 1990s.

More than 100,000 homicides occur in Latin America annually. According to the latest report on human security issued by the UNDP, there was an increase of 11 percent in the homicide rate from 2010 to 2011, while

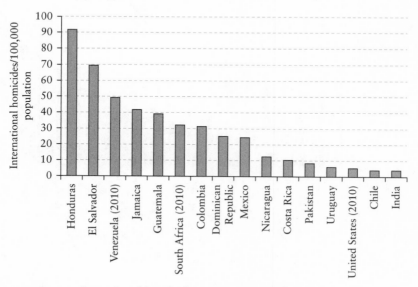

FIGURE 7.3 *Intentional homicides per 100,000 population, 2011*
Source: UNODC Homicide Rates (2011).

the rate was stable or decreased in the rest of the world. Latin America was the only region in the world where lethal violence increased between 2000 and 2010. Also, the same report stated that in the last decade, more than 1 million people died in the region because of violence. Yet, there is an important violence heterogeneity throughout the region.[6]

Two main types of violence are particularly worrisome to citizens in our region. First, 80 percent of Latin Americans consider intrafamily or domestic violence to be a significant problem. About two-thirds of those surveyed report knowing of cases of within-family violence against women, while one in every five people knows of violence against children or the elderly. Although domestic violence varies among countries, violence against women is greater everywhere than that against children and the elderly. Notably, younger women with greater educational attainment are more likely to formally report domestic violence than women with fewer years of education. A spiral of silence appears to be prevalent among low-income women, who not only suffer from gender violence but are the main victims of social and economic inequality.

Second, violent crimes appear to be the main threat afflicting the population at large, regardless of gender or income level. This involves crimes in public spaces that threaten people's physical integrity and private property. The category also includes crimes related to gangs and drugs.

In our region homicides are usually the result of gender violence, robberies, and organized crime. Homicides also tend to be concentrated in specific regions, cities, and neighborhoods, and the main types differ by country. For example, deaths in the Southern Cone are usually associated with gender violence. In Brazil, they derive from robberies and organized crime, while in Colombia and Venezuela, they are mainly the product of organized crime. In Central America, they derive from gangs and narcotrafficking. Even within countries there is great variation in the rate of violence. The main victims of this type of crime are young, low-income males. As a consequence, Brazil and Guatemala might soon have significantly fewer young males in their populations, which will in turn affect their demographic pyramid.

However, we must be aware that the accuracy of the numbers is subject to significant misrepresentation, given that agencies report conflicting statistics and that only 16 percent of criminal acts are formally reported. We continue to have institutional and structural flaws in the collection of data, in addition to insufficient coordination with subnational and international agencies fighting crime. To this I must add our generally weak police forces that respond slowly and often ineffectively to crime and investigative work. For these reasons, we must be aware of the possible underestimation presented by the current data. This means that we might be up against insecurity issues greater than what the numbers show.

Victimization, Fear, and Perception of Insecurity

In 2011, about one in every three Latin Americans or someone in their nuclear family was a victim of crime. Mexico, Peru, Argentina, Costa Rica, and Colombia are the countries with the highest rates of victimization. However, the perception of insecurity does not always follow the direction of the actual rate of victimization. There is actual insecurity, and there is the social perception of insecurity. The perception of insecurity depends on the initial level of crime, the rate of change in crimes, and the relative level of crime. The initial level is very important because it sets a reference point with which to compare the actual situation. We have a tendency to get used to different levels of violence. For example, a minor increase in victimization might have very different effects on the social perception of insecurity in Colombia, where people are more accustomed to violence, than in Uruguay, which has lower levels of violence.

The rate of change is significant because a large increase in the number of victims will receive greater attention from the media, generating a multiplier effect in the social perception of insecurity. News reporting of crimes with violence has a long-lasting effect on people's fears of being victimized. This is because, psychologically, we tend to vicariously experience a third person's experience with violence as if it were our own. Even when the probability of being a victim of violent crime is low, the concrete image of this possibility is already real in our minds. This generates a vicious cycle of fear generating more fear, even when actual victimization rates do not substantiate such levels of concern. This process takes place regardless of the individual's income level; however, women tend to have a higher perception of insecurity than men in our region.

Finally, I want to emphasize that the relative position is significant because it determines the importance of a given issue in society when compared to other issues. Currently, insecurity generates greater concern relative to other social issues such as education, health, or economic growth. This position is a moving target subject to change, which gives us some hope that improved capacity of state policies to deal with actual crime can reduce people's perception of insecurity.

Latin Americans deserve to live in an environment free of fear, where they can conduct their lives and prosper without concern for their own or their family's physical safety, and without fearing the loss of the property they have worked so hard to obtain. Our governments can no longer turn a blind eye to insecurity in the region. Eradicating crime and violence must become national priorities. A shared society is one in which all of our citizens feel fully and equally safe and secure to pursue their life dreams.

The Role of the State

For our democracies to develop deeper roots, our governments must be able to guarantee the safety of their citizens. It is one of government's most important and basic tasks. People cannot engage in a true social contract with a state that fails to protect them physically. The right to live is so ingrained in every individual's understanding of his or her political and civil rights that our democracies are severely weakened by the government's inability to eradicate violence and crime.

Not surprisingly, only one-third of the region's population have confidence in the police. This leaves a significant part of the population feeling vulnerable and defenseless in the face of a growing social perception of insecurity. This calls for the urgent need to reform the police, strengthen institutions and the rule of law, formulate more active government policies in the fight against crime, and establish better mechanisms to inform the public on actual victimization rates, rather than having the public rely on media reports to develop their perceptions of insecurity.

Let me make this clear: Latin Americans need to regain trust in the government's ability to protect their physical integrity and personal property against abusive acts of violence. Only then will we be able to walk the path toward a more sustainable and strengthened democracy.

NARCOTRAFFICKING: THE ACHILLES HEEL
OF LATIN AMERICAN DEMOCRACIES

Trafficking in narcotic drugs and psychotropic substances has emerged as one of the greatest threats to state capacity in Latin America and the greatest threat to the stability of its democracies. This is due to the increasing power of drug cartels, along with growing violence and crime. All this has left numerous governments unable to handle a problem of this magnitude. In this scenario there are notable bright and dark spots. For example, Colombia and Brazil have been able to strengthen their position against narcotrafficking, whereas the situation has dramatically worsened in Central America. Today Latin America faces the threat of a simultaneous increase in drug trafficking and illicit drug use.

Most transnational organized crime (TOC) starts on one continent and ends on a different one, often going through a third location before reaching its final destination. This makes TOC a truly global issue. In the case of our region, the bulk of cocaine production originates in the Andean countries, to later reach North America (via Central America) or Europe (via West Africa). More recently, the lower-quality cocaine produced in Bolivia has been directed toward the Southern Cone, generating growing issues of public health and crime.

In Latin America, narcotrafficking is largely based on the production and transportation of cocaine. Cocaine is produced in Colombia, Peru, and Bolivia. Historically, most cocaine shipments were directed to the US market, but this trend has declined steadily since the 1980s. In this period European demand has increased, rapidly compensating for the decline in the US market.

Until the 1990s, the Medellín and Cali cartels controlled narcotrafficking in the region. But the Colombian government's crackdown on organized crime was able to reduce their size and power. This vacuum created strong market incentives for the emergence of Mexican drug cartels because they are physically close to the US market. The shift to Mexico has led to a sharp escalation of violence in Central America.

Currently, cocaine is shipped from Colombia to Mexico and then transported by land to the United States. Colombian cartels are in charge of the production, while Mexican cartels are in charge of delivering cocaine to the United States. In 2008 figures, 196 tons of cocaine were necessary to meet US demand, representing a market value of US$38 billion. However, this US$38 billion was unevenly distributed. Coca farmers in the Andean region received only US$1.1 billion. Importing cocaine into Mexico generated profits of US$2.4 billion (excluding shipping costs), while Mexican cartels reaped US$2.9 billion in profits for transporting cocaine to the United States. But the greatest profits were made within the US market, accounting for US$29.5 billion. Market conditions clearly show the existing financial incentives preventing the eradication of narcotrafficking. It also shows the financial motivation behind drug wars in Mexico and the rest of Central America.

On the other hand, the number of cocaine users in Europe doubled from 2 million in 1998 to 4.1 million in 2008. In this period, the market value of cocaine going to Europe increased from US$14 billion to US$34 billion. Colombia is the main supplier of cocaine to Europe, followed by Peru and Bolivia. Shipments usually depart from Venezuela and Bolivia to West Africa before reaching the ports of Spain, Portugal, the Netherlands, and Belgium. From the total US$34 billion, Andean farmers receive only 1 percent, and cartels transporting it to Africa also receive only 1 percent of the total market value. The numbers show us that although small in terms of percentages, the revenue realized by cartels in our region constitutes a strong barrier to the eradication of narcotrafficking. We can also see that the profits made within the United States and Europe constitute the root of the problem. Eradicating narcotrafficking will be increasingly difficult as long as market incentives remain untouched. Attempts to eradicate cocaine production will be futile if little is done to eradicate the demand for drugs. Narcotrafficking is a global problem in need of global solutions.

The Direct and Indirect Impact of Narcotrafficking

The threats of organized crime are pervasive and highly destabilizing. In the big scheme of things, it is easy to overlook the negative effects of drug consumption in any given society, which involve serious physical and mental health problems, in addition to the negative externalities born by families and communities. In the case of Latin America, drug consumption is growing rapidly, especially in the Southern Cone countries. To start with, Latin American governments need to generate greater awareness among their own end users. But most importantly, developed countries must strive hard to generate greater awareness among their populations and end users of the real costs associated with their demand for drugs. We need to make it clear that when people in the United States and Europe consume cocaine, the people in our region suffer dearly. These costs and losses derive from the violence generated by narcotrafficking, drug wars between drug cartels, and the risks run by migrant smugglers. It is undeniable that drug use has undesirable consequences much greater than the mere act of consumption.

The indirect impact of organized crime is centered on its threat to state capacity, undermining the state's institutions and rule of law. In this regard, "traditional organized crime groups displace state authority by filling the governance niches neglected by the official structures and by co-opting whatever vestigial state agents remain."[7] Due to the financial profits derived from narcotrafficking, drug cartels tend to be powerful organizations that override the state and remain unaccountable to society.

Drug wars in Central America have led to the highest homicide rates in the world, surpassing the deaths caused by civil wars in the 1980s and 1990s. The arms and financial power of drug cartels have left governments in Mexico and Central America bewildered by their ability to buy public officials and silence the press. Whenever bribery and corruption fail to work, cartels increase their use of violence in order to threaten state capacity and nullify police enforcement of laws and regulations. Thus, Mexico's state capacity to crack down on drug cartels has been called into question. The growing waves of crime and violence decrease confidence in the state and affect the quality of democracy as citizens are left defenseless in the face of organized crime. In South America, narcotrafficking also threatens state capacity in countries that produce and transport drugs. In addition, narcotrafficking threatens the real economy across the region due to active money laundering activities. For all these reasons I argue that narcotrafficking has become Latin America's

Achilles heel. It weakens state capacity and threatens to undermine our democracies.

The fight against narcotrafficking requires not only strengthening state institutions and the rule of law but also focusing on decreasing opportunities for corruption and low enforcement of laws and regulations. We must also strengthen transnational cooperation and collaboration. Isolated efforts might reduce violence and the power of cartels in a specific region, but they will not root out the problem. This became clear in the case of Colombia and Mexico. The crackdown on Colombian cartels did not eradicate the production of cocaine; it simply led to the emergence of new drug cartels in Mexico. Violence and crime decreased in Colombia, while they got worse in Mexico and Central America. Thus, a holistic approach is necessary to target the underlying source of the problem, which is the high and profitable demand for cocaine in developed countries. We must also continue to dismantle the production and transportation of cocaine in South and Central America. This will require better transnational mechanisms and institutions to join forces in sharing information and resources in the fight against narcotrafficking.

Gangs

A report titled *Transnational Organized Crime in Central America and the Caribbean: A Threat Assessment*, prepared by the United Nations Office on Drugs and Crime (UNODC), defines street gangs as a variant of the classic territorial organized crime groups, whose main distinguishing feature is that they are comprised almost entirely of youth (with "youth" being extended into the twenties and even the thirties in societies where education and opportunities are limited). In the region, they are usually not classified as "organized crime groups" because their focus is not on financial gain.

Most of these street gangs lack the capacity to engage in pseudo-state functions, mainly because they are comprised of impulsive young people. They are not interested in being community servants (as many organized crime organizations are). However, they are strongly concerned with local affairs. For them, territorial control is about identity, respect, and their place in the world. These aspirations make them act against their own financial interests, feuding with similar groups over perceived insults or symbolic incursions into their "turf." Conflict seems to be a fundamental part of their existence, their group identity being rooted in those whom they oppose.

The "Maras" in Central America are street gangs. They do have an international origin and exist in several countries, but there is very little evidence that this has changed their central focus on local affairs. The two major factions—Mara Salvatrucha and Mara-18—both trace their origins to East Los Angeles, and their presence in Central America is almost certainly a result of the wave of criminal deportations from the United States to El Salvador, Guatemala, and Honduras after 1996. It is difficult to get an exact number of how many people belong to these street organizations. However, Figures 7.4 and 7.5, created by UNODC, give us a pretty good idea.

UNODC (2012) found that cocaine trafficking has undeniably catalyzed violence is some areas. The implementation of the new Mexican security strategy in 2006 interrupted cocaine supply to the US market, which disrupted US demand for the drug, but it has not yet reduced the violence associated with the flow.

In response to an increasingly inhospitable environment in Mexico, traffickers have shifted their focus to new routes along the Guatemalan/Honduran border and contesting new "plazas" throughout the region.

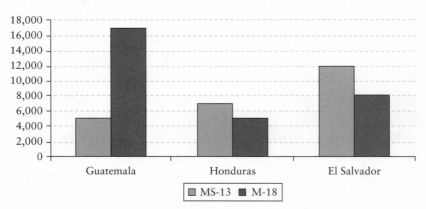

FIGURE 7.4 *Mara membership in the Northern Triangle, 2012*
Source: UNODC (2012).

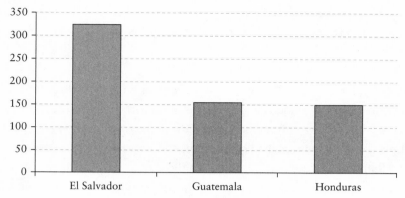

FIGURE 7.5 *Mareros per 100,000 population, 2012*
Source: UNODC (2012).

The contest today is between long-standing organized crime families that effectively govern the remote areas of the countries in which they operate.

Since 2007, the UNODC affirms that the Mara groups (MS-13 and M-18) play a minor role in transnational cocaine trafficking. However, the Maras, the Zetas, and other territorial groups appear to be involved in migrant smuggling, human trafficking, and the firearms trade. This involvement, according to the same report, may increase if cocaine revenues decline.

According to the UNDP (2013), where low-level criminal organizations exist, such as juvenile gangs, it is necessary to strengthen links between society and local authorities to prevent and control crime. Community policing is crucial in providing attention to at-risk populations. Providing educational programs that offer resources or technical training and arranging leisure activities in neighborhoods or communities can help strengthen the bond between these vulnerable groups and the rest of the community, as well as reduce risk factors linked to youth violence.

The presence of organized criminal groups requires highly targeted responses. The growing presence of drug trafficking networks or criminal groups dedicated to extortion or kidnapping, for example, requires a greater investment in investigation, intelligence work, and collaboration among the different security agencies. When organized crime permeates community dynamics deeply, it is necessary for the state to regain territorial control and strengthen local institutions, including public security forces.

SUMMING UP

This chapter explains the importance of measures to strengthen the weak institutional environment of our region. This is the way to break the vicious cycle of low enforcement of rules, de facto discretion over their implementation, entrenched corruption, and pervasive citizen insecurity.

Chapter 8 focuses on the social challenges to an inclusive society—namely, quality education, access to health services, addressing hunger and malnutrition, and decent housing. All of them are indispensable components of well-being.

Social Challenges to an Inclusive Society

MY VISION of a shared society and the multidimensional approach to addressing poverty suggest that to achieve the outcomes we care about, we must remedy income poverty and inequality. We Latin Americans know this, and we are making progress. But working on income issues alone is not sufficient. I believe the ultimate goal of Latin American societies is to have healthy, happy citizens; resilient social and economic structures; and stable and effective democracies. Such shared societies value and offer equal opportunity to all.

The keys to achieving this goal are the social services our governments deliver to all members of our societies. There is some disagreement about what should be included as essential in terms of social services. But there is widespread agreement that health and nutrition, access to schooling, and access to basic services (namely, drinkable water and power) are indispensable components of well-being. These elements of well-being are included in most of the new measures of poverty, as I discussed earlier. There is a rich empirical literature in the academic and development fields that shows that without access to these basic services, the chances a person has to develop a productive life are low to none. If governments are going to work toward the improved welfare of their citizens, then they will need to address all three of these areas.

Throughout this chapter I draw on a recent initiative by the World Bank to measure inequality in access to these services: the Human Opportunity Index (HOI). The HOI is intended to calculate how a child's personal circumstances—those things that are out of her control like gender, family wealth, race, and so forth—impact her probability of accessing those basic services so essential to developing the capabilities she needs to succeed.

The truth is that the inequality in income and wealth we have discussed is just the tip of the iceberg. We cannot break the cycle of poverty if we do not address inequality of opportunity. The HOI measures the average availability of services and then makes discounts on that average for how unfairly or unequally the services are distributed across the population. For instance, if two countries both have achieved 70 percent access to basic education, but in one country nearly all of the 30 percent without access are girls, or are indigenous, or live in rural areas, then it will have a lower HOI than its counterpart country where the 30 percent without access is distributed across different groups in the population.

We need new ways to measure progress toward the goals we really aim for. I found the HOI to be a compelling way to look at access to services. It is consistent with our capabilities and social inclusion paradigms. These areas—health, basic services, housing, and education—are nonnegotiable for achieving our vision, but Latin America faces tough challenges if we are to ensure that all of our citizens have access to them. Let's take a closer look at what is happening in our region with regard to these essential components of well-being.

THE SYNERGY BETWEEN EDUCATION AND HEALTH SERVICES

First, it may be helpful to understand that these areas are not actually separate issues but rather work synergistically. Health, education, and poverty are not only interrelated, but they are essential and self-reinforcing components. People who are educated are more likely to be healthy, and people who are healthy are more able to attend school, learn, and attain high levels of education. We know that people who are healthy and educated are more likely to be economically successful. They are also more likely to be involved actively in their country's political process, which contributes to the construction of vibrant, functioning democracies that work for the mutual progress of all.

We also know that the education of women leads to better health not only for themselves but also for their children. It is often women who are responsible for the welfare of children, including their nutrition and how often they see a health care provider. Above and beyond whether and how often they access health care, a woman who is educated is more likely to understand when treatment is necessary, seek treatment, and then feel empowered in her interactions with health service providers (Sperling 2005; Watkins 2000). This can enable her to demand better treatment from her health care providers. This, however, is not true only for women. In general, the better educated an individual is, the better equipped he or she is to become informed about both personal health status and health care options.

Health also plays a key role in schooling. Children's health affects their capacity to learn and therefore the likelihood of acquiring key skills and knowledge from the education they receive. Malnutrition or hunger diminishes the brain's ability to process the information it receives or to perform complex tasks. It also decreases children's ability to concentrate on their lessons or reading and suppresses energy levels (Del Rosso 1999; Dercon and Sánchez 2011; Outes-Leon, Porter, and Sánchez 2011). From these effects it seems obvious why malnourished children are more likely to drop out of school than healthy children and are more likely to miss class regularly if they are enrolled.

If education is the gateway to more and better employment as an adult, the implication is that malnourished children are unlikely to be able to develop the capabilities they need, or have the opportunities open to them, to make their own informed economic and political choices. And they are likely to stay poor as adults. The interrelationship comes full circle when evidence shows that the main cause of malnutrition is monetary poverty.

ACCESS TO BASIC HEALTH SERVICES

As in the case of both poverty and inequality, Latin America has made considerable progress in terms of improving access to basic health services and reducing the most common indicators of poor health. A significant proportion of the population, however, continue to be negatively affected by a lack of access to nutritious food and basic health care. One measure of overall access to health care is life expectancy. Latin Americans' life expectancy is slowly increasing. In 2003, average expected lifespan was 72.3 years, while in 2010 it was 74.1 years. In comparison, developed areas like the United States and Europe have life expectancies of 78.2 and 79.6 years, respectively, while a relatively underdeveloped region like South Asia has a life expectancy of 65.3 years (World Development

Indicators). Latin America seems to be quite close to the developed countries, but when the UNDP created a health-adjusted life expectancy index, Latin Americans' adjusted life expectancy fell to 65 years. This suggests that many people are living additional years but in ill health. This probably speaks to the fact that many of the biggest killers among health problems in Latin America are still chronic-type (many of them treatable) diseases of the poor—ultimately exacerbated by poor access to health care services.

While heart disease and cancer are the biggest killers in Latin America, the third largest cause of death is infection and parasitic diseases. And, although declining, tuberculosis is still one of the main causes of death in our region. Countries with large indigenous and/or rural populations, which tend to remain more excluded from access to basic services, still suffer the highest rates of death from this generally treatable and preventable disease.

Another test of access to health services is the access women have to basic services during pregnancy. Both carrying and giving birth to a child can be dangerous for both the mother and the child. The access women have to prenatal care and a skilled medical attendant at delivery and the number of women who die during childbirth are good indications of the extent of access to health care in a region.

In Latin America, approximately 85 women in 100,000 lose their lives while giving birth. This compares well with less developed regions like eastern and southern Africa, where 550 per 100,000 women die during childbirth, but it is still 3.5 times the 24 per 100,000 who die in the United States (Economic Commission for Latin America and the Caribbean [ECLAC] 2012). It is interesting that the mortality rate is so much higher than in the United States and Europe, when all three have approximately the same percentage of births attended by skilled health staff—about 90 percent (Vega et al. 2011). This raises issues about the quality aspect of health care services in the region rather than access alone.

After birth, young children remain more vulnerable to disease and the effects of malnutrition than older children or adults. The number of children who die before they reach 5 years of age is an important indicator of the quality of a country's health care and nutrition system. In Latin America as a whole, on average 2 percent of children die before they reach

5 years of age (19 out of 1,000 births). This is a great improvement over the 53 children per 1,000 who died in 1990 in the region (Vega et al. 2011). While all countries have made impressive progress in child mortality rates, in 2012, Bolivia still lost 5 percent of its children before they turned 5; Guatemala and Nicaragua lost around 3 percent; and Cuba, Chile, and Uruguay all lost less than 1 percent.[1]

THE SCOURGE OF MALNUTRITION

The continuing high child mortality rates are probably due largely to malnutrition. Malnutrition—a 100 percent preventable condition—is one of the main causes of poor health in Latin America. Malnutrition is a major public health concern in the region, especially as it relates to the effects it has on children: anemia, growth delay, being underweight, and more.

Figure 8.1 shows how the main indicators of child malnutrition and acute malnutrition vary across the region. As with all the other issues, the inequality within and across countries is striking. While these data are for 2008, the recent world crisis made it harder for the poor in Latin

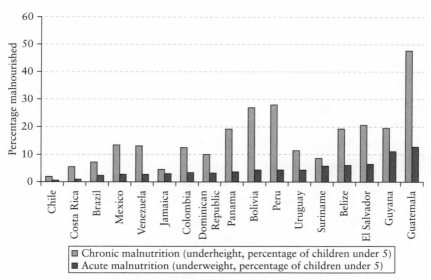

FIGURE 8.1 *Child malnutrition, 2007–2012*

Source: World Bank, World Development Indicators (database).
Note: Year varies by country.

America to get their nutritional needs met. The Economic Commission for Latin America and the Caribbean estimated that the food price crisis of 2006–2008 added 10 million people to the ranks of the extremely poor and 10 million more to the moderately poor. Another study of 19 Latin American countries found that poverty had increased by 4.3 percentage points, or by 21 million additional poor people (Robles et al. 2008). The poor are hit especially hard by food price increases because poor households can be expected to spend 50 to 80 percent of their income on food (Food and Agriculture Organization of the United Nations [FAO] 2010). This means that when prices increase dramatically but incomes stay the same, households are forced to cut food consumption; first, they generally cut down on the more nourishing (more expensive) foods, and then they tend to reduce the quantity and frequency of meals.

As might be expected from the patterns of inequality we saw in income, chronic malnutrition in children is high in many countries, but it is especially high among children in indigenous and rural communities. For instance, in Bolivia, Ecuador, and Peru, chronic malnutrition among nonindigenous children under 5 years old is a high 20 percent, 22 percent, and 20 percent, respectively. But among indigenous children this rises to a shocking 40 percent, 50 percent, and 45 percent (FAO 2010).

It is worth repeating that this is not "simply" a health issue: malnutrition in the early years has long-lasting, probably lifetime, effects on overall health as well as on children's cognitive and physical development. It is estimated that undernourishment and malnutrition account for nearly 11 percent of the total global disease burden and 35 percent of that among children under the age of 5 (de Pee et al. 2010). Undernourishment is particularly hard on children 0 to 24 months old and can have lifelong physical and cognitive development consequences. A recent study in Peru found that the global food price crisis in Peru between 2006 and 2008 had significant subsequent cognitive costs for children who were born during or shortly before that time (Outes-Leon, Porter, and Sánchez 2011).

ADDRESSING HUNGER AND MALNUTRITION

A well-thought-out food-security policy is the main element of a strategy to assure that all members of a society have access to adequate food.[2]

The evidence is strong that hunger and malnutrition are major results and causes of poverty. In my discussion of our educational strategy below, I stress again the important secondary effect that children cannot develop their capabilities in school on empty stomachs or without sufficient nutrients. Improving food security would not magically get rid of poverty, but it would likely go a long way toward reducing the intergenerational transmission of poverty by mitigating the negative effects poverty has on productivity. Thus, we consider addressing malnutrition as a way to invest in the minds of our people.

Food security can be seen as relating to both the availability (supply) of food and specific groups' vulnerability in access to food (demand). These can also be seen in terms of chronic food insecurity and transitory food insecurity. Over the past five decades, Latin America had largely solved the issue of food supply by around 1990. Indeed, when measured by the average daily requirement per person, the region has a surplus of food energy, as can be seen in Table 8.1.

However, despite the region having developed an adequate food supply, there are still millions of children and families who suffer from food insecurity and malnutrition. Thus, the main food security problem still facing Latin America today is one of access, not production. We have to make sure that low-income Latin Americans receive adequate nutrition. Eliminating hunger has to become a priority.

TABLE 8.1 *Food energy supply (kcal/person/day)*

Region	1990	2000	2005	2009
World	2,627	2,732	2,787	2,831
Africa	2,278	2,421	2,513	2,560
Americas	2,957	3,173	3,216	3,205
Central America	2,845	2,941	2,989	2,974
South America	2,579	2,782	2,873	2,951
Asia	2,421	2,591	2,635	2,706
Europe	3,378	3,248	3,369	3,362
Australia and New Zealand + (Total)	3,190	3,037	3,137	3,246

Source: Food and Agriculture Organization of the United Nations, FAOSTAT (2013).
Note: The average daily requirement is 2,200 kcal.

Some of our sister countries already provide models for how to move forward on this agenda. Brazil has developed a zero-hunger strategy, Fome Zero. This has motivated several other countries of the region to adopt similar strategies. Some countries (Argentina, Brazil, Ecuador, Guatemala, and Venezuela) have passed laws regarding food security. While most countries have not developed a coordinated strategy around "food security" per se, the issues of supply and demand are both being addressed as part of other policy initiatives, including small agriculture and rural development, social and food welfare, nutritional health assistance, and education and training on food and nutrition. The interrelated nature of food security, poverty, inequality, education, and agricultural policy means that these policy initiatives have worked to reduce food insecurity.

ACCESS TO BASIC SERVICES

Poverty does not only cause disease through malnutrition; it also makes people more likely to be exposed to diseases because the poor are much less likely to have access to safe drinking water and basic sanitation. Lack of sanitation facilities and unsafe drinking water have serious repercussions: they sicken and kill our fellow Latin Americans every day.

Latin America has managed to reach 86 percent of its population with piped, on-premises water—up from 73 percent in 1990 (UNICEF 2012). However, just as poverty is unequally distributed and concentrated in rural areas, so is the lack of access to safe water and sanitation.

When equity of access—how access is distributed across the population—is considered, the situation is much worse. The HOI measurements show that "at least one-third of the region's children do not have equitable access to water and sanitation opportunities" (Vega et al. 2011, 54). Although equitable access has grown by about 1.3 points per year since the mid-1990s, Figure 8.2 shows how access to safe water and basic sanitation is still largely dependent on how much money a household makes and where it is located—in urban or rural areas.

With regard to electricity, the situation is more equitable. Twelve out of 19 countries in Latin America and the Caribbean have an HOI for electricity higher than 90, and no country has less than a 55 HOI. This index has been growing by at least one point per year since the mid-1990s

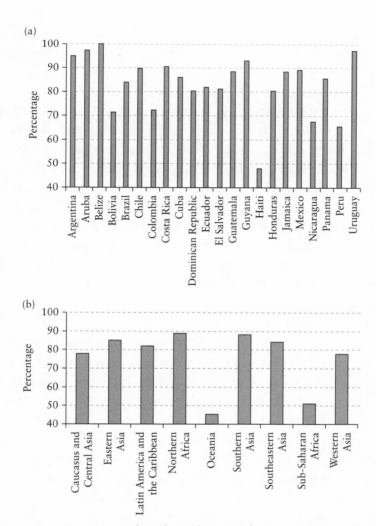

FIGURE 8.2 *Percentage of rural population with access to improved piped water: (a) by country; (b) by region*

Source: WHO/UNICEF Joint Monitoring Programme for Water Supply and Sanitation. http://www .wssinfo.org/.

(Vega et al. 2011). Remember that the HOI is a percentage of coverage discounted by inequalities in coverage; it ranges from 0 to 100, so a society that has achieved universal coverage of all services would score 100.

Across all "access to basic services" indicators, the inequality-of-opportunity is driven mainly by location (where a child lives) rather than by income or other personal circumstances. This means we need to consider the geographic inequalities in coverage, not just overall percentages.

DECENT HOUSING

Living in decent housing is a fundamental part of access to safe and sanitary living conditions. The Committee on Economic, Social and Cultural Rights (CESCR) defines as essential components of adequate, or "decent," housing legal security of tenure, availability of services, materials, facilities and infrastructure, affordability, habitability, accessibility, location, and cultural adequacy.[3] Home ownership can also be seen as playing a critical role in the strengthening of individual and community commitment to democratic institutions and to civic participation. Through decent housing, communities have greater safety, less drug use, less crime, and a more participative civil society. It can also strengthen local governments, because it is through local government that people address their community needs.

Access to decent housing can be measured best through proxies such as access to sanitation, potable water, and electricity (discussed above) and via measures of severe overcrowding. Severe overcrowding is a useful indicator because it is strongly linked to a number of issues we care about, including the likelihood of being exposed to unhygienic conditions, poor mental health, strained relationships between parents and children, lower educational attainment, and more.

Most of Latin America still has a long way to go when it comes to equitable access to uncrowded housing. Other than Brazil, Chile, and Costa Rica, all countries were more than ten points below the mean for European countries. They ranged from 7 to 8 percent of access to uncrowded housing in Guatemala and Nicaragua to 87 percent in Peru. In Peru, only 31 percent of the opportunities to access uncrowded housing are equitably distributed. In this measure, the large HOI gap between Latin America and Europe is almost fully attributable to inequality of opportunity levels that are nearly twice as high in our region.[4]

Migration from rural areas to the outskirts of urban areas is a major challenge when it comes to ensuring access to decent housing. Migrants almost universally locate in the outlying areas of large cities, where there is often little infrastructure for decent shelter, health care, schooling, recreational areas, or other services that are basic for inclusion and participation in society.

Almost all Latin American countries have implemented programs that try to ease the situation for migrants. Solutions attempted have included low-cost urbanization, providing minimal basics (e.g., paved streets, electricity, water, sanitation) and then letting migrants build their own houses. Despite these efforts, there is still not equitable or adequate access to decent housing for a large percentage of Latin Americans.

Improving and building decent housing for all, including the poor, can have a major benefit for our larger societies. If planned and financed prudently, building housing can create decent employment and increase skills in the low-income, lower-skilled labor force—precisely the population the programs are designed to help!

The second aspect of decent housing that could make a significant difference in the lives and wealth of Latin America's poor is ownership. This is important because there is an argument to be made that when families, especially low- and middle-class families, own their own homes, it increases their stake in making a democratic and participative society work, and it makes nondemocratic regimes less attractive (Carnoy 1962).

Hernando de Soto raised the additional argument that the poor often have assets that cannot function the way capital typically does:

They hold these resources in defective forms: houses built on land whose ownership rights are not adequately recorded, unincorporated businesses with undefined liability, industries located where financiers and investors cannot see them. Because the rights to these possessions are not adequately documented, these assets cannot readily be turned into capital, cannot be traded outside of narrow local circles where people know and trust each other, cannot be used as collateral for a loan, and cannot be used as a share against an investment.[5]

Together, these two arguments provide a sound basis for creating housing policies that ensure more equitable access to uncrowded housing with the essential basic services.

To do this, there is room for strengthened partnerships between government, private builders, banks, and the poor to increase the supply of affordable, safe, and sanitary housing. To gain all of the economic and democratic benefits, we need to pursue strategies that increase equitable access but also provide access to titles to low-income residents of houses that effectively belong to them but for which they have not established legal claim and provide credit funds for low-income families to invest in improving or buying their homes.

ACCESS TO QUALITY SCHOOLING

If we want an inclusive, shared society, we must invest in the minds of our people by providing a good-quality education for all. Education is arguably the most important tool a society has for increasing both social equality and economic growth. Every other aspect of development depends on education—and an educated populace—to be successful. Education is also one of the most important means by which we can strengthen democracy, enhance the benefits of development, and ensure participation in the twenty-first century's "knowledge economy."

To ensure equitable access to quality schooling, both the *access* and the *quality* aspects are essential—and neither is sufficient.

Access

Latin America has made substantial progress in increasing access to education for all of its children. In particular, in primary school, our region has done a good job of making sure our children get enrolled in school. Net enrollment—the percentage of children of official primary school age who are enrolled in school—was about 86.1 percent in 1980 but had risen to 95.3 percent in 2008 (World Bank Data Set; Vega et al. 2011, 54). Nearly all children who are of primary school age are enrolled in school.

However, despite this achievement, there are clear areas for improvement in access. First, the net intake rate for first grade in 2008 was only 72 percent (United Nations Educational, Scientific and Cultural Organization [UNESCO] 2011, 11). This means nearly one-third of our children do not enter school at the appropriate age. Additionally, we cannot ignore the fact that children who start later than the "normal" entry age have higher rates of grade repetition and are more likely to drop out of school than children who start on time.

This low net intake rate for first grade is probably related to the low preprimary school enrollment rates in the region. Preprimary education is receiving an increasing amount of attention because we are learning how important those early years are for cognitive development and how quality preprimary education has lasting effects throughout an individual's life—including on school achievement, health, and other indicators. In our region, only 65.3 percent of children, on average, are enrolled in preprimary school, and these enrollment data can mean only one year of preprimary school (kindergarten). While this is a significant increase over the 55.1 percent enrollment rate in 2000, we have a long way to go: six countries in Latin America and the Caribbean have enrollment rates lower than 40 percent, and only ten have rates above 80 percent (UNESCO 2011, 9).

Second, we are not doing as good a job as we should of ensuring that our children have access to school after primary school: net enrollment in lower secondary school is considerably lower than that in primary school. In 2008, net enrollment in secondary school for the LAC region was 72.8 percent (UNESCO 2011, 9). Furthermore, the likelihood of our children successfully completing secondary school is low by world standards: only about half (51.8 percent) of our 20- to 24-year-olds had completed secondary school in 2008. That is major progress compared to just 20 years ago, but it means that many youth are minimally prepared to take on the more complex lower-end jobs of the knowledge economy. And as with other figures, the percentage varies enormously among countries, with secondary completion rates in the poorer countries of Central America and Bolivia closer to 40 percent; of course, among rural populations in those countries, the rate is even lower.

This low completion rate is likely related to the biggest educational challenge we still face as a region: improving the quality of the schooling our children receive. In 2012, gross enrollments for Latin America and the Caribbean had risen to 116 percent. Gross enrollment is calculated by taking the total number of children enrolled in primary school divided by the number of children of primary school age. The fact that gross enrollments in primary school are more than 100 percent hides a lingering issue: while access has improved, quality has not always kept up. The gross enrollment ratio can be greater than 100 percent as a result of grade repetition and entry at ages younger or older than the typical age at that grade level.

The HOI report asserted that "LAC children have more chances to be enrolled in school than to complete the sixth grade on time." Enrollment, it seems, "is no synonym for learning" (Vega et al. 2011, 3). In other words, while we know access is necessary for our children to learn in school, it is not sufficient: the quality of education children receive in schools is of the utmost importance and remains a challenge for us.

Quality

We can think about quality of education in a number of ways—all of which are important for achieving our shared society. UNESCO's Education for All initiative defines quality through five dimensions: relevance, pertinence, equity, effectiveness, and efficiency (UNESCO 2011, 5). We focus on those most comparable across the region: effectiveness, equity, and efficiency. As with all aspects of education, these dimensions are highly interrelated. If you have an ineffective system (children do not learn the content), it is unlikely to be efficient (children will not complete the grade requirements). An inequitable system (one that only serves some children well) is both inefficient and less effective.

First, let's look at effectiveness. The results of international tests suggest that average education performance is not very high in our region. PISA is an exam administered in 65 countries that measures the knowledge and skills of 15-year-olds in reading, mathematics, and science. It asks students to apply what they have learned in both school and nonschool contexts and aims to assess the extent to which they have acquired the knowledge and skills they need to participate fully in their societies (Organisation for Economic Co-operation and Development [OECD] 2014). On the international PISA exams, Chile—the best-performing country of the eight Latin American countries that have taken the PISA test—was ranked 47th out of 65 countries in PISA 2012 reading and 51st in mathematics. Peru was ranked 65th in reading and 65th in mathematics. Over 50 percent of children in Brazil, Argentina, Colombia, and Peru were found to have difficulty performing the most rudimentary reading tasks (did not reach a level II on the exam). The good news, however, is that 15-year-olds in Brazil, Chile, Colombia, Mexico, and Peru among the countries that participated more than once in the PISA test have made substantial gains in the PISA mathematics test. All of that said, none of these scores are adjusted for the socioeconomic level of the students taking the test. Comparing students in Latin America who have similar family academic resources to students in developed countries reduces the gap in how well, say, Chilean or Mexican students perform compared to, say, students in Spain. Nevertheless, a large gap of about one-half a standard deviation remains, suggesting that either peer effects or the quality of schooling, or both, negatively impact student learning in Latin America.

Our region has also developed its own regional standardized evaluation of achievement. The SERCE (Segundo Estudio Regional Comparativo y Explicativo) was developed and administered by the Latin American Laboratory for the Assessment of Quality Education (LLECE by its Spanish acronym) in 2007. Sixteen Latin American countries took part: Argentina, Brazil, Chile, Colombia, Costa Rica, Cuba, Dominican Republic, Ecuador, El Salvador, Guatemala, Mexico, Nicaragua, Panama, Paraguay, Peru, and Uruguay. The test assessed the reading and mathematics knowledge and processes of third and sixth graders in each country.

On average, 36 percent of third graders and 23.3 percent of sixth graders did not reach at least a level II in reading (out of four possible levels). Achievement ranged widely. Over half of third- and sixth-grade students in Cuba read at the highest proficiency level (level IV), while around half of third graders in Guatemala, Paraguay, Ecuador, and Peru did not read at the level II proficiency. Figure 8.3 shows the percentage of third-grade students at each level of proficiency by country. The levels of achievement are similar in mathematics: on average, around 49.2 percent of third graders and 19.4 percent of sixth graders did not reach at least a level II in mathematics.

Basic levels of literacy and mathematics are necessary for the full participation of any individual in today's society. Without these skills, children are unlikely to be able to find decent work in a knowledge economy, but they are also disadvantaged in the daily tasks of their lives and in

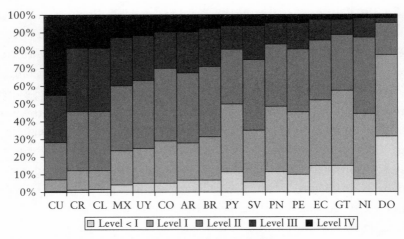

FIGURE 8.3 *Language proficiency of third graders*
Source: OREALC/UNESCO (2008).

their ability to gather and analyze information needed to make informed decisions about their household finances or about their elected officials.

Equity and Efficiency

When you account for per capita income and expenditure on education, Latin American countries perform worse than what would be predicted for them (Lora 2008). This is particularly troubling because the last decade has seen an increase in both economic growth and investment in and access to education. Increased investment has benefited our children in terms of increased access to *an* education, rather than increasing access to a quality education. However, as noted, Latin American secondary school students seem to be improving their performance from even lower levels ten years ago, at least as measured on the PISA test.

Like our wealth and income in the region, however, educational resources are still unequally distributed. Children in wealthy families attain much higher levels of education and better-quality education than children from poor families. Of course, this is also the case in the developed countries: lower-social-class students score much lower on international and national assessments than do higher-social-class children (Carnoy and Rothstein 2013). Indeed, the test score gap in Latin American countries is about the same as in the United States and Western European countries between the lowest-social-class students (where social class is measured by either books in the home or mother's education) and students from families with high human and cultural capital. One difference between Latin America and the developed countries is simply the proportion of students who come from homes with low parents' education levels and few academic resources, such as books. This means that most schools in Latin American countries are responsible for teaching students who have few academic resources at home.

Lower-social-class students are also highly concentrated in Latin American schools for two reasons: middle- and upper-middle-class families tend to send their children to private schools and to exclusively middle-class public schools. Highly unequal income distribution in Latin America also means highly segregated schools. However, a second apparent difference is the quality of schooling available even to high-social-class students. One effect of segregating lower-social-class students into their own schools is that these schools are generally caught in a low-achievement trap: they have more difficult working conditions for teachers, get fewer high-quality teachers and administrators, and get little political support from the more powerful middle class. Because these low-performing schools represent the majority of institutions in the educational system, schools catering to middle- and upper-middle-class children—even exclusive private schools—assume that they are doing well when their students score higher than this "comparison" group. Yet, consider this: in the PISA 2012, the highest-social-class students in Chile, representing only a low percent of the Chilean sample, scored lower in math and reading than an average student in Canada, a relatively high-scoring country but one with a much more equal income distribution than Chile.

Thus, income inequality reduces the quality of *all* schools in Latin America, not just those for students coming from poor families. Wealthier families send their children to much "better" schools, but they are lured into thinking that these exclusive public and private schools are good because they compare themselves to the substandard institutions that the public sector provides for poor children. In effect, because of the great inequalities in Latin America, wealthier families and the middle class "dumb down" their own children's schools by their unwillingness to fight for higher-quality public education for the mass of low-income children in their countries. As far as getting a really good education, an elite Chilean family would be better off sending their children to a middle-class school in Calgary or Winnipeg.

The inequality in income reproduces itself through the schooling system because the higher test results are rewarded economically. Our region has higher returns to education than most OECD countries, but there is also a higher correlation between parental education and child education—meaning a child's opportunity to access quality education is still highly dependent on circumstances outside of her or his control (Daude 2011, 26). Further complicating the situation is that, as discussed, a child's ability to take advantage of even poorer-quality education depends on her or his health, which is often also undermined in the case of poor children by malnutrition and treatable infections.

We are, however, seeing some improvement in equity. The Human Opportunity Index showed that since the mid-1990s, Peru has seen the most rapid expansion of the HOI for completing sixth grade on time—2.2 points annually—and Honduras has achieved a 1.3-point annual increase for school enrollment HOI (Vega et al. 2011, 55). Remember, these improvements are particularly impressive because they show increased equity in access and achievement between social groups, not just averaged increases.

Another way equity is assessed is through gender parity. In many countries in the world, girls still do not have access to the same quality of education as their brothers. Gender parity in education is measured by dividing the number of girls completing a grade by the number of boys. If the result is below 1, boys are at an advantage; if it is above 1, girls are at an advantage. We can look at gender parity over time by comparing the Gender Parity Index (GPI) across age groups. Figures 8.4 and 8.5 show the primary school GPI for 15- to 19-, 20- to 24-, and 25- to 29-year-olds, and the secondary school GPI for ages 20- to 24-, 25- to 29-, and 30- to 34-year-olds.

In primary school, most countries have achieved gender parity, or have at least made significant improvements in the younger populations; for

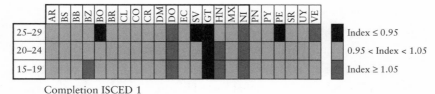

Completion ISCED 1

FIGURE 8.4 *Primary school Gender Parity Index*

Source: OREALC/UNESCO (2011, 19).

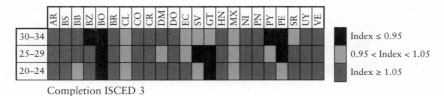

Completion ISCED 3

FIGURE 8.5 *Secondary school Gender Parity Index*

Source: OREALC/UNESCO (2011, 19).

instance, Bolivia, El Salvador, Peru, and Venezuela have all seen improvements in gender parity. However, Guatemala sticks out for its relatively stable inequity—with girls completing at lower levels than boys even in the most recent age cohort.

As a whole, our region is distinctive among developing regions for its high levels of gender parity at the primary school level. This is something we can be very proud of! At the secondary level, our region also is distinctive in the fact that at the secondary school level, we are seeing males at a disadvantage in terms of access to and completion of secondary school. This aspect of our gender parity is something we will need to keep an eye on, as true equity would not see males or females at a disadvantage. In terms of adult literacy, the region has achieved gender parity in the young population, though some inequalities (to the disadvantage of females) still exist in many countries. However, most continue to stress that functional literacy remains an issue in the region—as can be seen in our test results (UNESCO 2011, 18).

Overall, while great strides have been made in both social and gender equity in access to quality schooling, equity is still a huge cause for concern in our region, especially with regard to the relationship between wealth and access to quality education. The challenges in the effectiveness and equity components affect how efficiently our system is able to operate. One way we often think about school effectiveness is through the percentage of children who have to repeat a grade—the repetition rate—because a child having to enroll in the same grade for two consecutive years is a certain and direct waste of resources. UNESCO's EFA report estimates that 9.1 percent of first graders in the region repeat the grade. This is likely an underestimation of actual efficiency given that some countries have automatic promotion policies, but it does give us some sense of the challenge we face. Children are still starting later than the appropriate age and are having to repeat the first grade, both of which we know are associated with poorer future school performance.

If we are to make our leap forward, we must invest in the minds of our people. Low-quality schools will not develop the higher-level critical thinking and problem-solving skills required by the knowledge economy of the twenty-first century. They will not develop the skills and self-confidence Latin America's children need to participate in economic and political institutions in meaningful ways. Education—quality education— is an essential part of our vision of a socially inclusive society, and while we have made great strides in access, we now need to turn our attention toward equity in terms of quality.

Improving Access to Quality Education

Given that access is no longer the main challenge facing our education systems but rather quality is what we need to improve, there are a few priority areas we should look at. A better-educated population means more and better doctors, more and better teachers, and more of our people participating in the knowledge economy.

Experts at the World Bank, UNESCO, UNDP, IDB, and others have put together their recommendations, which overlap in large measure with the recommendations put forward by 20 former Latin American presidents, including myself, who gathered to discuss the most pressing social issues of our time and to develop a social agenda for Latin America in 2008.

Early childhood development and readiness to learn (IDB, World Bank, GCDD)

Low-income children in Latin America face many challenges when they enter school, including poor nutrition and access to basic services. To compound this, they are unlikely to have had exposure to the reading materials or other kinds of experiences they need to have prepared them for school. High-quality early child care education would help to reduce the huge differences in preparation that children from high-income and low-income families have.

Access, retention, and timely completion of schooling cycles; prioritizing low-income, rural, indigenous, Afro-descendants, and at-risk students (IDB, World Bank)

Class repetition and attendance are highly and negatively associated with students' performance and achievement in school. We need to find ways to make sure students—and teachers—are in school every day when they are enrolled. We also need to ensure that they have the resources they need to be able to get the most out of each day in the classroom.

Government-funded and -managed systems

In the 1980s and 1990s, there was a huge push for both privatization and decentralization of public services, including education. Instead of improving the system and making it more equal, they may have increased the inequality in performance between low-income and high-income students. In the Social Agenda, we noted how allowing privately run, publicly funded schools in Chile to select their students and charge tuition over and above the subsidy has likely increased the chances that students only attend schools with other students in their same social class. This creates huge inequities in the quality of education that is provided and probably reproduces income inequality. Daude gives a good overview of the effects of this situation:

In summary, the current education framework in the region promotes selection for those who can afford it. By itself selection tends to depress overall educational outcomes, and the region's private schools compound this by failing to make the most of their privileged intake. Nevertheless, selection succeeds in boosting the relative position of those in the upper layer. A system that under delivers and comes at the price of perpetuating inequalities will therefore continue to be something that parents aspire to—at least until policy provides them with an attractive alternative.[6]

A democratic government that aims for social inclusion must ensure that children's access to education is not dependent on their parents' income. To do this, we must take full responsibility for the education of all of our children. In 2009, Chilean legislation partially corrected the government policies that created large inequalities by awarding a 50 percent higher subsidy to low-income students in the first four grades of primary school. This apparently has had a significant positive effect on student achievement in low-income schools (Carrasco 2014).

Teacher quality and the interaction between teacher and other school factors that affect learning (GCDD, World Bank, UNESCO)
Most experts agree that educational systems cannot make large-scale increases in average student performance without improved teaching, and Latin America is no exception. UNESCO (2011) found that only teachers' experience, among all classroom variables, had a consistently positive impact on student performance. We need to increase the quality of preservice teacher training and improve the content and pedagogical expertise of both in-service and new teachers. We also need to make sure that *all* students have access to high-quality teachers—according to education and experience—regardless of where they live or their socioeconomic backgrounds. Teachers in communities where indigenous languages are spoken should speak the language of the community when they teach in school. Escuela Nueva, in Colombia, is an excellent example of a program that focuses on developing and preparing well-trained, knowledgeable teachers to teach in low-income and rural schools.

SUMMING UP

This chapter highlights three goals. First, if we want to achieve our vision of a shared, inclusive society, we have to address the multiple dimensions of poverty—not just income or monetary poverty. Second, health and nutrition, access to schooling, and access to basic services and decent housing are indispensable components of well-being. They are also fundamental to helping our citizens build the capabilities they need to make their own informed choices about their life options. Third, if we are to build equitable, shared societies that value and offer equal opportunity for well-being and inclusion to all, our governments must address all of these social areas.

Chapter 9 concentrates on state capacity. I take on the hardest nut of all: how to increase the capacity of Latin American states to carry out the many programs I propose throughout this book. In other words, how can the states deliver tangible, concrete, and measurable results? The bottom line of this analysis is that market-driven growth is crucial for continued development in the region, but it is not enough. I argue that government must not only ensure that the benefits of economic growth reach traditionally excluded groups on the lowest rungs of the socioeconomic ladder, but also that these groups must be active in generating growth and participating in an expanded democracy at the local and national levels.

CHAPTER 9

State Capacity to Deliver Tangible
and Measurable Results

IN THE PREVIOUS CHAPTERS, I described my vision for Latin America
and what we can and should achieve in the next 35 years by the middle
of the century, 2050. I have tried to show that we have many remaining
challenges to overcome in order to achieve inclusive economic growth
with decent jobs, while ending poverty; greatly reducing inequality; and
creating sustainable, environmentally friendly, and globally oriented development. At the same time, I am convinced (and hope that I have been
convincing) that we have an unparalleled opportunity to make the great
leap forward toward a shared society.

As I have discussed, rapid economic growth in the region has greatly
changed the possibilities of achieving this goal. However, the region is
still marked by institutional fragility that threatens its ability to deliver
the benefits of growth to the mass of Latin Americans who are still poor
and marginalized. This fragility is linked to corruption, citizen insecurity,
organized crime, and a weak judicial system that not only discourages
investment but also promotes and deepens the disillusion and despair of
the poor.

This challenge is exacerbated by the fact that growing segments of
our marginalized populations have access to cyber-technology, including
Internet and social media. Access to these technologies enables the poor
to observe on a daily basis the huge distance between the daily lives of
the rich and their own.

Most important, the weak capacity of central and local governments
to deliver tangible and measurable benefits of economic growth to these
increasingly aware marginalized populations is producing social turmoil. This social unrest risks interrupting the flow of national and external capital investment needed to sustain growth and undermining Latin
America's democracies.

Latin America now has the human capital capability to reverse this vicious cycle and build a regional consensus around strengthening our democratic institutions, particularly at the regional, provincial, district, and community levels, based on legal stability and social inclusion.

Evidence shows that in 2012, 64 million of the 600 million Latin Americans in the world lived outside the region and that many of them are highly skilled in various disciplines. We could repatriate this human capital by making the necessary changes in state policies that would create a more receptive professional environment and provide salary incentives for this vast Latin American talent living and working outside Latin America. We could make these highly trained professionals feel that they can contribute to Latin America's renaissance and make a difference in meeting the huge social and political challenges Latin America faces in the coming decades.

If we could develop the necessary incentives to bring back these Latin Americans to work outside the large urban areas, we could vastly improve the technocratic and administrative infrastructure desperately needed to diversify our growth and to deliver economic development to the rural areas and less developed urban communities, districts, and provinces in our respective countries.

WHAT IS THE "CAPACITY TO DELIVER"?

Building reliable infrastructure, promoting sustainable development, and creating equitable education systems are vastly different challenges that call for different sets of skills. What links them all together in a common framework is the fact that, to be successful, the state must have the capacity to deliver.

What do I mean by the "capacity to deliver"? Jim Yong Kim, the president of the World Bank, defines "delivery" as "getting goods and services to people in a way that meets their expectations." Kim explains that world leaders do already have a sense of the kinds of policies, or at least the broad policy directions, needed to reduce poverty or inequality and build a shared prosperity. In fact, many countries have policies and programs officially on the books that aim to achieve just that, and yet, "in country after country, sector after sector, the greatest challenge is delivery."[1] Without this capacity to deliver, even if small gains are made in only one or two areas, we will be unlikely to create a region of truly "shared prosperity."

He argues that what we need is a "science of delivery"—a focus on gathering the empirical evidence for how state institutions can get goods and services to their citizens in a timely, efficient way. A science of delivery would ask questions like: Which kinds of state institutions work best? In which contexts? With what kinds of incentives? Under what kinds of political regimes?

Francis Fukuyama labels the "capacity to deliver" as "state capacity,"[2] which consists of (1) human resources, in terms of officials who have appropriate technical, professional, and ethical skills; (2) the fiscal resources to support their activities; and (3) organizational and social capital that allows them to function properly. They need to be accountable to society but autonomous enough to be able to exercise judgment in the public interest.

In this book, we have discussed how important democracy is for creating a shared society, because democracy is meant to ensure that governments (the political regime) are responsive to the needs of their constituents: the majority of citizens. However, democracy alone does not actually ensure that the policies created to benefit the majority are implemented in ways that actually serve the majority. In fact, at times, authoritarian political regimes with high levels of state capacity deliver social services more effectively than democracies with low state capacity to deliver services (Hanson 2012).

While there is some empirical evidence that democracy is still more beneficial to the poor than autocracy, the relationship is complex and ambiguous (Hanson 2012). As I have mentioned earlier in this book, it turns out that "democracy," in terms of a right to vote, is not the same as inclusive political institutions and is relatively unrelated to whether state systems can effectively implement policies created by policy makers.

As we discussed in Chapter 3, many of our "democracies" have been what Larry Diamond calls "pseudo-democracies": political systems that may appear to be democracies but in which the ultimate power does not lie in the hands of the citizens. This could happen in a variety of ways—for instance, by having systems that are "rigged" so that leaders cannot be ousted by the voters or by having systems where the ultimate power lies in military or religious leaders rather than in the elected officials. In other words, it is not enough to set up a voting system. Voting alone does not a true democracy make. To be a liberal democracy, the whole political system must be inclusive and oriented toward serving citizens.

Acemoglu and Robinson's recent book (2012) explores the differential impact of inclusive and "extractive" political and economic systems and the ways they forge the success or failure of entire nations. They argue that it is extremely unlikely a country could have an inclusive economic system if there is an extractive political system, or vice versa. In their words, "It is the political process that determines what economic institutions people live under, and it is the political institutions that determine how this process works."[3]

They define extractive *economic* systems as those "designed to extract incomes and wealth from one subset of society to benefit a different subset."[4] In contrast, the kinds of inclusive economic institutions I want to see in Latin America will create a level playing field. They will encourage the participation of all individuals in economic activities that enable them to use their talents and skills and to make choices about their lives.[5] Similarly, an extractive *political* system puts true power in the hands of only a few. When there is an extractive political or economic system, states have little incentive to deliver services effectively because citizens do not hold the ultimate power over officials.

As we think about the capacity to deliver and its relationship with institutions, it is important to recognize the difference between "the state," which is the institutions that implement policy, and the "political regime," which is the way policy is made.[6] Every type of political regime—authoritarian, democratic, or otherwise—still needs to have state institutions that can effectively implement the policies it creates. The efficiency of the state is a separate issue from the way that the political system is organized.

Therefore, both democracies and authoritarian systems need state capacity; China's and Singapore's systems work well because they have a lot of state capacity, while many democracies lack state capacity. Latin

American democracies are faced with this situation on a daily basis, especially in the interior of our respective countries and, above all, in our rural areas.

Following up on Acemoglu and Robinson, we could say also that a democratic government can still be extractive, and it is much more likely to be extractive if its economic system is extractive—concentrating wealth in the hands of a few. Acemoglu and Robinson do not really pay any attention to state capacity in this sense; extractive for them means rent seeking or economically exploitative.

Let's be honest: we have a history of extractive and authoritarian rule in Latin America. This started with colonialism (or perhaps even before colonialism in some areas) and continues in large part today. While we are making progress, and our political systems are being organized to be much more democratic, we are still the most unequal region in the world. This means our wealth, and thus power, is more highly concentrated in fewer hands than in other regions. This is the best evidence we have that we have not created a shared society or inclusive economic and political systems.

If we are to continue our transition to being inclusive and democratic and achieve a truly shared prosperity, we must create mutually reinforcing paths between our economic, social, and institutional systems. While at first these may be "parallel paths," in reality they must become virtuous cycles that promote inclusivity and transform the extractive systems that only serve a few into systems that serve the vast majority.

It is essential that we do this now because we have learned from history that if democracies do not serve the majority, they will not last. As Larry Diamond notes, "Much more than dictatorships, democracies depend for their stability on legitimacy and voluntary compliance. . . . A democracy is, by nature, a system of popular consent."[7]

We are living in a technological age, and while technology is rapidly improving the lives of many, for better or for worse, technology is also making inequalities in our society more widely visible. What is wonderful about this visibility is that the power of knowledge is more widely shared. But if we do not begin addressing these inequalities quickly, economic growth will not be enough. Growth will be a double-edged sword if it is not shared: anger and frustration at the continued lack of shared growth will lead to social instability, as it did in the Arab Spring, with the *indignados* movement in Spain, and with movements of frustrated students and the rising middle class in our own region in Chile and Brazil.

We cannot avoid this dilemma created by the ever-expanding reach of technology—and we should not want to. It is undeniable that technological change and increasing access is shifting the balance of power toward the people, and this can support our movement toward a shared society. We can use it to both learn about what is needed by our people in their daily lives and to build support for the creation of policies that have a direct positive impact on the lives of the poor. But technology also makes it certain that social stability, effective inclusive development, and even the fate of our democracies depend on the ability of our democratic states to deliver on their inclusive policy promises.

Chapter 8 discusses the problems we are currently facing due to weak institutions. In the rest of this chapter, I look at what strong institutions actually are, what they do, and what challenges to creating strong institutions we currently face. Then I discuss the ways we can overcome these challenges to create a Latin America that has strong, inclusive, participatory state institutions that truly work for the benefit of all citizens.

WHAT IS A STRONG INSTITUTION?

We know that strong institutions are a necessary precondition for effective policy implementation. But what makes a strong institution? At its heart, a strong institution is simply, as Fukuyama asserts, "one that transparently and efficiently serves the needs of its clients—the citizens of the state."[8]

Naazneen Barma and colleagues elaborate on these ideas by creating three criteria for a successful institution: it delivers results according to its core mandate; it has attained legitimacy in the broader population it serves—legitimacy in terms of both public trust and performance; and it operates effectively despite internal and external change—in other words, it is durable and resilient across years and through transitions in internal and external leadership.

These definitions are clear. A strong institution is one that is dependable and efficient: it does what it is supposed to, when it is meant to, without too many delays or disruptions in service. But achieving this is not as straightforward as it may appear. Various components all have to work in harmony, and they must do so across different dimensions.

A useful framework for thinking about this was recently developed by Badru Bukenya and Pablo Yanguas (2013). They reviewed the literature on state capacity for inclusive development and derived two main components operating in two different domains: *effectiveness* (does the institution do what it is supposed to?) and *accountability* (does the institution ensure that public policy is not subverted by private incentives?). They argue that these components have to function in two different domains: *internal* and *external*. This means in order to achieve an effective, strong institution, one must consider each of the four dimensions of state capacity where the components and domains intersect. These are shown in Table 9.1.

Internally, to be effective, organizations must be *rational*. They need to perform administrative functions in an organized, hierarchical, rational, and technical manner. They also must be accountable or exercise *restraint*—that is, actors must be bound to act within formal, impersonal, and enforceable rules of conduct.

Externally, to be effective, institutions must be *embedded* within the social context in which they operate. In other words, there must be both interactions and two-way communication between stakeholders and bureaucratic actors, and the institution itself must be designed so as to take into account the social fabric, norms, and customs of the society in which it operates. To be accountable to its clients—in this case, this means the citizens it serves—it also must have the *institutional autonomy* to resist informal pressures from powerful political and economic actors.[9]

TABLE 9.1 *Dimensions of state capacity*

		Components	
		Effectiveness	*Accountability*
Domains	*Internal*	Rationality	Restraint
	External	Embeddedness	Autonomy

Source: Bukenya and Yanguas (2013).

Thus, any attempt to strengthen institutions needs to take into account both the internal issues of structure, management, and human resource motivation and capacity and the external issues of creating and managing partnerships that augment their scope and stability and establish and maintain relationships with their stakeholders and clients. Ignoring any one of these areas will result in weaker institutional capacity to deliver results according to its mandate.

According to Barma and colleagues, "Successful public institutions . . . have typically built internal mechanisms to monitor and evaluate their programs, attract and motivate skilled human resources, and communicate organizational goals effectively throughout the ranks."[10]

Such institutions, they continue, have the following characteristics:

- They emphasize reaching out to previously marginalized groups, including through a greater geographical coverage.
- They are adept at driving their own institutional agendas, particularly by using formal and informal partnerships to augment the scope, legitimacy, and stability of their mandates.
- They couple clear goals with sufficient commitments of resources.
- They identify and build on existing capabilities and social capital, while combining both short- and long-term interventions for institution building.

WHAT IS STANDING IN OUR WAY?

So if we know what makes for a successful institution, and we know what they should look like to promote inclusivity and shared growth, what is standing in our way? Why don't our institutions have the capacity to deliver in ways that promote sustainable, shared prosperity? The challenges we face in overcoming barriers to building them are both political and organizational.

Political

When I was trying to rebuild the badly damaged institutional structure in Peru during my five years as president (2001–2006), the most difficult challenges I faced were political. Daron Acemoglu and James Robinson note that "pluralism, the cornerstone of inclusive political institutions, requires political power to be widely held in society, and starting from extractive institutions that vest power in a narrow elite, this requires a process of empowerment."[11] It is almost self-evident that any change that involves power and money will result in some people who gain and some who lose. As Francis Fukuyama says, "The latter can be depended on to protect their relative positions."[12] Empowerment for some can make others feel they are losing their power. When you consider situations where power and money are highly concentrated in relatively few hands, as they are in Latin America, you can see how moving toward a political and economic system that is more inclusive will surely meet with stiff resistance.

In inclusive systems, economic growth is supported by technological change and creativity in a process that Schumpeter calls "creative destruction."[13] New ways of doing things are created and replace old, less efficient ways of doing things. But this only happens when people have incentives to increase their productivity and the space, time, and freedom to be thoughtful and creative. To give an extreme example, there is no reason for a slave to find ways to increase crop production (except for fear of being punished), because he will not share in the benefits of the increase. Fear works to keep people working but not to figure out ways to make large leaps in productivity.

Using Bukenya and Yanguas's framework, we can see that within each dimension there are competing, well-entrenched ways of organizing and managing institutions that would both push back against becoming rational, restrained, embedded, and autonomous and slow the process of creative destruction. Change becomes difficult politically because of these "different patterns of political contestation due to incentives for patrimonialism, corruption, oligarchy, and capture"[14] (see Table 9.2).

These four areas of political resistance are really the main obstacles to be overcome or circumvented by a public sector reform agenda. Their presence shows how extractive political and economic institutions can become mutually reinforcing. Serious resistance in any one of these areas, internally or externally, could make an institution dysfunctional. Worse, this resistance tends to be well rooted in Latin America's current set of

TABLE 9.2 *Definitions of the dimensions of state capacity and their opposites*

Domain	Dimension	Opposite
Internal	**Rationality** Performing administrative functions in an organized, hierarchical, rational, and technical manner	**Patronage** Staffing and remuneration of public bureaucracies on the basis of kinship or political clientelism
Internal	**Restraint** Actors bound to act within formal, impersonal, and enforceable rules of conduct	**Corruption** The use of public office for private gains—through appropriation of funds or through bribes for official duties
External	**Embeddedness** Two-way communication between stakeholders and bureaucratic actors (the institution itself is designed to take into account the social fabric, norms, and customs)	**Oligarchy** Subversion of public policies to benefit a few *societal* actors (who are not actually involved in governing)
External	**Autonomy** Ability to resist informal pressures from powerful political and economic actors	**Capture** Informal control of public policy by *political* actors who subvert the public policies to benefit a few

institutions. Changing them will require significant effort and inclusive reforms in both the political and economic realms.

Organizational Rationality/Management

Beyond political contestation, each of Bukenya and Yanguas's areas confront organizational and management challenges. First, at the very heart of our definition of a strong institution is that it delivers results with respect to its core mandate. But goals of organizations are not always straightforward. They can often be unclear or confusing, and at times an organization's goals can be mutually exclusive or in competition with one another.

Second, how do we generate the necessary process of monitoring and evaluating institutions? It is expensive, complex, and time consuming to implement such processes. Add in the problems of unclear desired outcomes or goals and the difficulty of measuring success in the public sphere, and it is easy to see why evaluating the effectiveness of institutions is often contested terrain. For example, we want our children to learn more in school, and we might be able to measure learning, but it is not so easy to figure out whether or not schools are effective. Further, change is seldom contained within a typical budget year. It is clear that monitoring and evaluating state institutions are difficult undertakings.

With public systems it is always complex, perhaps sometimes impossible, to gather the breadth and depth of the indicators we need to understand how well we are doing. Yet, without a sense of whether we are moving in the right direction, how can we estimate the effectiveness of our institutions?

Third, every organization faces the issue of what Fukuyama calls "delegated discretion," or the degree of autonomy and discretion that agents at different levels of the hierarchy must have to make key decisions. He explains that the rule of thumb in government work is that authority to make decisions at any level should correspond to the problems that are unique to the issues under its control. In the end, it really depends on the type of work being done at each level. However, the amount of discretion you can safely delegate depends on the capacity of the agents.

Where work cannot be easily routinized, more delegated discretion is necessary for being able to work efficiently; however, while decentralized organizations and higher delegated discretion at lower levels mean that organizations can react more rapidly to issues arising on the ground, any delegation of responsibility is also a delegation of risk. Almost all institutions working on public and social issues are confronting complex, nonroutine problems on the ground every day. For instance, teachers, doctors, and local government officials are dealing with nonroutine issues in governance every day, but the more authority that is delegated to actors closer to the ground, almost inevitably the more likely it is that we will see high levels of variation in performance. By nature, work that is not controlled centrally is likely to vary more, both due to greater responsiveness to local conditions and the variation in the skills that local actors bring to the task at hand.

Decentralization efforts across Latin America that have tried to delegate authority to local governments have confronted this issue. While in theory decentralization should have made them more responsive, often local governments did not have the capacity to evaluate all of the information and decisions they needed to make. As a result, they often took longer to make decisions than a centralized authority would, and there were huge variations in performance across districts and municipalities.

This issue is not unique to government institutions: all organizations—private, public, or otherwise—grapple with it. However, governments must make it possible for all of their citizens to receive the same level and quality of service. It is hard to ensure minimum standards of service delivery across very different contexts when there is no centralized control over the decisions being made. While local governments without centralized oversight may be able to respond more rapidly to local needs, delegating that authority to them creates opportunities for corruption, patronage, oligarchy, and capture at each site instead of only one site.

HOW DO WE DEVELOP SUCCESSFUL INSTITUTIONS WITH THE CAPACITY TO DELIVER?

I realize that many of these problems may seem insurmountable! The good news is that states that have been successful in creating more inclusive societies had almost never inherited the institutions that allowed them to do this. They built their capacities over time, with a strategic vision and "through purposeful leadership and the formation of strategic ties with citizens and business" (UNRISD).

The not-quite-as-good news is that this is going to require significant thought, energy, time, and political will, as well as resource mobilization, the shifting of institutional norms, and significant capacity building. In other words, it will be a lengthy process. If we are to achieve shared prosperity, it will also need to be an inclusive process that requires the establishment of a unique mix of formal mechanisms and informal norms. Processes like these take time, planning, and effort.

As such challenges would suggest, the long-term process also needs to take into account issues in both the internal and external domains. Internally, our institutions will need to establish visions and institutional missions and will need to build a team of people who can fulfill those missions and realize the larger vision. A useful classification of the internal work to be done was developed by World Bank researchers. They divided what successful organizations do into four categories.

1. *Develop an organizational mystique, or an internalized sense of mission and importance.* Being successful means creating a strong organizational culture that is oriented toward success. The challenge of delegated discretion that Fukuyama discusses is always easier in an organizational environment where workers share the same values, framework, and understanding of the mission. On the psychological side, we know that people who feel they are working on something that is meaningful are happier, more efficient, and more creative problem solvers. Creating a shared sense of purpose and meaning in the work that the institution is doing will benefit both the employees and the citizens who are benefiting from the services.

2. *Have flexible, equitable managers who are problem-solving and teamwork oriented.* Leaders are a main source of organizational culture.[15] If you do not have leaders who lead by example, the culture will never take root. Carol Dweck's work shows the importance of having managers who prioritize learning and problem solving and who encourage their team to grow and improve. Her work finds that people often bring either a fixed mind-set or a growth mind-set to different situations. A fixed mind-set assumes that some people are intelligent, skilled, or talented, and some are not. A growth mind-set believes that nearly everything can be learned and improved upon.

   In an organization, managers who believe an individual may or may not be talented or skilled will be afraid of failure and risk, will be more likely to hide poor performance and to lie about performance, and will not be able to take constructive criticism and change their behavior in response to that criticism. They will not encourage people to practice, learn, and grow and will make it difficult for staff to express doubt or uncertainty. Yet, it is by looking at problems as challenges rather than threats that we can create successful, flexible, and strong institutions.

3. *Have clearly defined performance expectations.* This is important on both institutional and team or individual levels. Just as it is imperative for an institution to have a goal and a vision that everyone can work toward, it is also important for different management teams and

individuals to have a sense of what their personal contribution will be to that larger mission. Without a sense of what is expected, either institutionally or individually, there is no way to know if progress is being made or if changes are required to achieve the larger goal. This also helps to fight corruption because with clear performance expectations comes more transparency about what each person's role is, what it takes to accomplish it, and what is and is not acceptable behavior within that role.

4. *Have some autonomy in personnel management that provides a facilitating context for the preceding three characteristics to be developed.* This highlights the importance of hiring well: starting with the leaders who can be free of external political and patronage pressure and focus on finding managers and employees who will be committed and passionate about their work. This works to minimize both the possibility for capture and, if well planned, allows a more rational and technical-bureaucratic institution to develop.

In addition to the internal organizational, cultural, management, and personnel issues, every institution is also embedded within a specific cultural, social, and larger institutional context. This means that each of our institutions needs to know how to work autonomously but also in a way that is dynamically connected with its environment. It is worth noting that Fukuyama is very skeptical about this technocratic model if it is implemented in isolation from local politics. As he told me in one of the many enriching discussions we had at Stanford, these kinds of technocratic models usually prove ineffective because they do not take account of political constraints, so we need to move from exclusively technocratic models to more political ones. That is why the World Bank and other international financial institutions have moved to more complex models of building capacity to deliver, where the impact on local politics is taken into account.

Successful institutions have leaders who recognize that the institution is not an island and can be more effective and able to navigate challenges if they build innovative partnerships with other organizations that work on related issues. Because each context is unique and because our demo-cratic, inclusive institutions are serving citizens themselves, successful institutions need to have both formal and informal mechanisms to be able to listen to stakeholders and beneficiaries. To be adaptive, interac-tive, and constantly evolving toward better service delivery, knowledge about what is working and what is not working can only be secured if there is constant communication. Creative solutions will come from col-laboration and joint problem solving.

It is vital that this be a truly inclusive process of communication and dialogue, not only because we are aiming for more inclusivity in our political and economic processes but also because it makes service de-livery itself more effective. Inclusivity is both intrinsically valuable and instrumental. As Kim notes, "One consequence of the interactive nature of delivery knowledge is that the quality of our knowledge depends on the inclusiveness of the debate. Excluding shareholders from the conver-sation deprives us of critical data. Thus, if grassroots community voices are not heard, our understanding of delivery processes will be distorted and incomplete."[16]

This is a key point of the "science of delivery" agenda.[17] Kim empha-sizes that solutions need to be grounded in the local level; no one "best practice" will fit across varied contexts. Good service delivery means working within and affecting complex social systems. The goals that good local administrators aim to achieve are inherently complex and interact with multiple human, cultural, social, and institutional systems that all mutually influence one another.

This does not mean we cannot learn from what works in other places and try to adapt and tailor it to local contexts. The key is being able to rigorously evaluate what we do with our objectives and to look at both our successes and our failures so we can learn from them. Just because something does not work the first time, it does not mean it is a bad idea. We must learn to be more process oriented and to truly create a "virtu-ous circle of learning" so we can understand the *why* and *how* of service delivery. It is only by exploring the mechanisms underlying the pro-cesses and results that we can truly develop a scientific understanding of delivery.

THE APPROACH

Addressing the internal and external domain issues can be approached in different ways. Knowing where we need to go still requires some consideration of how we will go about reforming our institutions. In my conversations with Fukuyama, we discussed three different approaches that could be taken to public sector institutional reform. These are not necessarily mutually exclusive, and we have to think about how we can weave them together, but they are three useful ways of thinking about reform.

1. *The business/technocratic approach.* In this approach, the challenge is framed as being one of organizational efficiency. It deals mainly with the internal domain. The focus is on bureaucratic and organizational change. Considering Bukenya and Yanguas's framework, these reforms would work to minimize patronage and corruption. Reforms aim to make organizations more rational and technocratic. Changes are focused on the structure of organizations, improving processes, changing incentive structures in pay scales, and so on.

2. *The political approach.* In this approach, the challenge is "It is not that the policies or institutions are designed badly but that politics get in the way." Often you hear the argument that the whole issue is simply that political actors are in the system and it is in their self-interest to keep it dysfunctional. In many ways, this is the same as the "oligarchy" and "capture" conflicts in Bukenya and Yanguas's framework. Reforms are focused on decentralization, creating autonomous agencies, and minimizing political interference in state bureaucratic matters.

3. *The classic state-building approach.* This approach frames the challenge as being a systemic one that requires a systemic solution. Reforms are focused on building an elite bureaucracy system using an elite educational system for those who will work within the bureaucracy and creating an incentive structure that encourages highly trained and motivated people to become involved in public administration, not just policy making. This is not simply about creating monetary incentives. We now know how important psychology is to success—of individuals and institutions—so the idea is to change the incentives not only

in terms of money but also in terms of recruiting people who want to be there for the "right" reasons and creating environments in which they can thrive.

The first two approaches have been the main focus of most reform programs by development agencies and developing countries over the last century. A major reason we are putting so much emphasis on this discussion here is because these reforms have not produced the results many thought would have happened by now. Despite all the resources available from rapid economic development in our region, using these old approaches has not produced the level of institutional reforms most analysts thought they would.

This is probably because it is not "simply" a bureaucratic or a political issue. As we have discussed in this chapter, institutions are comprised of, and embedded within, complex social, cultural, institutional, and historical systems. It is true that we have inefficient bureaucracies, but it is also true that in extractive systems we have significant political interference in institutional performance because shifting power dynamics create winners and losers, and the losers fight to keep their power.

The first approach sounds both reasonable to address and deceptively simple to achieve. But reforms focusing on bureaucracies have had very little impact. I think this is because, as the second reform approach would suggest, serious reform efforts have to begin by taking politics into account. Adverse incentives to change will need to be considered by reformers because if powerful stakeholders do not want reform, reformers will need to address this by either changing the incentives or mustering enough political and economic will to defeat them. But changing incentives alone does not solve the technical-bureaucratic issues.

While more difficult, and requiring more long-term dedication, the third option is the one that holds the most promise because it is the only one that can deal simultaneously with all the different potential obstacles to change. In Latin America, one can see examples of success of this approach in a number of our finance ministries and central banks. There is really no comparison in terms of what is happening now in our finance ministries and central banks with what was happening in the early 1980s and before. That is because we have focused on getting our economic house in order by making sure we had highly trained experts (if our systems were not ready to train them yet, they were sent to the best programs in the world), who were then given the opportunity and autonomy—the delegated discretion—to make the changes they believed would be best for those institutions.

Admittedly, some government institutions, such as educational and health care systems, pose more of a challenge for this approach than when there is one centralized agency (like a central bank), partly because of the delegated discretion we discussed earlier. Highly decentralized institutions require more delegated discretion, which means that if there are going to be universally high levels of service delivery across different local contexts, you need more people who are both highly trained and well aligned with the institutional values and missions. Just because it is more challenging, it does not mean it is not worthwhile. In fact, it may be the only way to create sustainable change.

In some instances this might mean actually "starting over" rather than tweaking an institutional system that has so many ingrained incentives that thwart change. Our old approaches have not worked, and we should view "quick fix" solutions with extreme skepticism. Building institutions takes a vision, time, political will, and commitment. But we also need new ways of thinking about how to create the inclusive political and economic systems needed to deepen our democracies and become a region of shared prosperity.

Below I offer an example of the kind of creative thinking we need in order to open the debate and begin considering our challenges in new and systemic ways.

A PROPOSAL

I explained at the beginning of the chapter that because political and economic institutions are mutually reinforcing, it will always be difficult (if not impossible) to create inclusive economic institutions when political systems are extractive (i.e., a "small" group of individuals do their best to exploit the rest of the population) and vice versa. This means if we want to create inclusive, shared societies, we need to have inclusive political *and* economic institutions. As Acemoglu and Robinson note, "Attempting to engineer prosperity without confronting the root cause of the problems— extractive institutions and the politics that keep them in place—is unlikely to bear fruit."[18] Extractive systems distort incentives and undermine our democratic principles and our aspirations for shared prosperity.

What are some ways we can begin to make extractive systems more inclusive? One way to think about this is by focusing on the relationship between the state and its citizens. For democratic institutions to work well, there must be a mutually beneficial and mutually dependent relationship between a state and its citizens. This means that the relationship between the state and the citizens, particularly in terms of resource mobilization, is incredibly important for creating a shared society and shared prosperity.[19] In a democracy, citizens give their consent to be governed not only through their votes but also by contributing part of their incomes to the state through taxes. Theoretically, it is through taxes that governments have the economic resources to implement their programs. Without citizens, governments are deprived of the economic power (and political legitimacy) to govern.

A powerful example of when this relationship is undermined is when a nation has the "curse" of natural resources. While one would perhaps think that a nation that is blessed with rich natural resources would be a wealthier, more prosperous nation, empirical evidence suggests the opposite. Nations that receive the bulk of their income from natural resources, even if they are rich by the numbers, tend to be the most unequal, least developed, and often authoritarian. They have a greater incidence of corruption, political and economic instability, and civil war.[20]

This seemingly odd relationship between natural resource abundance and negative social and political consequences was identified by Andre Gunder Frank in the 1960s[21] and again in the early 1990s[22] and has been the subject of considerable debate since. Larry Diamond has proposed a new explanation for why at its heart it may be a matter of the "curse" of natural resources subverting the relationship and balance of power between citizens and their governments. Basically, when unearned income— "rent" as economists call it—from natural resources replaces taxes as the main source of government funding, the relationship and social contract between the government and its citizens are undermined.[23] The government no longer needs its citizens to enjoy economic power, and because economic and political power go hand in hand, they often do not feel they require their citizens' consent to govern. The result is that natural resources do not result in public goods and services but rather in extractive economic systems that generate private and political goods instead.

If we want to save our democracies and make them more inclusive, and if we want to create a shared society and shared prosperity, we need new and creative ways of thinking about how to manage natural resource extraction in our region. We need to find ways to restore the power dynamics between citizens and the state and to ensure that *all* citizens benefit from the nation's resources.

In "Petroleum to the People," Larry Diamond and his coauthor Jack Mosbacher put forward a bold, paradigm-shifting proposition: Why not just give the money earned from oil directly to the citizens? In their model, payments would be directly deposited to citizens' bank accounts, which would be taxed as income back to the government. This article is not the first to support an "oil-to-cash" approach to the natural resource curse. Theoretically, it reestablishes the necessary balance of power between the citizens of a democracy and their elected leaders. It aims to "create a broad and active constituency of citizens who [are] directly affected by the government's management of their resources, in place of the often passive populations of corrupt, resource-cursed states. In a single step, it would build a broad domestic tax base—a fundamental piece of any modern, well-governed state."[24]

Now, that is an idea that will catalyze creativity and debate! When we began thinking about resources-for-cash in a more applied way and considering how to adapt it to the Latin American context, we came up with a three-stage plan of action that should accompany any new proposals for resource extraction. This is designed with the underlying concept of "zones of influence" or "zones of impact" in mind. It is often the people who are most directly impacted by mining and resource extraction activities who benefit the least. We wanted to think of ways in which the people locally affected by resource extraction activities become the first zone of impact, which receives the most benefits.

1. *The exploration phase.* When the areas where companies would like to explore for natural resources are identified, the first step would be to have the community and the company representatives design a memorandum of understanding (MOU), with the government acting as a "mediator" or "enforcer" to assure the community that the company will be held to its end of the bargain.

   The MOU will outline principal aspects of how the extraction will occur and what changes are foreseen to the environment and human ecologies of the area. The company will make a commitment to social investments requested by the community and also commit to providing employment opportunities to locals.

2. *Upon agreement to go ahead with extraction.* Once the company is committed to working in the area and the local communities have agreed to allow it to move forward with the extraction of resources, an official contract of "Impact and Benefits" will be signed between local community leaders and the company. Again, the state will be at the table, not as a beneficiary of the contract but rather as a guarantor that the company will be held responsible for fulfilling its commitments.

   This will be a more formal legal document that requires the company to outline the maximum environmental, social, and health impacts its extraction process will have on the area and its inhabitants. The document will specify the consequences should the impacts exceed the stated levels and list the ways the company will invest in the area to minimize the harmful effects of these impacts.

   Economic benefits to the community will be explicitly laid out; these will include large upfront investments, as well as more ongoing economic, environmental, educational, and other developmental investments. In addition, a plan will be put in place for how the company will move out of the area: what they will take with them, what will be left behind, and concrete ideas for ensuring that the profits from the extraction in that area will benefit local citizens even after the company is gone and that potential negative impacts will be mitigated.

   It is very important that these discussions occur and that significant social investment is made *before* any extraction begins. Much of the conflict between local communities and companies that extract natural resources arises because the community sees no benefit, only a destructive impact, when companies begin working in their area.

3. *Ongoing communication and investment in the local area—"directly into the vein."* The second and third "phases" are truly intertwined because a plan for this stage must be outlined in the contract between the company and the community. We have three propositions we want to explore in terms of a "directly into the vein" type of investment model that builds on Diamond and Mosbacher's proposal. We feel that the company should give the money directly to the communities rather than sending it to the national, regional, and local governments first. (Often in such cases, the money never reaches the community because resources are siphoned off through corruption and inefficiency at each of those levels.) We agree with Diamond that "the argument that poor people do not understand their best interests as well as bureaucrats and public servants do is a paternalist myth."

As a whole, this process is distinct from the current processes in a number of ways. However, the main difference is that in current processes the local communities rarely receive the benefits of extractive industries.

Besides simply being the "right" thing to do, this process will produce a more productive power balance among communities, governments, and natural resource companies, and it will have the added benefit of reducing resentment and conflict between mining companies and the local residents—thus increasing profits all around.

As we discussed in Chapter 5, cash transfer programs have been found to be incredibly effective at alleviating the worst effects of poverty, as they are normally used by families to support health, education, nutrition, and business investments. Plus, most of the money is spent locally, which stimulates community-level development and economic growth.

From these experiences, our multidisciplinary team has developed three different models that could be used to carry out this "directly into the vein" approach. We propose piloting the three different models to learn about which works best in which contexts.

"INTO THE VEIN" MODELS

A fundamental precept of each of these models is the active participation of local communities in deciding how to use the monetary resources that come from extractive industries for their community development. The goal is to grow true partnerships between the communities and the private enterprises that are extracting resources. Communities will begin to benefit directly from extractive industries that otherwise may disrupt their way of life. The truth is that there can be no sustained economic growth or sustainable development if communities and citizens do not participate in it. Business, government, and community need to work together to create a virtuous circle of development, with the aim of bridging the social divide not by giving but by empowering.

Whenever large sums of money are being discussed and transferred, corruption is a possibility. The first step is to minimize incentives for corruption, and the second step is to establish firm oversight mechanisms of transparency, inclusivity, and accountability. Each model has its own measures in place to ensure these three tenets are present.

Model 1

Vision. Communities are empowered to develop their community and make decisions about their shared future in ways that make sense to them. Some communities will choose to develop roads and other infrastructure, others might focus on water and sanitation, and still others on social development like schooling or job training. Community forums are established where every member has a voice, and an inclusive and transparent process for deciding on each project allows for lively debate and widespread buy-in on the final plan.

Project funding. A trust fund for the community (or communities) in the zone of impact where mining is going to occur would be created by using a portion of the fees and royalties from the mining company involved. The amount given to each community will depend on the stage of investment, or negotiations about investment, the mining project is in. In other words, is the investment already established and in operation? Is it at the exploration stage? Different protocols would be used for guiding the negotiations, depending on the stage.

Project development. The community could use the trust fund to finance community development projects of its choosing (e.g., water, roads, communication infrastructure, education, etc.). Each community would establish its own way of deciding which projects to invest in, but the requirement would be that the process is inclusive and transparent.

Project oversight. To assist the communities in the creation of development plans, the funds are administered by a committee of multidisciplinary professionals (e.g., a business administrator, economist, engineer, anthropologist, social communicator, etc.). This group is charged with advising each community on their development plans, as well as ensuring that funds are disbursed and used in transparent ways that benefit the community as a whole.

Model 2

Vision. Individual citizens are empowered to make decisions about their lives and the development of their community through direct monetary transfers. Individual members of the community are empowered to develop their community through a process of direct investment and universal participatory involvement in the development of plans and management of community projects.

Project funding. Along the lines of Diamond's proposition, in this model the money from the mining company would go directly to individual families within each community within the zone of impact. Each adult would receive an equal amount of the total, with a portion being transferred in a lump sum at the beginning of each year of the mining project and a portion being transferred in a monthly remittance.

Project development. Each individual and family would decide how to use the money they are given. However, each community is required to establish a community development forum, and each adult who receives benefits is required to participate. It would be recommended that citizens, members of each community, decide together on the projects they feel the community needs and how they will be funded.

Project oversight. In this model, there is less likelihood of corruption because the money is disbursed widely rather than to a centralized location, which makes it harder for an individual or a small group to access the funds for their own enrichment or benefit. However, smaller instances of fraud may occur, so an oversight panel will be in charge of checking that each individual adult is registered and is registered only once. In addition, there may still be a need for community development advisors, so a few different multidisciplinary groups of experts will be available to give advice and help with the management of development plans should the community request them.

Model 3

Vision. Both individual community members and a community forum are empowered to make decisions about their lives and the development of their community through direct monetary transfers and a community trust fund. Individuals can develop their own potential, and communities can make short-, medium-, and long-term development plans that benefit all. Multidisciplinary experts are available to support community committees, but the project is driven and managed by community members.

Project funding. For this model, approximately 20 percent of the resources would go directly to individual adults in the community through monthly transfers. The other 80 percent would be invested as annual lump sums into the community development trust fund.

Project development. As in the prior two models, individuals will be free to decide how to invest and spend their money as they see fit. At the community level, a community development committee with an inclusive and transparent process for making decisions about development projects will be established.

Project oversight. For the trust fund, a community development committee would be established, and a multidisciplinary team of experts would be in charge of advising the committee and disbursing the funds when the community has decided on its development projects and plan.

CONCLUDING THOUGHTS ON THE
CAPACITY TO DELIVER

While we have reduced poverty in the region, many of our member countries are highly reliant on extractive industries for their economic power. It is no coincidence that social discontent is predominantly concentrated in the areas where extractive industries are located. Economies that rely on extractive industries are more likely to have "extractive" economic and political systems, and Latin America is no exception. Our region confronts the enormous challenge of resolving coexisting high rates of economic growth with increasing social discontent about the extractive nature of current political and economic systems, despite the transition to democracy. We need to convert the curse of natural resources into an opportunity—this time for all. To transition from extractive to inclusive economic and political institutions, we need creative thinking and long-term planning if we are to overcome the challenges posed by patronage, corruption, oligarchy, and capture. We need a new, modern, rational technocracy and multidisciplinary bureaucracy to govern state institutions, and we need to find ways to include rural and currently marginalized communities in our economic and political systems. A simple focus on only the technical or the political, the internal or the external, challenges will not be sufficient. A classic state-building approach that develops our human capital and bureaucratic systems while methodically addressing the political challenges may be the only way to create sustainable, strong, inclusive institutions. But in the meantime, we need to establish immediate, creative, into-the-vein models for ensuring that individuals and communities benefit directly from the extractive industries that affect their lives and empower them to make decisions about their and their communities' life trajectories.

SUMMING UP

This chapter suggests ways to reverse the weaknesses of Latin American institutions and enable them to deliver measurable and tangible results. The state's incapacity to deliver results to the people has been the major hindrance to Latin America's economic and social development. I emphasize that Latin America now has the human capital capability to reverse this vicious cycle and build a regional consensus around strengthening our democratic institutions, particularly at the regional, provincial, district, and community levels, based on legal stability and social inclusion.

In Chapter 10, I discuss the importance of deepening and diversifying foreign trade and investments and how a reinvented Latin America can reposition itself in the global economy and polity and, in turn, how the

United States, Europe, and Asia should anticipate a very different relationship with the region than they have today. Finally, I examine the synergies and importance of the international agenda between the region, the United States, and Canada. I also explain the necessity of understanding the consequences of this new multipolar world for the region.

CHAPTER 10

Latin America Goes Global

BECOMING A GLOBAL PLAYER

As discussed in previous chapters, Latin America's investment, trade, and technology transfers with the rest of world have been at the heart of the growth and prosperity experienced in the past decade. In this period, the region diversified and expanded its export markets beyond the Western Hemisphere and took continuous steps toward becoming a more active global player. As trade with the United States declined, our region rapidly diversified to new export markets in China and Asia. This has helped strengthen our resilience to external market shocks and the vulnerability associated with the export of commodities.

However, Latin America needs to go beyond trade expansion; it needs to increase foreign investments in the region. At the same time, it is fundamental to diversify trade, investments, and sources of technology transfer, as well as human capital and training for social infrastructure programs. There has been a substantial change in the international arena, which has created a multipolar world, affecting relations among Latin America, the United States, Europe, and Asia. In fact, the United States is no longer the main investor in the region; the European Union took its place a decade ago. In third place is China, whose investments have increased at a staggering pace. Additionally, unlike other periods of economic growth, south–south trade and south–south cooperation have led this boom. We have worked to increase ties with our neighbors in the region and to forge new ties with countries in regions both close by and far away. The United States continues to be our natural geographical partner in investments, trade (free trade agreements), and technology transfers, as well as in fighting organized crime, narcotrafficking, and citizen insecurity.

To analyze the change in our international relations and its implications for future growth and development, I begin this chapter by reviewing how Latin America went from being a relatively closed region to one where international trade, foreign direct investments, and integration play a stronger role. Then I discuss the growing trade ties between Latin America and China, as well as the decline in trade between our region and the United States and Europe. I then explain the region's integration efforts, especially the rise of the Pacific Alliance. Finally, I explore the synergies and importance of the international agenda between the region, the United States, and Canada. I also explain the need to understand the consequences of this new multipolar world for our region.

FOREIGN DIRECT INVESTMENT IN THE REGION

Inflows of foreign direct investment to the region have steadily increased since the beginning of the twenty-first century. According to a recently published report by ECLAC, in 2012, foreign direct investment (FDI) flowing into Latin America and the Caribbean hit a new record high of US$174.546 billion (see Figure 10.1). This is 5.7 percent above the level posted in 2011 and confirms a consistent uptrend that began in 2010. These figures were set in a complex scenario of falling international FDI

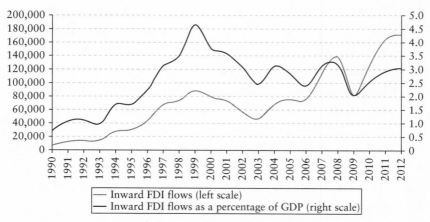

FIGURE 10.1 *Foreign direct investment flows, 1990–2012*

Source: Economic Commission for Latin America (ECLAC), on the basis of official figures and estimates as of April 29, 2013.

Note: FDI figures indicate inflows of foreign direct investment minus divestments (repatriation of capital) by foreign investors. The FDI figures do not include flows into the main financial centers of the Caribbean. These figures differ from those set out in the 2012 editions of *The Economic Survey of Latin America and the Caribbean* and the *Preliminary Overview of the Economies of Latin America and the Caribbean* because they show the net balance of foreign investment, that is, direct investment in the reporting economy (FDI) minus outward FDI.

flows throughout the year (13 percent) to levels close to those seen in 2009. Macroeconomic uncertainty in the United States and the European Union lay behind this fresh drop in global investment, which was sharpest when it came to flows to developed countries (22.5 percent). The developing countries as a whole also saw a decline in inward FDI, although the drop was much more modest (3 percent).[1]

In its report titled *Regional Economic Outlook: Western Hemisphere, 2014*, the IMF holds that net capital inflows remained relatively strong in 2013, despite jitters in global financial markets. Foreign direct investment inflows continue to exceed the current account deficit in most countries. Portfolio investment and other types of capital inflows also held up, despite some divestment by foreign mutual fund investors. In particular, the financially integrated economies have received a more resilient mix of inflows, with a greater share of foreign direct investment, and have used a larger share of those inflows to build up international reserves and private asset holdings overseas, while the widening of the current account deficit has been more contained. Nonetheless, the risk of a sudden stop of capital flows remains a concern.[2]

It is interesting to note that investments made by regional firms increased substantially in 2012 to 14 percent of all FDI entering the region. However, the United States and the countries of the European Union continue to be the largest investors in Latin America. Transnational corporations from the United States increased their share of FDI flowing into the region, while Spanish firms, which had ranked third in this respect in 2011, reduced their share heavily owing to divestments.[3]

Diversifying and increasing investments is crucial for inclusive growth and sustainable development. Why is it important to note the sectoral composition of FDI entering Latin America? I believe it is particularly significant because it indicates the extent to which investment is either driving change in the region's production structure or entrenching existing specialization patterns. As I mentioned before, it is also linked to the vulnerability of the region to external shocks with respect to the demand for and prices of commodities. In 2012, the sectoral distribution of FDI for the region as a whole was similar to the average for the previous five years, although the share going to services (the largest destination sector) edged up to 44 percent of the total in 2012. Manufacturing slid slightly but continues to account for 30 percent of the total. The proportion going to sectors based on natural resources was the same in 2012 (26 percent) as during 2007–2011.[4]

As I mentioned before, Latin America is not a homogeneous region, and this is also reflected in the different kinds of investments in the region (see Figure 10.2). In South America (excluding Brazil), FDI has been focused on natural resource–based sectors (51 percent in mining in 2012). Manufacturing and services accounted for 12 percent and 37 percent, respectively. The situation is different in Brazil, where the manufacturing sector represents a significant percentage of inward FDI at 38 percent of the total in 2012. However, this is lower than the average for the past five years. By contrast, natural resources were still a relatively small draw for FDI in Brazil in 2012 (13 percent of the total).[5]

Natural resources account for a smaller share of FDI in Mexico, Central America, and the Caribbean as well, and they have tended to hold steady: 10 percent in 2012 and over the previous five years. Manufacturing, conversely, despite the decline in absolute value in Mexico, was again the largest recipient of FDI (48 percent of the total). As for services, their share dropped sharply from 55 percent in 2007–2011 to 42 percent in 2012. Within this group of countries, the primary sector receives a substantial share in some economies of the Caribbean, such as Trinidad and Tobago and the Dominican Republic. In Mexico, the proportion of FDI going to this sector is very small because both mining and hydrocarbon extraction are in the hands of domestic groups.[6]

These investments can have a significant effect on the entrenchment or diversification of production patterns because of the substantial impact of FDI on host economies, measured approximately as the ratio of FDI to GDP. In 2012, the region captured flows equivalent to 3 percent of GDP (slightly more than in 2011). Chile stands out with an FDI-to-GDP ratio of 11.3 percent in 2012.[7]

Setting aside the current conditions, sectoral patterns of FDI are leaning increasingly toward natural resource exploitation, especially in South America, and are thus entrenching the region's existing production

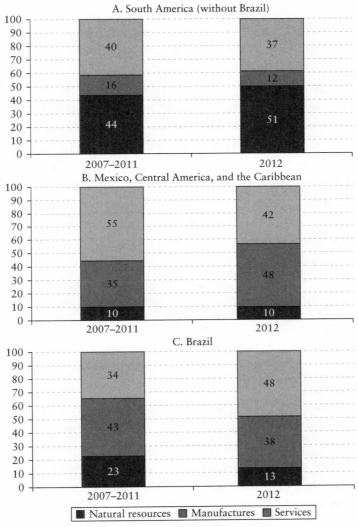

FIGURE 10.2 *Sectoral distribution of foreign direct investment by subregion, 2007–2011 and 2012*

Source: ECLAC, on the basis of official figures and estimates as of April 19, 2013.

structure. Generally speaking, manufacturing accounts for quite a limited share of FDI flows, except in Brazil and Mexico.[8]

As I mentioned in Chapter 5, the goals of increasing foreign investment and decent jobs are intrinsically related. What really matters is observing what kind of jobs our people can choose as a consequence of the new investments. Commerce and construction investments create the most jobs (seven per US$1 million invested), followed by the manufacturing industry and services (three per US$1 million invested). Mining (including oil) creates one job for every US$2 million. Labor-intensive manufacturing creates seven jobs per US$1 million invested; engineering-intensive manufacturing (including the automobile industry) creates four, similar to the food industry. Other natural resource–intensive activities (excluding food) are less employment intensive, creating two jobs per US$1 million invested.[9]

DEEPENING AND DIVERSIFYING
TRADE WITH THE WORLD

Understanding Latin America's International Trade History

Our region's economies remained relatively closed during much of the twentieth century, especially during the period of import substitution industrialization (ISI). As we saw in previous chapters, ISI sought to protect infant industry by imposing tariffs on manufactured goods, while facilitating the import of capital goods to develop national industry. This process was often linked to overvalued currencies that made it easier to acquire machinery and equipment. As countries in the region focused on developing their national economies, trade with the rest of the world remained limited.

Until the 1970s, governments used their own resources as well as loans from international development banks to support ISI policies and infrastructure projects. But things started to change with the 1973 OPEC oil embargo and the subsequent increase in oil prices. Petrodollars flooded the international banking system, and commercial banks, which until that period had shown little interest in the region, started offering governments and businesses easy access to financing. Not surprisingly, private and public debt rose sharply.

High levels of sovereign debt, coupled with rising interest rates, led to Mexico's sovereign default and then to the restructuring of sovereign debt throughout the region. This marked the end of ISI and the beginning of what would come to be known as the Washington Consensus. Structural reforms followed suit, as well as the opening of Latin American markets through open trade policies.

The 1980s and 1990s saw the region's comeback in international markets through the export of energy, mineral, and food commodities. However, historically low commodity prices and dependency on only a few markets made our region vulnerable and growth sluggish. But this began to change in the first years of the new century, with the emergence of a commodities "supercycle" led by China's strong demand for energy, mineral, and food commodities. A decade-long period of rising commodity prices offered our region an unparalleled period of economic stability and prosperity. Let's analyze the causes of this commodity "supercycle."

What Caused the Recent Commodity Supercycle?

China has been the main driver behind commodity demand in the last decade and the subsequent rise in commodity prices. This can be explained, in part, by its rapid industrialization and urbanization process, which requires large quantities of energy and mineral commodities. In addition, rising incomes have also fueled the demand for food commodities, especially meat, soybeans, and corn.

Historical studies show that countries tend to enter a commodity-intensive stage of development when their GDP per capita ranges from $3,000 to $20,000.[10] Looking at historical commodity prices, especially in minerals and energy, higher prices correlate with periods of industrialization and urbanization. Western countries experienced this process in the eighteenth and nineteenth centuries and during the postwar recovery period of the 1940s and 1950s. These periods show strong hikes in commodity prices. But as developed countries graduated into a more service-oriented stage of development, coupled by improvements in technology, there was a sharp decline in the demand for commodities, followed by historically low prices during the 1980s and 1990s. Not surprisingly, this led to underinvestment in commodities.

Within this context, there are three factors that can explain the commodity "supercycle" experienced in the first decade of the twenty-first century. First, the entrance of China and other populous countries into a new industrialization and urbanization phase ramped up demand for commodities. Second, this new demand was matched with underinvestment in the energy and mineral markets, given the historically low prices experienced in the 1980s and 1990s. Demand greatly surpassed supply, leading to further increases in price. Third, investment in mineral and energy commodities is costly and long term in nature, which explains the lag in supply response. The 2008 global financial crisis further enhanced this process, as costly investment in this field was delayed, increasing prices even further.

China's demand for commodities is estimated to have peaked in 2011, and while demand is expected to subside, it will still be higher than that experienced in the last two decades of the twentieth century. China is still undergoing a strong industrialization and urbanization process, which is likely to continue to fuel commodity demand. In the past decade, 12 countries have entered a commodity-intensive stage of development. Of them, China, India, the Philippines, and Vietnam are the largest economies. Their contribution to global GDP increased from 22 percent to 44 percent.[11] In addition, other large emerging economies are also expected to contribute to future commodity demand. Thus, estimates suggest that although commodity prices peaked in 2011, they are expected to remain relatively constant for the short and medium terms.

The central argument of this book is that the "time factor" is crucial. *We need to make an urgent and drastic shift in the composition of Latin America's economic growth while the prices of commodities are still high.* Let us not wait any longer because we will miss the train that could free us from vulnerability to external factors.

This means that our region is likely to continue benefiting from international trade, but our governments will need to manage resources wisely. In the past decade, revenue increased as commodity prices rose. But in the years ahead, revenue is likely to remain more or less stable, and our governments will need to use it efficiently in order to ensure adequate investment in education, health, and infrastructure. For this reason, and as

I will discuss in the next sections, many countries in the region have commenced efforts to expand export markets and diversify export products in an attempt to capture untapped sources of trade revenue.

Increasing South–South Trade

South–south trade has increased dramatically over the last decade. By *south–south trade*, we mean the exchange of goods and services among developing countries, as opposed to traditional north–south exchanges. As I said above, south–south trade between our region and Asia has been a game changer, leading to a decade-long commodity "supercycle."

Our trade with the rest of the world has tripled to more than $1.9 trillion, leading to a proliferation of trade agreements within and outside the region. As we can see in Figure 10.3, commodities constitute 74 percent of our exports; 34 percent of this is food, 31 percent is fuel, and 27 percent is mineral commodities.[12]

More specifically, exports from Latin America to China increased from 1 percent in 1992 to 7 percent in 2012. In this period, China has become the main trading partner of Peru, Brazil, and Chile, displacing the United States and Europe. Not surprisingly, China holds the potential to become the region's main export destination by 2030.[13]

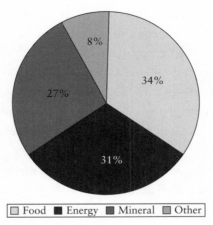

FIGURE 10.3 *Commodity exports*

Source: Loes (2013).

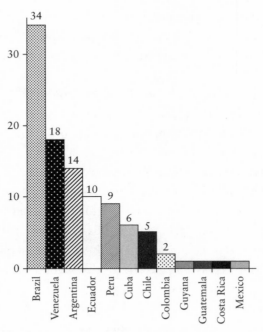

FIGURE 10.4 *Chinese outbound direct investment to Latin America (%), 2011*

Source: Laidler et al. (2013).

In addition to the export of commodities, relations with China also involve public and private sector investment in our region. There has been a sharp increase in Chinese outbound direct investment (ODI) in the last decade, making Latin America the second largest recipient after Asia. Due to greater domestic competition and slower growth in developed countries, Chinese firms and banks have begun exploring new markets, acquiring new technologies, and securing raw materials. The distribution of Chinese ODI to our region can be seen in Figure 10.4, where the five largest recipients of ODI in our region are Brazil, Venezuela, Argentina, Ecuador, and Peru.

Chinese development lending to the region is greater than that of multilateral organizations such as the IMF and Inter-American Development Bank.[14] Led by China Development Bank and China Ex-Im Bank, this lending has centered around three main areas: infrastructure, mining, and energy. But in order to understand the nature of Chinese investment in the region, we need to take a sectoral approach and analyze its impact in each sector.

Energy Sector

Chinese investment in energy, mining, and infrastructure projects represents 65 percent of the $84 billion outbound direct investment to Latin America. This process has been led by both Chinese state-owned enterprises (SOEs) and China's private sector.

In order to meet future energy needs derived from projected GDP growth, it is estimated that our region will need a 26 percent increase in its power generation. This process has been supported by Chinese investments, especially in the development of infrastructure for hydropower, wind, and solar facilities. Chinese banks have provided long-term financing for projects that would otherwise not have been viable.

Chinese investment in Ecuador's hydropower sector stands out, with seven projects awarded to Chinese contractors.[15] In the wind energy sector, Hydrochina is completing the 15-MW Qollpana project, which is the first wind farm in Bolivia, and negotiating a 50-MW project with the Chinese firm Sinomach.[16] In the solar energy sector, China has seen Chile as a strong market for the entry of Chinese construction firms and the export of components. There are other billion-dollar projects in Costa Rica and Mexico.[17] Regarding electricity generation, Chinese State Grid was awarded a $438 million contract to build the electrical infrastructure that connects the Belo Monte dam to the Brazilian power grid. As we can see, China has been an active player, financing the development of infrastructure in our region's energy sector.

Mining and Infrastructure Sector

China is the main destination of Peru's mining exports, 40 percent of which are copper, 21 percent silver and zinc, and 18 percent lead. The three major Chinese-led mining projects in the country consist of the US$1.5 billion investment by Shougang Corporation in the Marcona iron ore expansion, the US$1.3 billion investment in the Toromocho copper mine under construction by Chinalco, and the US$240 million copper, iron ore, and zinc project by Shouxin.[18] Finally, Minmetals and Chinalco have submitted a

$5.9 billion bid for the Las Bambas copper mine in Peru.[19] Not surprisingly, China is expected to become the largest investor in Peru's mining industry. Chinese mining companies have also expanded to Brazil's iron ore industry.

Automobile Sector

Chinese automobile exports started in the 1990s, at first focusing on smaller and less developed car markets in the region and establishing assembly plants. Chinese producers have an auto market share of 23 percent in Uruguay, 15 percent in Peru, 9 percent in Paraguay, and 7 percent in Chile. The Chinese companies Chery and Lifan have assembly factories in Uruguay and Dongfeng in Paraguay.[20] Chinese companies have also begun to venture into larger regional markets such as Brazil, Mexico, and Argentina. Of these, Brazil is the largest recipient of Chinese auto exports in the world. Companies investing in these markets include First Automotive Works (FAW), Foton, Chery, JAC, and Geely.

Fishmeal Sector

Peru is the world's largest fishmeal and fish oil producer. In 2011, it produced 30 percent of global fishmeal and 33 percent of global fish oil. China is the main export market for this industry, accounting for 56 percent of total exports in 2012. China Fishery Group Ltd. acquired Norwegian-listed Peruvian fishmeal and fish oil producer Copeinca, the second largest Peruvian fishmeal company, with an investment of $800 million.[21] This acquisition made China Fishery Group the world's largest fishmeal producer.

Bank Lending Sector

Chinese development lending has totaled $85 billion since 2005, targeting a few countries and specific sectors. Cumulatively, China Development Bank provided 80 percent of lending, and China Ex-Im Bank supplied 9 percent of lending. Both institutions offer more lending than other multilateral organizations such as the IMF, World Bank, and Inter-American Development Bank combined.[22] Lending peaked in 2011 with loan commitments of more than $35 billion, which later decreased to $10 billion in 2012. More than half of the lending was allocated to Venezuela, and the rest distributed mainly to Brazil, Argentina, and Ecuador. Loans tend to be worth $1 billion or more and have been devoted to financing infrastructure, mining, and energy projects.

Different types of conditionality apply to this lending. China Development Bank's conditions tend to be more stringent than those of other lending institutions, while China Ex-Im Bank usually offers lower interest rates. Chinese loans usually require the purchase of equipment and sometimes oil sale agreements.[23]

LATIN AMERICA AND ASIA: THE CHALLENGES IN A FURTHER CHINA–LATIN AMERICA INTEGRATION

In addition to business investments, China has also invested in developing cultural ties with our region. China has opened 32 new Confucius Institutes throughout the region to help promote Chinese language and culture and facilitate cultural exchange. In the past decade, China has also increased its political ties with the region. Presidential visits hosted in China and in Latin America have become more and more frequent, signaling the growing importance of ties between our regions.

In addition, in 2004, China gained permanent observer status at the Organization of American States, and since 2008, it has been a member of the Inter-American Development Bank. However, further integration between China and Latin America is not free of challenges. Next we will analyze some of them.

Regarding economic challenges, in recent years, there has been a growing concern about Latin America's possible dependency on China as a key recipient of our exports and, more recently, as a key investor in our region. The slowdown in China's GDP growth has already led to a decline in commodity prices, which appear to have peaked in 2011. But a sharp decline in China's GDP would negatively affect trade with the region and severely dampen our growth prospects. A strong decline in commodity demand would cause international commodity prices to plummet. Slow growth in China would decrease foreign investment and lending to our region, which would further negatively affect growth. Analyzing this worst-case scenario is crucial because it underscores the importance of continuing our region's diversification process. As I mentioned before, the more diversified our production and export markets are, the better we can protect ourselves from negative external shocks. However, a more realistic medium-term scenario is one in which China continues its urbanization and industrialization processes, sustaining demand for commodities. As a result, prices will be lower than the levels seen at the commodity peak in 2011 but still high compared to the low prices experienced in the 1980s and 1990s.

Another pressing concern is the challenge posed by cheap manufacturing imports from China. Brazil and Mexico have already voiced their concern over a deindustrialization process, because the region may not be able to compete with China's economies of scale and low prices. Brazil has even denounced the "currency war" in relation to an artificially undervalued renminbi, which makes Chinese exports more attractive, while negatively affecting the international competitiveness of the region's manufacturing products. Countries around the world have expressed similar concerns, and these issues are likely to remain a challenge in the future.

Concerns over food security have restricted China's landownership in the region by imposing new regulations, especially in Brazil, Argentina, and Uruguay, where investors are encouraged to enter farming partnerships instead of acquiring landownership.[24] As we have discussed in previous chapters, climate change and a growing world population will put further strains on our natural resources. Thus, our region will need to be strategic about protecting its natural resource endowment and its capacity to become the "farm of the world" by 2030. Otherwise, we run the risk of endangering our capacity to meet the future needs of our population.

Unlike trade relations with other regions, which have been supported by historical, cultural, and language ties, relations between China and Latin America are very new. As a growing and powerful global player, China might still need to win hearts and minds in the region. As we have seen earlier in this chapter, it has already taken active steps in this direction by introducing Confucius Institutes and supporting cultural exchanges. But more will probably need to be done on these grounds to strengthen ties between the two regions. The next section examines how some Latin American companies have already begun taking steps to diversify and expand their markets globally, reducing dependence on one sole trading partner.

APEC AND THE OPPORTUNITY FOR
PERU TO BECOME THE HUB OF THE
AMERICAS FOR THE PACIFIC

The Asia-Pacific Economic Cooperation Association (APEC) was created as an informal ministerial-level dialogue group with 12 members in 1989. However, today APEC is made up of 21 countries, 3 of them Latin American (Mexico, Peru, and Chile). APEC is the premier Asia-Pacific economic forum, and its primary goal is to support sustainable economic growth and prosperity in the Asia-Pacific region.

APEC's 21 member economies comprise a market of 2.77 billion consumers (40 percent of the global population), account for 44 percent of world trade, represent 55 percent of global economic output (more than $38 trillion in 2011), and represent 53 percent of world real GDP in purchasing power parity (PPP) terms ($35.8 trillion).[25] The organization has been pretty successful in its aims. Since APEC was created, average tariffs in the region have fallen from 16 percent to 5 percent. As a consequence, intra-APEC merchandise trade (exports and imports) has grown from $1.7 trillion in 1989 to $9.9 trillion in 2010, nearly a sixfold increase, now accounting for 67 percent of APEC's total merchandise trade. By June 2011, 48 FTAs had been signed between APEC members; there are currently 42 FTAs in force between APEC member economies.[26]

APEC's main goals are building a dynamic and harmonious Asia-Pacific community by championing free and open trade and investment, promoting and accelerating regional economic integration, encouraging economic and technical cooperation, enhancing human security, and facilitating a favorable and sustainable business environment.[27]

Some Latin American countries are already benefiting from being part of this organization. Peru has many comparative geographic, economic, and political advantages to enable it to become the hub for the Pacific in Latin America. As I said before, we cannot miss the train of history.

PACIFIC ALLIANCE—A PROMISING
MULTILATERAL TRADING BLOC

While most trade negotiations with China and Asia have been conducted on a bilateral basis, a new Latin American trade and economic integration bloc is emerging. The Pacific Alliance was established by the governments of Chile, Colombia, Mexico, and Peru in June 2012. Pacific Alliance members are among the most competitive, fastest-growing, and most attractive economies in our region. The initiative seeks to deepen integration among its members in order to enhance trade with the rest of the world, especially with Asia. The bloc has a population of 209 million people, which represents 36 percent of the region's population, giving it greater leverage for negotiating with larger trading partners.

The four countries have democratic governments, are open to international trade, and have a positive investment environment. The Pacific Alliance's GDP accounts for 35 percent of the region's GDP, 50 percent of its international trade, and 41 percent of incoming foreign investment. If the Pacific Alliance were a country, it would be the world's eighth largest economy and the seventh largest exporter.[28] The four countries also have the highest rankings in 2014 for "ease of doing business," as measured by the World Bank.

Pacific Alliance members share a strong interest in international trade, which is reflected in their engagement with countries inside and outside the region. All members have signed free trade agreements with the United States and with one another and have numerous overlapping trade commitments. As we can see in Figure 10.5, Chile has signed 22 trade agreements with 60 countries, followed by Mexico with 17 free trade agreements with 44 countries, Peru with 16 free trade agreements with 50 countries, and Colombia with 10 free trade agreements with 30 countries.[29] From its inception, member countries have demonstrated their full commitment through regular meetings taking place every six months, which is no mean feat for a nascent organization. The Alliance has also shown its resilience to changes of heads of state, as was the case in Peru, Chile, and Mexico, showing the strength of the Alliance's shared interests and values.

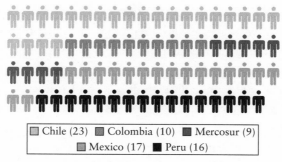

Chile (23)   Colombia (10)   Mercosur (9)
Mexico (17)   Peru (16)

FIGURE 10.5 *Free trade agreements*
Source: García (2013).

Since 2012, the Pacific Alliance has achieved significant goals. The bloc has eliminated 92 percent of import tariffs among its members; eliminated business and tourist visa requirements; established a platform for academic and student mobility, including more than 100 scholarships per country; signed a tourism cooperation agreement to strengthen tourism among country members; and created the Pacific Alliance Business Council and four trade promotion agencies (ProMexico, Promperu, Pro-Chile, and Proexport).[30]

In addition, Chile, Colombia, and Peru have linked their stock markets, and Mexico is expected to join in 2014. Known as the Integrated Latin American Market (MILA), it will compete with Brazil's as the largest stock market in Latin America. These remarkable achievements can be in part attributed to its "harvest approach," which enables agreements to be approved piecemeal rather than having to wait for all points to be approved before an agreement can be reached.[31] Its pragmatic approach sets the Alliance apart from other organizations in the region.

One of the main goals of the Pacific Alliance is to implement regulatory reforms to improve the trade, investment, and governance structures of its members in order to make it one of the most competitive trading areas in the world, using collective action to negotiate with Asia. The Pacific Alliance has the potential to become the main driver of trans-Pacific trade integration, and, not surprisingly, the Association of Southeast Asian Nations (ASEAN) and China have already expressed interest in the bloc.

The Pacific Alliance has accepted Costa Rica as a full member, and the number of observer states has grown rapidly, including representation in all regions including China, Japan, Korea, France, Spain, Portugal, Turkey, Australia, New Zealand, Canada, United States, Guatemala, Honduras, Dominican Republic, El Salvador, Costa Rica, Panama, Ecuador, Paraguay, and Uruguay.

The Pacific Alliance's prospects are promising, but its future will depend on the consolidation of its trade agreements and the selective integration of observer states. Its selectivity is important because it will help preserve its pragmatic approach geared toward increased trade and growth. The Pacific Alliance needs to take note of errors made by other trade unions in the region, such as Mercosur, which has superposed political needs on commitments to free markets and the rule of law.

TRADE WITH THE UNITED STATES

Although trade between the United States and Latin America has decreased in recent years, the United States is still the recipient of 40 percent of Latin America's exports, it provides 40 percent of the region's FDI, and it is the source of 90 percent of the remittances received by the region. Furthermore, the United States is the first or second trading partner of every country in the region. The US presence in the region has decreased over the last decade, but its influence should not be understated (see Figures 10.6 and 10.7).

The United States is spearheading the Trans-Pacific Partnership (TPP), an ambitious international initiative that seeks to bring deeper trade and diplomatic integration among some members of APEC. The TPP includes 11 countries that are members of APEC: Australia, Brunei, Canada, Chile, Malaysia, Mexico, New Zealand, Peru, Singapore, the United States, and Vietnam. Together they represent close to 30 percent of world GDP and a fifth of total world exports.

The Pacific Alliance and TPP have a lot in common, from shared member countries to their strong interest in enhancing trade between both sides of the Pacific. TPP is a much larger initiative, with the potential to become the largest regional trading bloc in the world. Its potential is grand, but so are the stumbling blocks standing between the idea and the

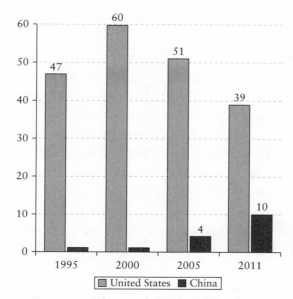

FIGURE 10.6 *Exports to China and the United States*

Source: Loes (2013).

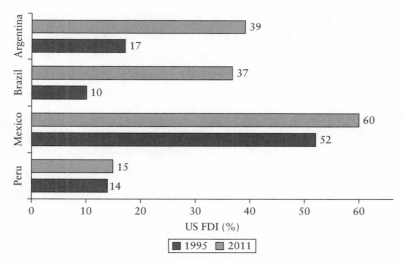

FIGURE 10.7 *US foreign direct investment*

Source: García (2013).

realization of the idea. Free trade negotiations between the United States and ten countries across the Pacific are likely to stall, especially regarding sensitive topics such as labor, agriculture, environment, and human rights. Ratification of an agreement by the US Senate will probably be long and hard. Hence, the Pacific Alliance stands as a more immediate and feasible alternative to free trade across the Pacific.

Given their similarities, TPP and the Pacific Alliance are complementary initiatives rather than mutually exclusive ones. Thus, in the years to come we are likely to see stronger advocacy efforts by the United States to strengthen free trade throughout the region and to increase the number of participating members. The success of these endeavors will depend on multiple factors, such as political will, economic conditions, and the ability of its members to reconcile competing regulations and requirements imposed by the spaghetti bowl of trade agreements between countries inside and outside the region.

LATIN AMERICAN BUSINESSES
WITH A GLOBAL REACH

Latin American companies have also increased their investments in China, but this process has taken place at a slower pace than Chinese ODI in our region. For instance, Brazil has invested $300 million in China since 2006, compared with the $25 billion invested by China in Brazil.[32]

Trade relations between Latin American companies and China began in the 1970s, but they have intensified in the past decade. The first company to venture into China was Vale, a Brazilian iron ore producer. Similarly, Tenaris, an Argentinean pipe maker, started exporting to China in the 1970s, with plans to later open an office and a capacity facility there.

More recently, a new set of Latin American multinational companies have expedited their global expansion. These companies have come to be known as *multilatinas*. Their internalization process is based on key competitive advantages such as the targeting of low-income consumers, expertise in challenging distribution systems, and an understanding of politically unstable settings and complex regulatory environments, as well as lessons learned from domestic competition imposed by foreign companies.[33] Interestingly, multilatinas have not only expanded their tar-

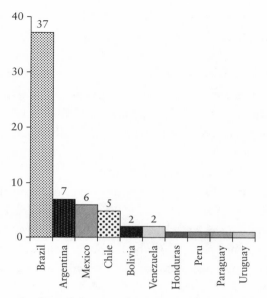

FIGURE 10.8 *Outbound direct investment to China (%), 2012*
Source: Laidler et al. (2013).

get markets but also have diversified their production to areas of higher value-added.

Due to historical, cultural, and geopolitical ties, Europe has been the largest source of FDI in the region, with investments representing close to 10 percent of the region's GDP.[34] Spain has contributed with 40 percent of this FDI. However, the aftermath of the global financial crisis has led to a decrease in European investment in our region. Some companies even began to dispose of noncore assets in order to free up resources from Latin America, which have totaled $28 billion since 2011.

This trend has presented new opportunities for Latin American companies interested in expanding to Europe or purchasing Latin American assets from European companies. Such transactions have totaled more than $16 billion. America Movil expanded into Europe with the purchase of KPN and Telekom Austria, as have other companies in Brazil, Chile, Colombia, and Mexico.

Although much of the region's international trade advances have taken place on a bilateral basis, we will see in the next section that new multilateral efforts have emerged to strengthen and increase the region's negotiating power vis-à-vis its trading partners.

LATIN AMERICAN REGIONAL INTEGRATION

In this past decade we have also seen increasing integration efforts, in an attempt to enhance trade and cooperation within Latin America, and to increase our region's leverage as an international player. These new regional organizations include ALBA in 2004, UNASUR in 2008, CELAC in 2011, and the Pacific Alliance in 2012.

The Bolivarian Alliance for the Peoples of Our America (ALBA) was founded in 2004 by Venezuela and Cuba as a counterpart to the US-led Free Trade Areas of the Americas (FTAA). To date, seven countries have joined the organization: Antigua and Barbuda, Bolivia, Dominica, Ecuador, Nicaragua, Saint Vincent, and the Grenadines. In 2008, a new and more comprehensive bloc, the Union of South American States (UNASUR), emerged, which integrated two preexisting trade unions, Mercosur and the Andean Community of Nations (CAN). Whereas ALBA and UNASUR have a more political agenda, CELAC and the Pacific Alliance are focused on investment, trade, technology transfer, innovation, and technology.

The Community of Latin American and Caribbean States was formally established in 2011 and consists of 33 countries from South America, Central America, and the Caribbean. Its purpose is to deepen integration throughout Latin America and the Caribbean. Although similar in scope, CELAC stands out from the Organization of American States in the sense that it has excluded the participation of Canada and the United States in order to reduce the United States' influence in the region and to generate a true Latin American integration free of foreign interference. As a bloc, CELAC has a population of 600 million people and a joint GDP of more than $7 trillion. If it were a country, it would be the third largest economy in the world. The size of its combined population and GDP gives it leverage in international affairs to negotiate with larger trading partners and with other regional blocks.

Out of these organizations, CELAC and the Pacific Alliance hold the greatest potential to enhance Latin America's position as a global player in international affairs and trade. In January 2013, in Chile, CELAC held the 7th Bi-Regional Summit of EU-LAC Heads of State and Government, with representatives from 61 countries and 46 heads of state. This was the first time that CELAC represented its members as the EU's counterpart.

In addition, CELAC offers some advantages to negotiating with Asia and China. Two of the main challenges facing China when expanding investment and trade with the region are dealing individually with each country and entering a region with historically strong ties to the United States.[35] At CELAC's second annual meeting in January 2014, member countries agreed to create the first China-CELAC summit in an attempt to develop a mechanism to interact with China collectively.[36]

Some of the challenges include articulating the plurality of political drivers and economic interests into one consolidated bloc. For China, the challenge will also be advancing its interest in the region without jeopardizing its relations with the United States. Thus, a clear balancing of political and economic interests will likely mark the future outcomes of China-CELAC summits.

CAN BRAZIL LEAD LATIN AMERICA'S CONSOLIDATION AS A GLOBAL PLAYER?

Brazil is the sixth largest economy in the world, the fifth largest country by size of territory, and the largest in the Southern Hemisphere. Due to its status as a large emerging economy, Brazil has played a key role representing Latin America in new associations such as BRICS, IBSA, and trade negotiations at international summits. Brazil delivers the opening address at the United Nations General Assembly every September, and, along with Japan, it has been elected ten times as a member of the UN Security Council.[37]

Since 2003, Brazil has adopted a more open stand toward foreign policy. In this period, Brazil opened 40 new embassies, with a total of 140 embassies worldwide, as opposed to 164 from the United States.[38] In Africa alone, Brazil inaugurated 20 embassies, with a total of 37 embassies. Brazil has more embassies in Africa than the United Kingdom does.[39] Lula undertook 12 official visits to 23 African countries, while his minister of foreign affairs undertook 67 official visits to 34 countries in

Africa.[40] In this period, the number of foreign service officers increased to 1,400 worldwide.[41]

Since 2010, it has been part of BRICS, an association that consists of Brazil, Russia, India, China, and South Africa. Combined they have a population of close to 3 billion people, a GDP of about $32.5 trillion, and an estimated $4 trillion in foreign reserves. They are considered the biggest and fastest-growing emerging economies and are members of the G20, with significant influence in regional and global affairs.

In addition to BRICS, Brazil has engaged with India and South Africa in the establishment of IBSA, launched in 2003. Its mission is to promote a democratic development model and to forge a new approach of south–south cooperation in order to improve their negotiating capacity in many issues ranging from trade to international security. IBSA's role in the international concert of nations is not marginal. For instance, IBSA led the opposition bloc to developed countries at the World Trade Organization (WTO) Summit in Cancun, Mexico, and played a crucial role in changing the negotiating model of the organization.[42]

One of their main objectives is to reform the UN Security Council. All IBSA members are advocating an expansion in the number of Security Council members, and each one wants a permanent seat. In 2011, all three countries held temporary seats on the Security Council, which offered a unique opportunity to advance their efforts.

In 2008, IBSA countries started holding joint naval exercises off the coast of South Africa in a marine security effort known as IBSA-MAR. Cooperation among all countries has also covered other areas, such as Indian officials' study of Brazil's Bolsa Família in support of India's efforts to introduce a conditional cash transfer system in the country. In turn, Brazil has sought cooperation from South Africa to learn about its policy toward taxpayers.[43]

But the future of IBSA will depend on the success of their democratic models at home in order to sustain the aim of advocating democratic development across the developing world. This could prove to be a challenge in the face of slow growth, insecurity, corruption, and popular protests. Further integration will also need increased trade relations. Although trade has increased from the 2003 level of $4 billion and is expected to total $40 billion in 2015, it pales in comparison to trade between IBSA countries and external members.

South–south cooperation has been at the heart of Brazil's foreign policy from the Doha Round of trade negotiations in 2003, the formation of the G20+ group of developing countries on agriculture, the IBSA initiative, and the emergence of the BRICS group.[44] Brazil's nonconfrontational diplomacy has relied on being a link between north and south, west and east. However, President Rousseff has been preoccupied with domestic affairs, so Brazilian foreign policy efforts have been relegated to the back burner. Thus, questions remain regarding the sustainability of Brazil's role in leading the region's global efforts.

TECHNOLOGY TRANSFERS

As I mentioned at the beginning of this book, limited innovation in Latin American countries impairs the region's sustained and inclusive economic growth. It comes as no surprise that technological change, and not only factor accumulation, is critical to growth; economists have known this since the seminal research of Solow in 1957. According to a recent report by the World Bank, the region does not invest sufficiently in innovation, nor does it always use scarce resources efficiently. With the exception of Brazil, the majority of countries in Latin America and the Caribbean invest less in research and development (R&D) than other countries with similar income levels. Moreover, as shown in Figure 10.9, less than 50 percent of R&D investments are financed by private industry, which contrasts with the experience of dynamic global innovators such as China, Korea, and the United States.[45]

Public funding of research in Latin America and the Caribbean has emphasized the generation of conceptual knowledge but has been less efficient at energizing technological innovation such as the production of patents (see Figure 10.10a). Collaboration between industry and universities is limited, hindering the transformation of new knowledge into innovation (see Figure 10.10b). Universities and industries must deal with different incentives and cultures discouraging productive research collaboration. Insufficient knowledge sharing by universities in the region prevents the productive sector and society from benefiting from the research being

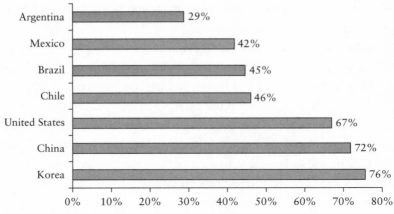

FIGURE 10.9 *Private participation in R&D*

Source: Lasagabaster and Reddy (2010).
Note: Percentage of R&D financed by the private sector.

conducted by the academic community. The establishment of technology transfer offices (TTOs) by universities helps address this challenge by acting as intermediaries in innovation systems and facilitating the transfer of knowledge generated by universities and research centers to industry.[46]

Governments should stimulate the formation of these alliances and help to address several market failures, including coordination failures and the inability to appropriate all of the benefits derived from the R&D. This support needs to be extended on a multiyear basis because the alliances have to undertake R&D work of a long-term nature. Awareness of the importance of innovation is growing at the public and private sector levels. Public initiatives are underway to start addressing these challenges.[47]

While investing in R&D is important, countries in Latin America and the Caribbean can also attain important productivity gains through the acquisition of existing technologies, especially in sectors where industry is far from the technology frontier. However, for the most part, the region has not built efficient support systems for technology extension and dissemination. We will come back to the importance of this topic in the region's agenda with the United States and Canada.

Aligned with the proposal of the Sustainable Development Goals, I believe Latin America needs to enhance regional and international co-

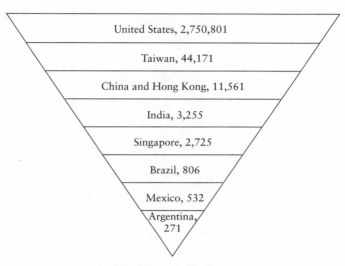

FIGURE 10.10A *Level of patenting (cumulative 2004–2009)*

Source: Lasagabaster and Reddy (2010).

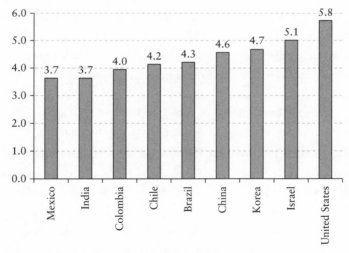

FIGURE 10.10B *Industry-university collaboration*

Source: Lasagabaster and Reddy (2010).
Note: Weighted average. Rating is from 1 to 7, with 7 meaning highest collaboration.

operation for science, technology, and innovation and solutions-oriented research, and to enhance knowledge sharing, including through north–south, south–south, and triangular cooperation. For instance, the promotion of transferring and disseminating clean and environmentally sound technologies to our region is crucial. Also, the region needs to strength its institutions and building capacities to undertake research, development, and adaptation of technologies.

We already have attempted to reverse the trend, and we have been successful. The Trade Facilitation and Productivity Improvement Technical Assistance project—implemented by the government of Peru and supported by World Bank financing—illustrates mechanisms that can be developed to facilitate technology extension, with a focus on increasing enterprise productivity and access to export markets. The project helped strengthen a network of technological innovation centers (Centros de Innovación Tecnológica, or CITEs), following the model of technology centers in Spain. The ownership and governance structure varied. Some were built on public-private partnerships, and others were privately or publicly owned. In 2010, 14 CITEs operating in Peru provided services to more than 4,000 firms in the agribusiness, wood, furniture, and garment industries; logistics; and metal machinery sectors.[48]

LATIN AMERICA'S INTERNATIONAL AGENDA IN A MULTIPOLAR WORLD

It should be clear by now that Latin America needs to go beyond trade expansion; we also need to increase foreign investment, cultural exchange, technology transfer, and joint efforts to fight narcotrafficking and organized crime. As I have mentioned many times, we need to diversify production and rapidly shift into a knowledge economy in order to contribute to this global changing economy. Moreover, the items on Latin America's agendas with respect to the United States, Europe, and Asia will also have to change in light of the knowledge acquired in this multipolar world in which we live.

We should note with a higher degree of concern that China, as a part of Asia, is not the only destination of our commodities. China has aggressively begun to purchase land in several countries in Latin America—Brazil and Peru, among others—in anticipation of its food security challenge.

Again, Latin America is not a homogeneous region. Not only are there large variations in the pace of economic growth and trade and differences in the social faces of our societies, but there are also some outliers in terms of the consolidation of democracy and the manner in which these countries articulate their foreign policies. As I mentioned before, some countries may hold regular elections without necessarily having a genuinely democratic system.

In this period, the region has asserted its foreign policy directives even when they stood in opposition to its partners in the north. Such was the case of Chile's and Mexico's opposition to the second Iraq war in the United Nations Security Council.[49] Brazil partnered with Turkey to negotiate a deal with Iran to prevent harder sanctions over its nuclear program.[50] Ecuador provided diplomatic asylum to Wikileaks founder Julian Assange, who has lived in the Ecuadorian Embassy in London since 2012, thus avoiding extradition to Sweden. Similarly, Bolivia led the developing countries' position on climate change negotiations, refusing to sign the Copenhagen Accord.

In this new multipolar era, the rapid growth of China and India, which represent 40 percent of the world's population, has opened the door for greater diversification of investment and market opportunities, as I explained at the beginning of this book. Thus, diversification in economic growth, investments, trade, and the introduction of science and technology are imperative if Latin America is to seize this unique opportunity.

However, this new world order does not alter the historic and geographic relationship that the Latin American region has with the United States. Every country in the Americas would benefit from strengthened and expanded economic relations with the United States, with improved access to each other's markets, investment capital, and energy resources.[51] The United States is a market of approximately 300 million people, with a GDP per capita of US$51,749[52] and a shared culture of democratic values. Also, the United States' $16 trillion economy[53] is a vital market and a source of capital (including remittances) and technology for Latin America, and it could contribute more to the region's performance. Latin America is also an interesting market for the United States. Taking advantage of the Latin American middle classes' higher purchasing power, the United States should increase trade and promote tourism from Latin America to the United States, and vice versa.[54]

With a rapidly expanding US Hispanic population of more than 50 million, the cultural and demographic integration of the United States and Latin America is proceeding at an accelerating pace, setting a firmer basis for hemispheric partnership.[55] The 53 million–plus Latin American diaspora sent over $50 billion in remittances back home in 2013. Remittances remain one of the largest sources of foreign exchange in the region, in many countries exceeding foreign direct investment (FDI) and development assistance (ODA) combined. In Mexico, Central America, and the Caribbean, remittances often account for over 10 percent of GDP.[56]

Washington and Ottawa will always be partners in helping the region to capitalize on this historic opportunity. I am convinced that the United States and Canada, major players in the world economy, will collaborate with us to meet the challenges of inclusive economic growth, sustainable development, and technology transfers, as well as those involved in combating drug trafficking and organized crime. Yet, I insist that the critical variable is time. This is the moment to make the decisive leap from commodity export growth to effective investment of the resources from these commodities exports in the minds of our people. If we do not do this now, we will miss the train.

It is also important to note that Latin American should not expect the United States to fix the region's problems. We have matured through our own mistakes and our human capital building, and although we still have a long path to walk, we can stand on our own feet. We have learned to put our economic house in order.

It is crucial now that we take advantage of the stock of human capital within the region and dispersed in the diaspora, especially to manage the social and infrastructure investment programs outside our respective national capitals. Around 5.5 million Latin Americans have BA, MA, and PhD degrees in the diaspora around the world.[57]

We do not confront the challenge of building human capital only to manage our economic ministries or assign professional bureaucrats to run the central banks, the tax collection agencies, or our ministries of foreign affairs. We also need this alliance between Latin America and the

United States and Canada to help us construct the urgently needed human capital for strengthening the decentralization state reform that some countries have already initiated, as well as to deliver concrete, measurable, and tangible results to the poorest of the poor in our respective countries.

There are many other areas where the region needs this human capital. As the last UNDP report on human security stated, the successful enforcement of preventive strategies (against crime, violence, and fear) requires the professionalization of the staff involved. This can be both complex and costly, as in the case of treating addiction and psychosocial interventions directed at young people who have committed crimes. The state should create alliances with the private sector and universities to promote professionalization. The same report posited that in Latin America, valuable experiences have been developed to prevent and mitigate the impact of violence and crime by means of strengthening the capacities of the state and encouraging active, responsible citizen participation.

There are other ways in which a synergistic international agenda between the United States and the region can collaborate to improve human capital. Brazil has been a constructive partner in the Domestic Finance for Development (df4d) program, created by the State Department in 2011 to address looming budget crises in smaller economies by improving the collection of public revenues, introducing budget transparency, and reducing corruption. The premise of the project is that the elites and the new middle classes will not pay taxes, and informality will persist, unless taxpayers are convinced that their funds will not be siphoned to offshore bank accounts and will instead be used for agreed-upon public purposes.[58]

We are looking at these new relationships with our neighbors in the north in a more horizontal and equal manner. Latin America needs to assume its responsibility as a mature region. At the same time, we are aware that we have a long way to go and unavoidable challenges to confront. The need for technology transfer is a good example of this. The use of technology in rural areas is crucial if we are to increase the productivity, output, and competitiveness of these communities so the poor will not depend on their capital city. Developing their skills and productivity and empowering them will allow the poor to claim their rights and the opportunity to learn how to fend for themselves. While poverty in the last decade has been gradually reduced as a consequence of economic growth in some delivered social programs, such as direct cash transfers, inequality has not been reduced significantly. It needs to be said loudly and clearly: the poor in Latin America are losing patience with continuing to be poor. To a large extent, their new stance has to do with accessibility to cell phones and new cyber-technologies. The poor know the differences between the haves and the have-nots. I like to remind my entrepreneur friends that the rate of return on investing in empowering the poor is excellent. As I said before, empowering and training the poor will induce them to be partners of the business community. Therefore, there will be less social turmoil, and country risk will decrease; consequently, the interest rate will be lower. However, more important, enabling the poor to have decent and good-paying jobs expands the market for the goods that entrepreneurs produce. All of this will be conducive to a prosperous shared society.

I agree with the last report published by the Inter-American Dialogue on the bilateral relations between the United States and Latin America.[59] Five pressing topics must be included in the US–Latin America agenda. The first is immigration issues: the current immigration system affects Latin America more than any other part of the world. Second, the fight against drugs and organized crime needs to be revised and tackled, together with the European Union, in a more innovative way (where arms traffickers are a crucial component of this challenge). Third, the US embargo against Cuba and other restrictions on US-Cuban relations that are widely rejected in the region need to be lifted. Fourth, we must confront the challenge of avoiding nuclear proliferation and terrorism. The region has proved its political and material commitment—through training, mutual military exercises, technology transfers, intel information cooperation, and so on—to fight against these problems together with our neighbors to the north. Last, we need the United States to take a long, hard look to the south.

I have no doubt that nowadays the relationship between the United States, Canada, the European Union, and Latin America can be complementary. New challenges are bringing us together in a multipolar world.

Distances and borders have no importance regarding the most pressing issues on the international agenda. Whatever happens today in Peru, Paraguay, South Africa, Vietnam, China, or Spain is a matter of mutual concern.

I could continue enumerating common challenges, but it is important to understand that all of these problems are intrinsically interrelated. I believe the primary goal of our agenda should be the achievement of human security (as I explained in Chapter 8) in order to guarantee the flow of capital investments, ensure sustained and inclusive economic growth, and deepen the quality of democracy in the region.

CONSOLIDATING ACHIEVEMENTS

In the years to come, countries in the region will face the challenge of maintaining high growth rates and more prudent fiscal balances without depending necessarily on a rise in international commodity prices. This underscores the importance of continuing current efforts to diversify production, increase productivity, and expand domestic markets, international investment, and trade markets. To achieve this, the need to increase production and productivity will become crucial. As we have seen in previous chapters, improving productivity involves investing more in quality of education and health care. By this I mean investing in the minds of our people, improving our infrastructure, and accessing technology, innovation, and connectivity. This also implies becoming fully aware of the social and environmental responsibilities of our nations and our entrepreneurs. Greater innovation will be key to the development of our region.

Strengthening integration efforts within the region will help increase intraregional investment, trade, and trading blocs, and facilitate the sharing of our experiences with social programs, such as direct conditional cash transfers. Here the Pacific Alliance and CELAC have the potential to increase their members' leverage when dealing with larger trading partners in Asia and the North. More technology, innovation, national and international investment, international trade, and diversity in the destination of exports will not only help the region lessen its vulnerability and dependency but will also help it become more resilient to external market shocks.

South–south cooperation will also become increasingly important, especially in relation to joint efforts devoted to climate change prevention and mitigation, international security and narcotrafficking, technology transfers, and the sharing of knowledge and best practices.

Climate change prevention and mitigation initiatives, as well as disaster prevention initiatives, are becoming increasingly interconnected given that events taking place in one area tend to affect multiple other areas. We have seen improved Latin American and international efforts to monitor and share information regarding tsunamis, hurricanes, fires, and earthquake alerts. The recent magnitude 8.2 earthquake that struck northern Chile led to a rapid tsunami alert extending from Chile's Pacific coast all the way to the Hawaiian Islands.

International efforts such as the Extractive Industries Transparency Initiative (EITI) seek to support resource-rich countries in the transparent management of natural resource revenues. Institutional capacity-building efforts range from supporting countries' ability to negotiate fair extraction contracts to making such contracts publicly available to transparency in the allocation of payments to national governments and subsequent disbursements to subnational governments (see Chapter 9). Greater transparency and accountability help governments to use natural resource revenues wisely, and transparency reduces the uncertainty and risk faced by foreign companies investing in these sectors. Our nations' effective capacity to deliver the natural resource revenue to those who need it most will help support our region's commitment to eradicate poverty and reduce inequality by investing these resources in potable water, sanitation, quality of education, health care, and decent and well-paid jobs for our population, particularly for youth.

Similarly, the wave of insecurity and illicit drug trafficking afflicting our region will require greater and more integrated international efforts to share information and resources. Cooperation among international agencies will need to be better integrated, with mechanisms for detecting and monitoring illegal activities. Narcotrafficking is a global business spreading across all continents, and thus its eradication will require truly joint international measures.

FINAL REMARKS

Throughout this chapter I stress that Latin America needs to go beyond trade expansion; it needs to increase foreign investment, technology, cybernetics, and strong democratic institutions, including civil society and political parties. We need to emphasize all of them in order to generate sustainable development, create decent and well-paid jobs, and establish a democracy that delivers. There has been a substantial economic and political shift in this multipolar world in the relationship between Latin America, the United States, Europe, and Asia.

Latin America has learned from its mistakes, has learned to put its economic house in order, and has matured enough to confront its own challenges, although, admittedly, we still have a long way to go. However, there are many areas of opportunity, shared challenges, and complementarities among Latin America, the United States, and Europe. Technology transfer and building human capital are crucial areas of common interest in the Americas.

I am aware that it is always easier to forecast the past than the future because we have the data on the facts. I am taking the risk of looking at the future without having the data. The time has come to put our vision, inspired literature, commitment, courage, leadership, and state policy decisions together independently of our nationalities or the skin color of our people.

I am convinced that with mutual respect for our biocultural diversity, faith in the power of pooling our efforts will vastly improve the outlook for our children—and the children of our children 35 years from now—when we reach 2050.

Conclusion

IN THESE PAGES I have spelled out a vision for our economically and culturally rich region's future, and I have tried to point to some specific and sensible policies for achieving it. This is not rocket science. After years of political instability and on again, off again economic growth, Latin America is well into an era of sustained democracy and economic development. Our economies barely missed a beat in the 2008–2009 recession and global financial crisis that so deeply impacted North America and Europe. We are on our way to building a large middle class and have the potential to become truly developed, culturally diverse societies in the next generation.

We have a great opportunity, but that does not mean our future is assured. Latin America's leaders will need to make some hard choices and many smart decisions, and in saying that, I am not trying to peddle platitudes. The decisions our countries need to make will be politically difficult, and they will require considerable vision, medium- and long-term decisions and policies, courage, determination, and inspiring leadership to confront powerful players: domestic elites with their long-held notions of privilege, international extractive industries, drug cartels, organized crime, and many others who stand to make high short-term profits on environmentally and socially costly projects.

In my view, the major barrier standing in the way of realizing our potential is Latin America's deeply entrenched economic and social inequality. Our rapid economic growth over the past two decades is the engine necessary for eradicating poverty and reducing inequality in the region. Yet, should the incredibly large differences between the wealthiest few percent of Latin Americans and the poorest 40 percent also continue to characterize our societies, democracy in the region could be eroded. If that happens, our economic growth would also stall, just as it did for a generation in the second half of the twentieth century. We must continue working on a democracy that delivers in both Latin America and the world, with the explicit participation of civil society and a strong, accountable political system.

An underlying theme of my argument is that reducing inequality is not all that is required to strengthen our region's democratic institutions. Along with helping to deepen the political rights we have long fought for, reducing differences between the poor and the rich, men and women, and the diverse cultural and racial groups that live in Latin America is *morally the right thing to do* and *economically the smart thing to do*. How can our national constitutions affirm the fundamental dignity and equality of all individuals when, in practice, our political and social institutions consistently provide our economically and ethnically marginalized citizens far less protection and much less access to public resources? How many highly productive individuals have our economies lost because we did not invest in their early health and education? How much more effective would our local government organizations be if we developed local talent among these excluded groups?

Economists have long argued whether greater income and wealth inequality have positive or adverse impacts on economic growth. It is a basic fact that a nation's economic development is perceived very differently by those at the top and those at the bottom of the pyramid when inequality is rampant. When income and wealth are more evenly distributed, even minor improvements can unleash an enormous amount of human, social, and cultural capital. For instance, the gradual equalization of income in Latin America in the past five years has reduced poverty more rapidly than in the past for every percent increase in growth. If more serious efforts were made to bring about high-quality health, education, water, and sanitary services; design community-based security programs for low-income areas; reduce corruption; and increase the quality of the police and court systems to deal more justly across social classes, the impact would be even more spectacular.

I believe in this story because it is *my* story. Without the pure luck of meeting a few people who wanted to help me, my ability to contribute to society would have been much diminished. I admit that as I was working on this book I thought of the tens of millions of poor young people like me everywhere in Latin America who are barely scraping by, playing soccer with worn-out shoes, attending crowded schools, and wanting desperately to succeed. The path to poor education, intermittent work, low wages, drugs, crime, early pregnancy, and hopelessness is so much wider for these young people than the road to good educational opportunities, decent jobs, and running their own business with access to loans and social networks.

This is what I want desperately to change. I want to change the width of these two paths. I want to do whatever it takes to narrow the path to insecurity and despair for all Latin American youth and build in its place a four-lane highway to quality education, health, and opportunities. I also want to ensure that the Latin America they grow up in is not ravaged by climate change, unclean water and air, and food shortages.

I believe that by accomplishing these objectives, we can make Latin America both a better place and a leading region of the world, with fantastic cultural contributions, and create the kinds of societies where people want to live, feel confident in their children's futures, feel secure, feel they have collective control of their political destinies, and feel proud of being who they are, whatever their local heritage and their gender.

Latin American leaders of my generation will not see this Latin America of 2050, but that should not deter them from making the difficult decisions that will eventually create it. We truly can realize such a long-term vision if we keep it clearly in mind and work every day, step by step, to implement the policies that synergistically can shift the course of our history.

For the rest of the days that God gives me, I have decided to dedicate my life to fighting with the force of my convictions to free people from poverty and inequality in Latin America and in the world, while defending my belief in democracy, freedom of the press, and human rights. I believe that democracy does not have a nationality, human rights do not depend on a person's color, and a dissident voice cannot be silenced.

Acknowledgments

THIS BOOK SYNTHESIZES, with my own imperfections, the knowledge, insights, and inspiration I have gained from a variety of institutions and people around the world during five decades of studying what I call, perhaps somewhat pretentiously, the "political economy of democracy and social inclusion," nourished with some first-hand experience of different parts of the world.

In this book, unlike my previous writings, I risk a forward-looking perspective, with a strong conviction that, in this changing world, Latin America is *the* promising continent of the next 35 years, *but* one that is not free of monumental challenges in several crucial areas that we need to face with decisiveness and inspiring leadership.

In writing this book, as well as my previous one about Peru (*Growing for Inclusion, 2001–2006*), I have enormous debts of gratitude to several institutions and many thoughtful individuals.

Both books benefited from the accumulated knowledge, wisdom, and decisive support of the Center on Democracy, Development, and the Rule of Law (CDDRL) under the leadership of its director, Professor Larry Diamond, whom I thank from the bottom of my heart.

I would also like to register my gratitude to Professor Coit D. "Chip" Blacker, former Stanford University president Gerhard Casper, and my friend Professor Michael McFaul, all of whom are also directors or fellows at Stanford's Freeman Spogli Institute for International Studies (FSI), of which CDDRL is a part. Their kindness, support, and intellectual stimulation have meant much to me over the years, particularly during the period from September 2012 to August 2014.

Special thanks go to my friend and colleague Professor Francis Fukuyama of FSI-CDDRL for his support and kind words of endorsement and, above all, for having given me his precious time to read several drafts of this book. In the same vein, I will be indebted for the rest of my life to former US president Bill Clinton and to Fernando Henrique Cardoso, the former president of Brazil, for having read the last version of this book and for offering me their warm and kind endorsements. I also want to thank the president of the World Bank, Jim Yong Kim, for the insights he shared during a conversation about the crucial challenges facing developing countries and state capacities to deliver concrete and measurable results, particularly to the most disadvantaged segments of our populations. Similarly, I would like to thank my friend and president of the Inter-American Development Bank, Luis Alberto Moreno, for the insights in his book *The Decade of Latin America and the Caribbean: A Real Opportunity*. I have greatly benefited from its content. I also learned a great deal from the meetings of global leaders on emerging markets organized and headed by my friend Enrique Garcia.

Heartfelt thanks go also to Professor Steven Levitsky of Harvard University for his thoughtful suggestions and profound knowledge of Latin America, and Peru in particular.

I also want to explicitly record my gratitude and admiration for biology professor and director of the Stanford University Center for Latin American Studies, Rodolfo Dirzo, for sharing with me his knowledge and convictions about one of the crucial challenges the Latin American region will inevitably have to confront: the irreversible negative effects of climate change on our biodiversity.

I am especially thankful to Stanford University provost John Etchemendy for his friend-ship and support during my presidency of Peru and afterward. Stanford also played a key role in preparing me for that enormous privilege of leading my country back to democracy. The merits of my government belong to all those generous persons, collaborators, and institutions, inside and outside Peru, who helped me grasp that momentous opportunity. The mistakes of my presidency are my sole responsibility; the successes and accomplishments belong to my collaborators. Let history be the judge of that.

Let me, dear reader, pay special tribute to one person, to his entire family, and to Stanford University, home for about 55 years to Professor Martin Carnoy of the Graduate School of Education. Professor Carnoy has shaped the path of my life in more than one way, but especially in developing my academic, professional, and personal understand-ing of the world as an ongoing search, in democracy, for equality, inclusion, and human rights, through equal access to nutrition, health care, and education, beginning with the poorest of the poor.

Professor Carnoy took the risk of believing in me. He believed in this young Peruvian of Andean descent, born at 12,000 feet above sea level, one of 16 brothers and sisters, whose parents migrated from the Andes to a poor fishing village on the coast of Peru when he was five years old.

Owing to the generosity of a young couple who were Peace Corps volunteers, Joel and Nancy Meister, and several statistical accidents, that young man won a scholarship to study economics at the University of San Francisco. At the conclusion of his undergradu-ate studies, he was encouraged to go on to do graduate work. He was accepted to several prestigious universities in the United States and Europe, but lacked the financial resources to pursue his MA and PhD.

That is when Professor Carnoy stepped up and vouched for this young Indian man, who later became an academic and teacher and president of Peru: the only member of his family to attend a university anywhere. Dear Martin: Thank you from the bottom of my heart for believing in me without knowing what would come out of that experiment. Thank you for being my mentor, my advisor during my studies, after my studies, and dur-ing and after my presidency.

Thank you for taking the time to read and make valuable suggestions for several drafts of this book. My hope is that if this publication serves as just a small inspiration to many other disadvantaged young women and men, regardless of their skin color or where they were born, to seek similar opportunities to attend the best universities in the world and tackle with courage and determination the formidable challenges of the globe, then this book will have made a useful contribution.

Finally, this book would not have come about had I not had the undeserved luck of knowing such brilliant graduate and undergraduate students at Stanford, who generously collaborated with me as research assistants: Erin Raab, Nuria Moya Guzman, Emmanuel Ferrario, Luis Alberto Chavez, and Allen Xu. To all of you, my deep thanks: you all are part of this book. I also want to express my great appreciation and thanks forever to Al-ice Kada and Alice Carter of FSI-CDDRL for their immense contribution to the logistics of this book.

The publication of this book is one of the projects of the Global Center for Development and Democracy (CGDD)—which I have the privilege to chair in Latin America, the United States, and the European Union. This book project was conducted from the Peru headquarters for Latin America under the leadership of former social policy minister, Executive Director Ana Maria Romero. To her and her staff, many, many thanks. This book has greatly benefited from the experience, lessons, wisdom, and intelligent inspiration of all my fellow former presidents of Latin America and other presidents and personalities around the globe, who honor us with their membership on the International Advisory Council of the GCDD. We will be forever indebted to them. (Please visit our websites at http://cgdd .org/ and http://cgdd.org/en/who-we-are/international-advisory-council.)

In that connection, I feel particular admiration for Dr. Carl Gershman, president of the National Endowment for Democracy; Kenneth Wollack of the National Democratic Institute for International Affairs; the Carter Center; and the International Republican Institute, as well as their respective senior staff, for the tireless work they do to strengthen democracy around the world and for their ongoing support for the work of the GCDD in Latin America.

Almost last, but not least, I want to thank Stanford University Press. With enormous diligence, professionalism, and generosity, my editor, Dr. Eric Brandt, and his colleagues John Feneron, Fran Andersen, and Friederike Sundaram, undertook to publish this book under very demanding time constraints. Many thanks to all of you. I also want to thank my agent, Scott Mendel, for his professionalism and effectiveness, and Jonathan Cavanagh, who did a great job editing my English in the final version of my manuscript.

Finally, I dedicate this book, from the bottom of my heart and soul, to the companion of not just my, but our dreams, as we work together on the same challenges facing Latin America and the world: poverty, equality, empowering indigenous people, biodiversity, climate change. . . . That person is my wife, Elaine Karp-Toledo. With her by my side, I am the happiest man on earth.

Alejandro Toledo

Notes

CHAPTER ONE

1. Club de Madrid, "Call to Action" (Club de Madrid, Madrid), 20.

2. I am grateful to Stanford professor Rodolfo Dirzon for his notes on this section.

3. I am grateful to Stanford professor Rodolfo Dirzon for his notes on this section.

4. While it is a challenge to come up with a precise figure for the number of Latin Americans in the diaspora with BA, MA, and PhD degrees, we based our estimates on the Current Population Survey of the United States and the Economically Active Population of the European Union, 2010.

CHAPTER TWO

1. "In the space of one hundred and seventy-six years the Lower Mississippi has shortened itself two hundred and forty-two miles. That is an average of a trifle over one mile and a third per year. Therefore, any calm person, who is not blind or idiotic, can see that in the Old Oolitic Silurian Period, just a million years ago next November, the Lower Mississippi River was upwards of one million three hundred thousand miles long, and stuck out over the Gulf of Mexico like a fishing-rod. And by the same token any person can see that seven hundred and forty-two years from now the Lower Mississippi will be only a mile and three-quarters long, and Cairo and New Orleans will have joined their streets together, and be plodding comfortably along under a single mayor and a mutual board of aldermen. There is something fascinating about science. One gets such wholesale returns of conjecture out of such a trifling investment of fact." Mark Twain, *Life on the Mississippi*, http://www.twainquotes.com/Mississippi.html.

2. Brian Snowdon, "Three Cheers for the 'Progressive State': Ben Friedman on the Moral Consequences of Economic Growth," *World Economics* 9, no. 1 (2008): 97.

3. Ibid., 102.

4. Ibid.

5. Larry Diamond and Leonardo Morlino, "The Quality of Democracy: An Overview," *Journal of Democracy* 15, no. 4 (2004): 20.

6. The "self-coup," or power-grab by the executive. We have seen a trend in the region for the executive to bypass the legislature and judiciary by calling for popular referenda that seek to constitutionally eradicate term limits. These circumventions of the checks and balances of power threaten to undermine the democratic system.

7. Fishlow's observations were largely ignored until recently, when the conditions in Asian countries and their high rates of growth have been contrasted with those in Latin America.

CHAPTER THREE

1. "Life after the Commodity Boom," *The Economist*, March 29, 2014.

2. Economic Commission for Latin America and the Caribbean (ECLAC), *Economic Overview of Latin America and the Caribbean* (Santiago: ECLAC, 2014), 21.

3. A longer version of this section appeared in Global Center for Development and Democracy (GCDD), *Social Agenda for Democracy in Latin America for the Next Twenty Years* (Lima: GCDD, 2009). Thanks to Jeff Puryear and Mariellen Malloy Jewers for their contribution. See also ECLAC, *Time for Equality* (Santiago: ECLAC, 2010).

4. Other dimensions of fiscal policy, such as promoting growth and stabilizing the economy in good times and bad, are also important for the poor. For a discussion, see, for example, Nancy Birdsall, Augusto de la Torre, and Rachel Menezes, *Fair Growth: Economic Policies for Latin America's Poor and Middle-Income Majority* (Washington, DC: Brookings Institution Press, 2008), chaps. 1 and 2.

5. Alain de Janvry and Elisabeth Sadoulet, "Making Conditional Cash Transfers More Efficient: Designing for Maximum Effect of the Conditionality," *World Bank Economic Review* 20 (2006): 1–29.

6. See Armando Barrientos and Claudio Santibáñez, "New Forms of Social Assistance and the Evolution of Social Protection in Latin America," *Journal of Latin American Studies* 41, no. 1 (2009): 1–26; Armando Barrientos and Jocelyn DeJong, "Reducing Child Poverty with Cash Transfers: A Sure Thing?" *Development Policy Review* 24, no. 5 (2006): 537–552; Paul Gertler, Ingrid Woolard, and Barbara Barungi, "The Impact of Conditional Cash Transfers on Human Development Outcomes: A Review of Evidence from PROGRESA in Mexico and Some Implications for Policy Debates in South and Southern Africa" (Southern African Regional Poverty Network, Pretoria, South Africa, 2005); and Nanak Kakwani, Fabio Soares, and Hyun H. Son, "Cash Transfers for School-Age Children in African Countries: Simulation of Impacts on Poverty and School Attendance," *Development Policy Review* 24, no. 5 (2006): 553–569.

7. Amber K. Gove, "The Optimizing Parent? Household Demand for Schooling and the Impact of a Conditional Cash Transfer Program on School Attendance and Achievement in Brazil" (PhD diss., Stanford University, 2005).

8. Elizaveta Perova and Renos Vakis, *Más tiempo en el programa, mejores resultados: Duración e impactos del programa Juntos en el Perú* (Washington, DC: World Bank, 2009).

9. Simone Cecchini and Aldo Madariaga, *Conditional Cash Transfer Programmes: The Recent Experience in Latin America and the Caribbean* (Santiago: ECLAC, 2011).

10. Centro Global para la Democracia y el Desarrollo (CGDD), *Agenda social para la democracia en Latinoamérica para los próximos veinte años* (Estoril, Portugal: CGDD, 2009), 4.

11. Sam Daley-Harris, "A Deeper Vision for Microfinance: Restoring People's Honour and Worth," *Journal of Social Business* 1, no. 3 (2011): 22.

12. International Labour Office, *Key Indicators of the Labour Market*, 5th ed. (Geneva: ILO, 2007), 4.

13. "More Jobs, Less Poverty: Two Goals Post 2015" (Working Group 1A, Club de Madrid Annual Conference, Brisbane, Australia, December 2013), 4.

14. UN A/68/202.

15. "More Jobs, Less Poverty," 8–9.

16. Ibid., 2.

17. Ibid., 3.

18. CGDD, *Agenda social para la democracia*, 80.

19. "A Focus on Youth: In Rescue of a Generation" (Club de Madrid Annual Conference, Brisbane, Australia, December 2013), 1.

20. Ibid., 230.

21. International Labour Organization (ILO), *Global Employment Trends for Youth 2013* (Geneva: ILO, 2013).

22. "Focus on Youth," 5–7.

23. World Bank, *World Development Report 2013: Jobs* (Washington, DC: World Bank, 2013).

24. "Employment: Contributing to Security and Peace" (Club de Madrid Annual Conference, Brisbane, Australia, December 2013), 3; and Henrik Urdal, "A Clash of Generations? Youth Bulges and Political Violence," *International Studies Quarterly* 50 (2006): 607–629.

25. "Focus on Youth," 6–7.

26. Ibid., 8.

27. There is some counterevidence for this assertion when schools are organized around children's work schedules (see Pamela Sud, "Can Non-Formal Education Keep Working Children in School: A Case Study from Punjab, India" [unpublished honors thesis, Stanford University, 2008]). However, this is rarely the case.

28. "Green Jobs for Sustainable Growth" (Club de Madrid Annual Conference, Brisbane, Australia, December 2013), 9–11.

29. Ibid., 8.

30. Ibid., 6.

31. Ibid., 7.

32. ILO/UNEP/IOE/ITUC, *Working towards Sustainable Development: Opportunities for Decent Work and Social Inclusion in a Green Economy* (Geneva: ILO, 2012).

33. "Green Jobs for Sustainable Growth," 9–10.

34. Ibid.

CHAPTER FOUR

1. Manuel Alcantara Saez, "El origen de los partidos políticos en América Latina" (Working Paper 187, Institut de Ciències Polítiques i Socials, Barcelona, 2001).

2. Samuel P. Huntington, *The Third Wave: Democratization in the Late Twentieth Century* (Norman: University of Oklahoma Press, 1993).

3. Mark P. Jones, "The Diversity of Latin American Democracy," *World Politics Review*, March 20, 2012.

4. Luis Alberto Moreno, *La década de América Latina, una oportunidad real* (Washington, DC: Inter-American Development Bank, 2012).

5. Jones, "Diversity of Latin American Democracy."

6. The ISI model was developed by Raul Prebisch and Hans Singer when Prebisch became the director of the Economic Commission for Latin America and the Caribbean (ECLAC) in 1948. The Prebisch-Singer model argued that because they were dependent on commodity exports, less developed countries were at a permanent terms of trade disadvantage in their relations with the developed countries. The only escape was through tariff protection of nascent manufacturing industries in Latin America.

7. Jones, "Diversity of Latin American Democracy."

8. Jaime de Althaus, *La promesa de la democracia: Marchas y contramarchas del sistema político en el Perú* (Lima: Planeta, 2011).

9. Jones, "Diversity of Latin American Democracy."

10. Larry Diamond, *The Spirit of Democracy: The Struggle to Build Free Societies throughout the World* (New York: Henry Holt, 2008), 171–189.

11. Ibid., 22.

12. Corporación Latinobarómetro, *Informe 2013* (Santiago: Corporación Latinobarómetro, 2013).

13. Guillermo A. O'Donnell, "Democracy, Law, and Comparative Politics," *Studies in Comparative International Development* 36, no. 1 (2001): 7–36.

14. Corporación Latinobarómetro, *Informe 2013*, 30.

15. Ibid., 32.

16. Julio F. Carrión and Patricia Zárate, *Cultura política de la democracia en el Perú, 2010: Consolidación democrática de las Américas en tiempos difíciles* (Lima: Instituto de Estudios Peruanos / Vanderbilt University, 2010).

17. Jaime Daremblum, "La democracia puesta a prueba en América Latina," http:// pjmedia.com/blog/la-democracia-puesta-a-prueba-en-america-latina.

18. Corporación Latinobarómetro, *Informe 2011* (Santiago: Corporación Latinobarómetro, 2011).

19. Steven Levitsky and Lucan A. Way, *Competitive Authoritarianism: Hybrid Regimes after the Cold War* (New York: Cambridge University Press, 2010).

20. Steven Levitsky and Lucan A. Way, "Elections without Democracy: The Rise of Competitive Authoritarianism," *Journal of Democracy* 13, no. 2 (2002): 53.

21. Ibid., 53–54.

22. Corporación Latinobarómetro, *Informe 2011*.

23. Ibid.

24. Nelson Manrique, "Democracia: Quién la califica," http://www.larepublica.pe /columnistas/en-construccion/democracia-quien-la-califica-19-02-2013.

25. Corporación Latinobarómetro, *Informe 2013*, 37.

26. Carrión and Zárate, *Cultura política de la democracia en el Perú, 2010*, 47.

27. Ibid., 77.

28. Adam Przeworski, "What Makes Democracies Endure?" *Journal of Democracy* 7, no. 1 (1996), cited in Carrión and Zárate, *Cultura política de la democracia en el Perú, 2010*, 47–48.

29. Carrión and Zárate, *Cultura política de la democracia en el Perú, 2010*.

30. Indice de Desarrollo Democrático Centroamericano, Fundación Konrad Adenauer, Instituto Centroamericano de Estudios, Guatemala City, Guatemala, 2006.

31. Corporación Latinobarómetro, *Informe 2011*, 47.

32. Ibid.

33. Ibid., n.p.

34. Corporación Latinobarómetro, *Informe 2013*, 5.

35. Moreno, *La década de América Latina*.

36. Ibid.

37. World Bank, *Economic Mobility and the Rise of the Latin American Middle Class* (Washington, DC: World Bank, 2013), xi.

38. Augusto de la Torre and Jamele Rigolini, *MIC Forum: The Rise of the Middle Class* (Washington, DC: World Bank, 2013), 2.

39. Corporación Latinobarómetro, *Informe 2013*, 74.

40. According to the quarterly survey by the two institutions, which is given to 138 specialists from 18 countries: http://peru21.pe/economia/clima-negocios-latinoamerica -sube-su-mejor-nivel-18-meses-2118272.

41. International Bank for Reconstruction and Development / World Bank, "Doing Business," http://espanol.doingbusiness.org/~/media/GIAWB/Doing_Business/Documents /Annual-Reports/Foreign/DB13-spanish.pdf.

42. Moreno, *La década de América Latina.*

CHAPTER FIVE

1. Amartya K. Sen, "Democracy as Universal Value," in *The Global Divergence of Democracies*, ed. Larry Diamond and Marc F. Plattner (Baltimore: Johns Hopkins University Press, 2001).

2. Quoted on the United Nations Development Programme (UNDP) website, http:// hdr.undp.org/en/humandev/.

3. Christine Lagarde, "Innovation, Technology and the 21st Century Global Economy" (speech delivered at Stanford University, Stanford, CA, February 2014), 4.

4. World Bank, Databank (2012).

5. UNDP, *Informe regional sobre Desarrollo Humano para América Latina y el Caribe 2010. Actuar sobre el futuro: Romper la transmisión intergeneracional de la desigualdad* (New York: UNDP, 2010), 21.

6. Enrique Vásquez, "When Deprivation and Differences Do Matter: Multidimensionality of Poverty in Latin America and the Caribbean" (working paper, Department of Economics, University of the Pacific, Lima, 2013), 17.

7. Branko Milanovic and Rafael Muñoz de Bustillo, "La desigualdad de la distribución de la renta en América Latina: Situación, evolución y factores explicativos," *América Latina Hoy* 48 (2008): 24.

8. Vásquez, "When Deprivation and Differences Do Matter," 17.

9. Ibid., 5.

10. The MPI was developed by the Oxford Poverty and Human Development Initiative (OPHI), which is part of Oxford University, and the Human Development Report Office of the UNDP.

11. Vásquez, "When Deprivation and Differences Do Matter," 11; and Sabina Alkire and Maria Emma Santos, "Acute Multidimensional Poverty: A New Index for Developing Countries" (Working Paper 38, Oxford Poverty and Human Development Initiative, Oxford University, Oxford), 7.

CHAPTER SIX

1. The World Wildlife Fund (WWF; www.worldwildlife.org) defines an *ecoregion* as a "large unit of land or water containing a geographically distinct assemblage of species, natural communities, and environmental conditions." In this definition, the boundaries of an ecoregion are not fixed and clearly defined, such as with nation-states, but rather "encompass an area within which important ecological and evolutionary processes most strongly interact."

2. Jorge M. Rodriguez Zuñiga, "Paying for Forest Environmental Services: The Costa Rican Experience" (FAO Corporate Document Repository, 2002), http://www.fao.org /docrep/005/y4744e/y4744e08.htm.

CHAPTER SEVEN

1. The Brady Plan is the set of principles that were first articulated by US Treasury Secretary Nicholas F. Brady in March 1989 to address the so-called developing countries' debt crisis of the 1980s.

2. Larry Diamond, *The Spirit of Democracy: The Struggle to Build Free Societies throughout the World* (New York: Henry Holt, 2008).

3. Ibid.

4. Ibid.

5. United Nations Development Programme (UNDP), *Citizen Security with a Human Face: Evidence and Proposals for Latin America* (New York: UNDP, 2013).

6. Ibid.

7. United Nations Office on Drugs and Crime (UNODC), *The Globalization of Crime: A Transnational Organized Crime Threat Assessment* (Vienna: UNODC, 2010).

CHAPTER EIGHT

1. http://data.worldbank.org/indicator/SH.DYN.MORT.

2. Global Center for Development and Democracy (GCDD), *Social Agenda for Democracy in Latin America for the Next Twenty Years* (Lima: GCDD, 2009), 56.

3. Office of the United Nations High Commissioner for Human Rights, *The Right to Adequate Housing*, Fact Sheet 21/Rev. 1 (Geneva: Office of the United Nations High Commissioner for Human Rights, 2009), 3–5.

4. José R. Molinas Vega, Ricardo Paes de Barros, Jaime Saavedra Chanduvi, Marcelo Giugale, Louise J. Cord, Carola Pessino, and Amer Hasan, *Do Our Children Have a Chance? A Human Opportunity Report for Latin America and the Caribbean* (Washington, DC: World Bank, 2011).

5. Hernando de Soto, *The Mystery of Capital: Why Capitalism Triumphs in the West and Fails Everywhere Else* (New York: Basic Books, 2000), 6.

6. Christian Daude, "Ascendance by Descendants? On Intergenerational Education Mobility in Latin America" (Working Paper 297, OECD Development Centre, OECD, Paris, 2011), 31, http://www.oecd.org/dev/latinamericaandthecaribbean/47237039.pdf.

CHAPTER NINE

1. Jim Yong Kim, "Delivering on Development: Harnessing Knowledge to Build Prosperity and End Poverty" (keynote speech delivered to the World Knowledge Forum [World Bank], Seoul, October 8, 2012).

2. Francis Fukuyama, "What Is Governance?" *Governance* 26, no. 3 (2013): 347–368.

3. Daron Acemoglu and James A. Robinson, *Why Nations Fail: The Origins of Power, Prosperity, and Poverty* (New York: Crown, 2012), 36.

4. Ibid., 70.

5. Ibid., 68.

6. Badru Bukenya and Pablo Yanguas, "Building State Capacity for Inclusive Development: The Politics of Public Sector Reform" (Working Paper 25, Effective States and Inclusive Development Research Centre, University of Manchester, Manchester, October 2013).

7. Larry Diamond, *The Spirit of Democracy: The Struggle to Build Free Societies throughout the World* (New York: Henry Holt, 2008), 99.

8. Francis Fukuyama, *State-Building: Governance and World Order in the 21st Century* (Ithaca, NY: Cornell University Press, 2004), 26.

9. Bukenya and Yanguas, "Building State Capacity for Inclusive Development," 7–8.

10. Naazneen Barma, Elisabeth Huybens, and Lorena Viñuela, *Institutions Taking Root: Building State Capacity in Challenging Contexts* (Washington, DC: World Bank, 2014).

11. Acemoglu and Robinson, *Why Nations Fail*, 70.

12. Fukuyama, *State-Building*, 33.

13. Ibid.

14. Bukenya and Yanguas, "Building State Capacity for Inclusive Development," 2.

15. Fukuyama, *State-Building*, 80.

16. Kim, "Delivering on Development."

17. Ibid.

18. Acemoglu and Robinson, *Why Nations Fail*, 68.

19. Diamond, *Spirit of Democracy*.

20. Ibid., 99.

21. See Andre Gunder Frank, "The Development of Underdevelopment," *Monthly Review* 18, no. 4 (1966): 17–31.

22. See Terry Lynn Karl, *The Paradox of Plenty: Oil Booms and Petro States*, Studies in International Political Economy (Berkeley: University of California Press, 1997).

23. Diamond, *Spirit of Democracy*, 99.

24. Larry Diamond and Jack Mosbacher, "Petroleum to the People—Africa's Coming Resource Curse—And How to Avoid It," *Foreign Affairs* 92, no. 5 (2013): 86–98.

CHAPTER TEN

1. Economic Commission for Latin America and the Caribbean (ECLAC), *Foreign Direct Investment in Latin America and the Caribbean* (Santiago: ECLAC, 2012), 9.

2. International Monetary Fund (IMF), *Regional Economic Outlook: Western Hemisphere, 2014* (Washington, DC: IMF, 2014), 17.

3. ECLAC, *Foreign Direct Investment*, 10.

4. Ibid.

5. Ibid.

6. Ibid., 10–11.

7. Ibid., 10.

8. Ibid., 16.

9. Ibid., 11.

10. Paul Bloxham, Andrew Keen, and Luke Hartigan, *Commodities and the Global Economy: Are Current Prices the New Normal?* (Sydney: HSBC Bank Australia, 2012).

11. Ibid.

12. Ben Laidler, Qu Hongbin, Todd Dunivant, Simon Francis, Thomas Hilboldt, and Andre Loes, *South–South Special: What a Globalizing China Means for LatAm* (New York: HSBC Securities [USA], 2013).

13. Ibid.

14. Ibid.

15. Evan Ellis, "Are Big Chinese Energy Investments in Latin America a Concern?" *Manzella Report*, November 23, 2013.

16. Ibid.

17. Ibid.

18. Laidler et al., *South–South Special*, 20.

19. Ibid., 38.

20. Ibid., 24.

21. Ibid., 25.

22. Ibid., 28–29.

23. Ibid., 29.

24. Ibid., n.p.

25. US Department of State, http://www.state.gov/r/pa/prs/ps/2013/10/215195.htm.

26. http://www.apec.org/About-Us/About-APEC/Member-Economies.aspx.

27. Ibid.

28. Moisés Naim, "The Most Important Alliance You've Never Heard Of," *The Atlantic*, February 17, 2014.

29. M. Angeles Villarreal, *The Pacific Alliance: A Trade Integration Initiative in Latin America* (Washington, DC: Congressional Research Service, 2014).

30. Ibid.

31. Carlo Dade and Carl Meacham, *The Pacific Alliance: An Example of Lessons Learned* (Washington, DC: Center for Strategic and International Studies, 2013).

32. Laidler et al., *South–South Special*.

33. Inter-American Development Bank, *From Multilatinas to Global Latinas: The New Latin American Multinationals* (Washington, DC: Inter-American Development Bank, 2008).

34. Ben Laidler, Alexandre Gartner, Juan Carlos Mateos, and Francisco Machado, *LatAm Equity Insights* (New York: HSBC Securities [USA], 2012).

35. Evan Ellis, "China's Strategy in Latin America Demonstrates Boldness of President Xi," *Manzella Report*, February 19, 2014.

36. Ibid.

37. Jorge Heine, "Latin America Goes Global," *Americas Quarterly* 7, no. 2 (2013): 42.

38. Ibid.

39. Ibid.

40. Ibid.

41. Ibid.

42. Daniel Kurtz-Phelan, "What Is IBSA Anyway?" *Americas Quarterly* 7, no. 2 (2013).

43. Heine, "Latin America Goes Global," 42.

44. Ibid.

45. World Bank, "Supporting Innovation in Latin America and the Caribbean: Successful Examples of Technology Transfer Promotion," http://siteresources.worldbank.org/INTLAC/Resources/257803-1269390034020/EnBreve_164_Printable.pdf.

46. Ibid.

47. Ibid.

48. Ibid.

49. Heine, "Latin America Goes Global," 42.

50. Ibid.

51. Inter-American Dialogue, *Remaking the Relationship: The United States and Latin America* (Washington, DC: Inter-American Dialogue, 2012), 3.

52. World Bank, "Supporting Innovation in Latin America and the Caribbean."

53. US Bureau of Economic Analysis, "Gross Domestic Product, Fourth Quarter and Annual 2013 (Advance Estimate)" (US Bureau of Economic Analysis, Washington, DC, January 30, 2014).

54. José Fernandez, "Speaking a Common Language with Latin America: Economics," *Americas Quarterly* 8, no. 2 (2014).

55. Inter-American Dialogue, *Remaking the Relationship*, 3.

56. Fernandez, "Speaking a Common Language with Latin America."

57. While it is a challenge to estimate a precise figure for the number of Latin Americans in the diaspora with BA, MA, and PhD degrees, we based our estimations on the Current Population Survey of the United States and the Economically Active Population of the European Union, 2010.

58. Fernandez, "Speaking a Common Language with Latin America."

59. Inter-American Dialogue, *Remaking the Relationship*, 3.

Bibliography

Acemoglu, Daron, Simon Johnson, and James A. Robinson. 2001. "The Colonial Origins of Comparative Development: An Empirical Investigation." *American Economic Review* 91 (5): 1369–1401.

———. 2002. "Reversal of Fortune: Geography and Institutions in the Making of the Modern World Income Distribution." *Quarterly Journal of Economics* 117 (4): 1231–1294.

Acemoglu, Daron, and James A. Robinson. 2012. *Why Nations Fail: The Origins of Power, Prosperity, and Poverty*. New York: Crown.

Alcantara Saez, Manuel. 2001. "El origen de los partidos políticos en América Latina." Working Paper 187, Institut de Ciències Polítiques i Socials, Barcelona.

Alkire, Sabina, Adriana Conconi, and José Manuel Roche. 2013. "Multidimensional Poverty Index 2013: Brief Methodological Note and Results." Oxford Poverty and Human Development Initiative, Oxford University, Oxford.

Alkire, Sabina, and James Foster. 2011. "Understandings and Misunderstandings of Multidimensional Poverty Measurement." Working Paper 43, Oxford Poverty and Human Development Initiative, Oxford University, Oxford.

Alkire, Sabina, and Maria Emma Santos. 2010. "Acute Multidimensional Poverty: A New Index for Developing Countries." Working Paper 38, Oxford Poverty and Human Development Initiative, Oxford University, Oxford.

Barrientos, Armando, and Jocelyn DeJong. 2006. "Reducing Child Poverty with Cash Transfers: A Sure Thing?" *Development Policy Review* 24 (5): 537–552.

Barrientos, Armando, and Claudio Santibáñez. 2009. "New Forms of Social Assistance and the Evolution of Social Protection in Latin America." *Journal of Latin American Studies* 41 (1): 1–26.

Birdsall, Nancy, and Juan Luis Londoño. 1997. "Asset Inequality Matters: An Assessment of the World Bank's Approach to Poverty Reduction." *American Economic Review* 87 (2): 32–37.

Boix, Carles. 2003. *Democracy and Redistribution*. Cambridge: Cambridge University Press.

Brusco, Valeria, Marcelo Nazareno, and Susan C. Stokes. 2004. "Vote Buying in Argentina." *Latin American Research Review* 39 (2): 66–88.

Carnoy, Alan. 1962. *Democracia Sí! A Way to Win the Cold War*. New York: Vantage Press.

Carnoy, Martin, and Richard Rothstein. 2013. *What Do International Tests Really Show about U.S. Student Performance?* Washington, DC: Economic Policy Institute.

Carothers, Thomas. 2006. *Promoting the Rule of Law Abroad: In Search of Knowledge*. Washington, DC: Carnegie Endowment.

———. 2007. "The 'Sequencing' Fallacy." *Journal of Democracy* 18 (1): 12–27.

Carrasco, Alejandro. 2014. "Selección de estudiantes y desigualdad educacional en Chile: Qué tan coactive es la regulación que la prohíbe?" (FONIDE 711286, Fondo de Investigación y Desarrollo en Educación, Ministerio de Educación, Santiago).

Carrión, Julio F., and Patricia Zárate. 2010. *Cultura política de la democracia en el Perú, 2010: Consolidación democrática de las Américas en tiempos difíciles*. Lima: Instituto de Estudios Peruanos / Vanderbilt University.

Cleary, Matthew R., and Susan C. Stokes. 2006. *Democracy and the Culture of Skepticism: Political Trust in Argentina and Mexico*. New York: Russell Sage Foundation.

Club de Madrid Annual Conference. 2013. "Employment: Contributing to Security and Peace." Brisbane, Australia.

———. 2013. "A Focus on Youth: In Rescue of a Generation." Brisbane, Australia.

———. 2013. "Green Jobs for Sustainable Growth." Brisbane, Australia.

———. 2013. "More Jobs, Less Poverty: Two Goals Post 2015." Issues for Working Group 1A, Brisbane, Australia.

Coatsworth, John H., and Alan M. Taylor. 1978. "Obstacles to Economic Growth in Nineteenth-Century Mexico." *American Historical Review* 83:80–100.

———. 1998. *Latin America and the World Economy since 1800*. Cambridge, MA: Harvard University Press.

Collier, George A., Renato I. Rosaldo, and John D. Wirth. 1982. *The Inca and Aztec States 1400–1800: Anthropology and History*. New York: Academic Press.

Collier, Paul. 2001. "Implications of Ethnic Diversity." *Economic Policy* 16 (32): 129–166.

———. 2006. "Economic Causes of Civil Conflict and Their Implications for Policy." Oxford Economic Papers, Oxford University, Oxford.

———. 2007. *The Bottom Billion: Why the Poorest Countries Are Failing and What Can Be Done about It*. Oxford: Oxford University Press.

Collier, Paul, Anke Hoeffler, and Dominic Rohner. 2007. "Beyond Greed and Grievance: Feasibility and Civil War." Oxford Economic Papers, Oxford University, Oxford.

Collier, Ruth B. 1999. *Paths toward Democracy: The Working Class and Elites in Western Europe and South America*. Cambridge: Cambridge University Press.

Corporación Latinobarómetro. 2011. *Informe 2011*. Santiago: Corporación Latinobarómetro.

———. 2013. *Informe 2013*. Santiago: Corporación Latinobarómetro.

Dahl, Robert A. 1956. *A Preface to Democratic Theory*. Chicago: University of Chicago Press.

———. 1969. *Pluralist Democracy in the United States: Conflict and Consent*. New York: Rand McNally.

———. 1982. *Dilemmas of Pluralist Democracy: Autonomy vs. Control*. New Haven, CT: Yale University Press.

Daremblum, Jaime. 2013. "La democracia puesta a prueba en América Latina." http://pjmedia.com/blog/la-democracia-puesta-a-prueba-en-america-latina/.

Daude, Christian. 2011. "Ascendance by Descendants? On Intergenerational Education Mobility in Latin America." Working Paper 297, OECD Development Centre, OECD, Paris. http://www.oecd.org/dev/latinamericaandthecaribbean/47237039.pdf.

de Althaus, Jaime. 2011. *La promesa de la democracia: Marchas y contramarchas del sistema político en el Perú*. Lima: Planeta.

Del Rosso, Joy Miller. 1999. *School Feeding Programs: Improving Effectiveness and Increasing the Benefit to Education. A Guide for Program Managers*. Oxford: Partnership for Child Development.

de Pee, Saskia, Henk-Jan Brinkman, Patrick Webb, Steve Godfrey, Ian Darnton-Hill, Harold Alderman, Richard D. Semba, Ellen Piwoz, and Martin W. Bloem. 2010. "How to Ensure Nutrition Security in the Global Economic Crisis to Protect and Enhance Development of Young Children and Our Common Future." *Journal of Nutrition* 140 (1): 138S–142S.

Dercon, Stefan, and Alan Sánchez. 2011. "Long-Term Implications of Under-Nutrition on Psychosocial Competencies: Evidence from Four Developing Countries." Working Paper 72, Young Lives, Oxford. http://www.dfid.gov.uk/r4d/PDF/Outputs/Younglives/wp72_long-term-implications-of-under-nutrition.pdf.

de Soto, Hernando. 2000. *The Mystery of Capital: Why Capitalism Triumphs in the West and Fails Everywhere Else*. New York: Basic Books.

Diamond, Larry. 1992. "Economic Development and Democracy Reconsidered." *American Behavioral Scientist* 15 (4–5): 450–499.

———. 1999. *Developing Democracy: Toward Consolidation*. Baltimore: Johns Hopkins University Press.

———. 2008. *The Spirit of Democracy: The Struggle to Build Free Societies throughout the World*. New York: Henry Holt.

Diamond, Larry, and Richard Gunther. 2001. *Political Parties and Democracy*. Baltimore: Johns Hopkins University Press.

Diamond, Larry, and Seymour Martin Lipset. 1988. *Democracy in Developing Countries*. Boulder, CO: Lynne Rienner.

Diamond, Larry, and Leonardo Morlino. 2004. "The Quality of Democracy: An Overview." *Journal of Democracy* 15 (4): 20–31.

Economic Commission for Latin America and the Caribbean (ECLAC). 2010. *Time for Equality*. Santiago: ECLAC.

———. 2012. *Panorama social de América Latina*. Santiago: ECLAC.

———. 2013. *Natural Resources: Status and Trends towards a Regional Development Agenda in Latin America and the Caribbean*. Santiago: ECLAC.

———. 2014. "The Governance of Natural Resources in Latin America and the Caribbean." http://www.cepal.org/prensa/noticias/paginas/7/51947/ECLAC_RRNN.pdf.

Food and Agriculture Organization of the United Nations (FAO). 2011. *The State of Food Insecurity in the World: Addressing Food Insecurity in Protracted Crises*. Rome: FAO.

Fukuyama, Francis. 1995. *Trust: The Social Virtues and the Creation of Prosperity*. New York: Free Press.

———. 2000. "The March of Equality." *Journal of Democracy* 11 (1): 11–17.

———. 2004. *State-Building: Governance and World Order in the 21st Century*. Ithaca, NY: Cornell University Press.

———. 2006. "Identity, Immigration, and Liberal Democracy." *Journal of Democracy* 17 (2): 5–20.

———. 2008. *Falling Behind: Explaining the Development Gap between Latin America and the United States*. New York: Oxford University Press.

———. 2011. "Is There a Proper Sequence in Democratic Transitions?" *Current History* 110 (739): 308–310.

———. 2011. *The Origins of Political Order: From Prehuman Times to the French Revolution*. New York: Farrar, Straus and Giroux.

———. 2013. "What Is Governance?" *Governance* 26 (3): 347–368.

Fukuyama, Francis, and Nancy Birdsall. 2011. *New Ideas in Development after the Financial Crisis*. Baltimore: Johns Hopkins University Press.

García, Leani. 2013. "Latin America's Changing Global Connections." *Americas Quarterly* 7 (2).

Geddes, Barbara. 1996. *Politician's Dilemma: Building State Capacity in Latin America*. Berkeley: University of California Press.

Gellner, Ernest. 1987. *Culture, Identity, and Politics*. Cambridge: Cambridge University Press.

———. 2006. *Nations and Nationalism*. 2nd ed. Ithaca, NY: Cornell University Press.

Gerschenkron, Alexander. 1962. *Economic Backwardness in Historical Perspective*. Cambridge, MA: Harvard University Press.

Gertler, Paul, Ingrid Woolard, and Barbara Barungi. 2005. "The Impact of Conditional Cash Transfers on Human Development Outcomes: A Review of Evidence from PROGRESA in Mexico and Some Implications for Policy Debates in South and Southern Africa." Southern African Regional Poverty Network, Pretoria, South Africa.

Global Center for Development and Democracy (GCDD). 2009. *Social Agenda for Democracy in Latin America for the Next Twenty Years*. Lima: GCDD.

Haber, Stephen. 1997. *How Latin America Fell Behind: Essays on the Economic Histories of Brazil and Mexico, 1800–1914*. Stanford, CA: Stanford University Press.

Haber, Stephen, and Jeffrey Bortz. 2002. *The Mexican Economy, 1870–1930: Essays on the Economic History of Institutions, Revolution, and Growth*. Stanford, CA: Stanford University Press.

Hanson, Jonathan. 2012. "Democracy and State Capacity: Complements or Substitutes?" Working paper, Syracuse University, Syracuse, NY.

Hausmann, Ricardo, Lant Pritchett, and Dani Rodrik. 2005. "Growth Accelerations." *Journal of Economic Growth* 10 (4): 303–329.

Huntington, Samuel P. 1965. "Political Development and Political Decay." *World Politics* 17 (3): 386–430.

———. 1966. "Political Modernization: America vs. Europe." *World Politics* 18 (3): 378–414.

———. 1991. *The Third Wave: Democratization in the Late Twentieth Century*. Norman: University of Oklahoma Press.

———. 2004. *Who Are We? The Challenges to America's National Identity*. New York: Simon and Schuster.

———. 2006. *Political Order in Changing Societies*. New Haven, CT: Yale University Press.

International Labour Office. 2007. *Key Indicators of the Labor Market*. 5th ed. Geneva: ILO.

International Labour Organization (ILO). 2013. *Global Employment Trends for Youth 2013*. Geneva: ILO.

International Labour Organization / United Nations Environment Programme / International Organization of Employers / International Trade Union Confederation. 2012. *Working towards Sustainable Development: Opportunities for Decent Work and Social Inclusion in a Green Economy*. Geneva: ILO.

International Monetary Fund (IMF). 2014. *Regional Economic Outlook Western Hemisphere*. Washington, DC: IMF.

Jones, Mark P. 2012. "The Diversity of the Latin America Democracy." *World Policy Review*, March 20.

Kakwani, Nanak, Fabio Soares, and Hyun H. Son. 2006. "Cash Transfers for School-Age Children in African Countries: Simulation of Impacts on Poverty and School Attendance." *Development Policy Review* 24 (5): 553–569.

Kaufman, Herbert. 1960. *The Forest Ranger: A Study in Administrative Behavior*. Baltimore: Johns Hopkins University Press.

Kaufmann, Daniel. 1997. "Corruption: The Facts." *Foreign Policy* 107:114–131.

Kawata, Junichi. 2006. *Comparing Political Corruption and Clientelism*. Aldershot, UK: Ashgate.

Kennedy, Paul M. 1987. *The Rise and Fall of the Great Powers: Economic Change and Military Conflict*. New York: Random House.

Lagarde, Christine. 2014. "Innovation, Technology and the 21st Century Global Economy." Speech delivered at Stanford University, Stanford, CA, February.

Laidler, Ben, Qu Hongbin, Todd Dunivant, Simon Francis, Thomas Hilboldt, and Andre Loes. 2013. *South–South Special: What a Globalizing China Means for LatAm*. New York: HSBC Securities (USA).

Lasagabaster, Esperanza, and Rekha Reddy. 2010. "Supporting Innovation in Latin America and the Caribbean: Successful Examples of Technology Transfer Promotion." *En Breve* 164. https://openknowledge.worldbank.org/bitstream/handle/10986/10144/596020BR IoEnBr10BOX358286B01PUBLIC1.pdf?sequence=1.

Levitsky, Steven, and Lucan A. Way. 2002. "The Rise of Competitive Authoritarianism." *Journal of Democracy* 13 (2): 51–65.

———. 2010. *Competitive Authoritarianism: Hybrid Regimes after the Cold War*. New York: Cambridge University Press.

Linz, Juan J. 2000. *Totalitarian and Authoritarian Regimes*. Boulder, CO: Lynne Rienner.

Linz, Juan J., and Alfred Stepan. 1978. *The Breakdown of Democratic Regimes: Crisis, Breakdown and Reequilibration. An Introduction*. Baltimore: Johns Hopkins University Press.

Lipset, Seymour Martin. 1959. "Some Social Requisites of Democracy: Economic Development and Political Legitimacy." *American Political Science Review* 53 (1): 69–105.

———. 1963. *The First New Nation*. New York: Basic Books.

———. 1981. *Political Man*. Baltimore: Johns Hopkins University Press.

Loes, Andre. 2013. *In the Spotlight . . . LatAm Trade Flows: Expanding, Diversified and Increasingly South–South*. São Paulo: HSBC Bank Brasil.

López-Calva, Luis F., and Nora Lustig. 2010. *Declining Inequality in Latin America: A Decade of Progress?* Washington, DC: Brookings Institution Press.

Lora, Eduardo. 2008. *Beyond Facts: Understanding Quality of Life*. http://www.iadb.org /en/research-and-data/publication-details,3169.html?pub_id=B-632.

Milanovic, Branko, and Rafael Muñoz de Bustillo. 2008. "La desigualdad de la distribución de la renta en América Latina: Situación, evolución y factores explicativos." *América Latina Hoy* 48:15–42.

Moreno, Luis Alberto. 2012. *La década de América Latina, una oportunidad real*. Washington, DC: Inter-American Development Bank.

Neckerman, Kathryn M., and Florencia Torche. 2007. "Inequality: Causes and Consequences." *Annual Review of Sociology* 33:335–357.

Ñopo, Hugo. 2012. *New Century, Old Disparities: Gender and Ethnic Earnings Gaps in Latin America and the Caribbean*. Washington, DC: Inter-American Development Bank.

Nye, Joseph S., Jr. 1967. "Corruption and Political Development: A Cost-Benefit Analysis." *American Political Science Review* 61 (2): 417–427.

O'Donnell, Guillermo A. 1973. *Modernization and Bureaucratic Authoritarianism: Studies in South American Politics*. Berkeley: University of California Press.

———. 2001. "Democracy, Law, and Comparative Politics." *Studies in Comparative International Development* 36 (1): 7–36.

Olson, Mancur. 1965. *The Logic of Collective Action: Public Goods and the Theory of Groups*. Cambridge, MA: Harvard University Press.

———. 1982. *The Rise and Decline of Nations*. New Haven, CT: Yale University Press.

———. 1993. "Dictatorship, Democracy, and Development." *American Political Science Review* 87 (9): 567–576.

OREALC/UNESCO. 2008. *Primer reporte SERCE: Los aprendizajes de los estudiantes de América Latina y el Caribe*. Santiago: Regional Bureau of Education for Latin America and the Caribbean OREALC/UNESCO.

———. 2011. *Regional Report on Education for All in Latin America and the Caribbean*. Santiago: Regional Bureau of Education for Latin America and the Caribbean OREALC/UNESCO.

Organisation for Economic Co-operation and Development (OECD). 2008. *Latin American Economic Outlook, 2009*. Paris: OECD.

———. 2014. *PISA 2012 Results in Focus*. Paris: OECD.

Organisation for Economic Co-operation and Development (OECD) / Economic Commission for Latin America and the Caribbean (ECLAC) / Inter-American Center of Tax Administrations (CIAT). 2012. *Revenue Statistics in Latin America*. Paris: OECD. http:// dx.doi.org/10.1787/9789264183889-en-fr.

Outes-Leon, Ingo, Catherine Porter, and Alan Sánchez. 2011. "Early Nutrition and Cognition in Peru: A Within-Sibling Investigation." Working Paper IDB-WP-241, Inter-American Development Bank, Washington, DC.

Oxford Poverty and Human Development Initiative (OPHI). 2013. http://www.ophi.org .uk/wp-content/uploads/OPHI-UNSC-2012.pdf?oa8fd7.

Przeworski, Adam. 1996. "What Makes Democracies Endure?" *Journal of Democracy* 7 (1). Cited in Carrión and Zárate, *Cultura política de la democracia en el Perú, 2010*.

———. 2009. "Conquered or Granted? A History of Suffrage Extensions." *British Journal of Political Science* 39 (2): 291–321.

Przeworski, Adam, Michael Alvarez, José Antonio Cheibub, and Fernando Limongi. 2000. *Democracy and Development: Political Institutions and Well-Being in the World, 1950–1990*. Cambridge: Cambridge University Press.

Przeworski, Adam, Susan C. Stokes, and Bernard Manin. 1999. *Democracy, Accountability, and Representation*. Cambridge: Cambridge University Press.

Putnam, Robert D. 1993. *Making Democracy Work: Civic Traditions in Modern Italy*. Princeton, NJ: Princeton University Press.

———. 2000. *Bowling Alone: The Collapse and Revival of American Community*. New York: Simon and Schuster.

Ribe, Helena, David A. Robalino, and Ian Walker. 2012. *From Right to Reality: Incentives, Labor Markets, and the Challenge of Universal Social Protection in Latin America and the Caribbean*. Washington, DC: World Bank.

Robles, Marcos, José Cuesta, Suzanne Duryea, Ted Enamorado, Alberto Gonzales, and Victoria Rodríguez. 2008. *Rising Food Prices and Poverty in Latin America: Effects of the 2006–2008 Price Surge*. Washington, DC: Inter-American Development Bank.

Rose-Ackerman, Susan. 1979. *Corruption: A Study in Political Economy*. New York: Academic Press.

———. 1999. *Corruption and Government: Causes, Consequences, and Reform*. Cambridge: Cambridge University Press.

Schmitter, Philippe C., and Guillermo O'Donnell. 1986. *Transitions from Authoritarian Rule: Comparative Perspectives*. Baltimore: Johns Hopkins University Press.

Schumpeter, Joseph. 1947. *Capitalism, Socialism, and Democracy*. 2nd ed. New York: Harper.

Sen, Amartya K. 1999. *Development as Freedom*. New York: Knopf.

———. 2001. "Democracy as Universal Value." In *The Global Divergence of Democracies*, edited by Larry Diamond and Marc F. Plattner. Baltimore: Johns Hopkins University Press.

Skidmore, Thomas E., and Peter H. Smith. 2004. *Modern Latin America*. 6th ed. New York: Oxford University Press.

Sperling, Gene B. 2005. "The Case for Universal Basic Education for the World's Poorest Boys and Girls." *Phi Delta Kappan* 87 (3): 213–216.

Stepan, Alfred C., Juan J. Linz, and Yogendra Yadav. 2010. "The Rise of 'State-Nations.'" *Journal of Democracy* 21 (3): 50–68.

Stepan, Alfred C., and Graeme B. Robertson. 2003. "An 'Arab' More Than a 'Muslim' Democracy Gap." *Journal of Democracy* 14 (3): 30–44.

Stokes, Susan C. 2005. "Perverse Accountability: A Formal Model of Machine Politics with Evidence from Argentina." *American Political Science Review* 99 (3): 315–325.

Toledo, Alejandro. 1990. *Peru and Latin America in Crisis: How to Finance Growth*. Lima: Instituto de Desarrollo Economico, Escuela de Administración de Negocios para Graduados.

———. 2003. *Cartas sobre la mesa*. 2nd ed. Lima: Instituto de Investigación para el Desarrollo.

———. 2014. *Crecer para incluir: Lo hicimos juntos, 2001–2006. Cinco años en los que se sembró el futuro* [Growing for inclusion: We did it together, 2001–2006. Five years in which we planted the future]. Lima: Planeta.

UNICEF. 2012. *Children in an Urban World: The State of the World's Children*. New York: UNICEF.

UNICEF/ECLAC. 2010. *Child Poverty in Latin America and the Caribbean*. LC/R.2168. Santiago: ECLAC.

United Nations Development Programme (UNDP). 2010. *Informe regional sobre Desarrollo Humano para América Latina y el Caribe 2010. Actuar sobre el futuro: Romper la transmisión intergeneracional de la desigualdad*. New York: UNDP.

———. 2013. *Citizen Security with a Human Face: Evidence and Proposals for Latin America*. New York: UNDP.

United Nations Office on Drugs and Crime (UNODC). 2010. *The Globalization of Crime: A Transnational Organized Crime Threat Assessment*. Vienna: UNODC.

———. 2012. *Transnational Organized Crime in Central America and the Caribbean: A Threat Assessment*. Vienna: UNODC.

Urdal, Henrik. 2006. "A Clash of Generations? Youth Bulges and Political Violence." *International Studies Quarterly* 50:607–629.

Vásquez, Enrique. 2013. "When Deprivation and Differences Do Matter: Multidimensionality of Poverty in Latin America and the Caribbean." Working paper, Department of Economics, University of the Pacific, Lima.

Vega, José R. Molinas, Ricardo Paes de Barros, Jaime Saavedra Chanduvi, Marcelo Giugale, Louise J. Cord, Carola Pessino, and Amer Hasan. 2011. *Do Our Children Have a Chance? A Human Opportunity Report for Latin America and the Caribbean*. Washington, DC: World Bank.

Watkins, Kevin. 2000. *The Oxfam Education Report*. Oxford: Oxfam GB.

Wilkinson, Richard, and Kate Pickett. 2011. *The Spirit Level: Why Greater Equality Makes Societies Stronger*. New York: Bloomsbury.

Wodon, Quentin, and Shlomo Yitzhaki. 2002. "Evaluating the Impact of Government Programs on Social Welfare: The Role of Targeting and the Allocation Rules among Program Beneficiaries." *Public Finance Review* 30 (2): 102–123.

About the Author

DR. ALEJANDRO TOLEDO was democratically elected president of Peru in 2001. During his five-year term, the central aim of Toledo's presidency was the fight against poverty through investment in health care and education. As a result of sustained economic growth and deliberate social policies directed to the poorest of the poor, extreme poverty was reduced by 25 percent in five years, and employment rose at an average rate of 6 percent from 2004 to 2006. From 2001 to 2006, the Peruvian economy grew at an average rate of 6 percent, making it one of the fastest-growing economies in Latin America.

Before becoming president, Dr. Toledo worked for the World Bank and the Inter-American Development Bank in Washington, DC, and the United Nations in New York. He first appeared on the international political scene in 1996 when he formed and led a broad democratic coalition that eventually brought down in 2000 the autocratic regime of Alberto Fujimori.

Toledo was born in a small and remote village in the Peruvian Andes, 12,000 feet above sea level. He grew up in extreme poverty in a family of 16 siblings. At the age of six, Toledo worked as a street shoe shiner and also sold newspapers and lottery tickets to supplement the family income. Owing to a series of accidental opportunities, he was able to escape from extreme poverty and attend the most prestigious academic centers of the world, later becoming one of the most prominent democratic leaders of Latin America. Dr. Toledo is the first Peruvian president of indigenous descent to be democratically elected in 500 years.

Toledo received a BA in economics and business administration from the University of San Francisco. He has an MA in economics, and an MA and PhD in the economics of human resources from the Stanford Graduate School of Education, Stanford University. During his academic career, Dr. Toledo was a visiting scholar at Harvard University and a research associate at Waseda University in Tokyo.

After finishing his term as president, Toledo returned to Stanford for three years, where he was a Distinguished Fellow in Residence at the university's Center for Advanced Study in the Behavioral Sciences, and also a Payne Distinguished Visiting Lecturer at the Freeman Spogli Institute for International Studies' Center on Democracy, Development, and the Rule of Law. Simultaneously, Dr. Toledo founded and continues to serve as the president of the Global Center for Development and Democracy (www.cgdd.org), which is based in Latin America, the United States, and the European Union. In 2009–2010, Dr. Toledo was a Distinguished Visiting Scholar at the School of Advanced International Studies at Johns Hopkins University in Washington, DC, and also a Non-Resident Senior Fellow in Foreign Policy and Global Economy and Development at the Brookings Institution in Washington, DC.

In recent years, Dr. Toledo has published on policy-oriented academic issues related to economic growth, inclusiveness, and democracy. Most recently, he has led several electoral observation missions with the National Democratic Institute and the Carter Center, in Nicaragua, Ecuador, and Tunisia.

Dr. Toledo has lectured in more than 45 countries on issues related to economic growth, poverty and inequality reduction, and democracy, as well as on the benefits of human capital investment. He has received 62 honorary doctoral degrees from prestigious universities in Peru and around the world.

Index

Italic page numbers indicate material in figures or tables.